Festivals
U.S.A. & Canada

Also by Robert Meyer, Jr.

FESTIVALS U.S.A.

FESTIVALS EUROPE

LOW COST TRIPS FOR THE WHOLE FAMILY

THE STARS AND STRIPES
   STORY OF WORLD WAR II

FESTIVALS
U.S.A. & **
CANADA *

** Robert Meyer Jr.

Ives Washburn, Inc.
New York ***

FESTIVALS U.S.A. AND CANADA

To: NATALIE APPLEGATE, PEGGY BARRY, ADELE BERNIUS, JOAN CHAMBERS, IRENE CHIARUTTINI, BERTHA DEAN, RUTH DE GROSBOIS, FRANCES DE GUERRE, JEANETTE LE BEUF DUFOUR, ALICE DUNN, LEONA FERGUSON, HILDA FRIEDLANDER, LOUISE GARCIA, KAREN GOODKIND, ROSAMOND GOODMAN, EDA GORMAIN, ANN & LENA HUDSPITH, PATRICE MANAHAN, GRACE LE TOURNEAU, FRANCES BRYSON MOORE, SALLY MORRIS, WILHELMINA ROYES, GAIL STARR AND CYNTHIA SQUIRE.

LIBRARY OF CONGRESS CATALOG CARD NUMBER: 67-22014
MANUFACTURED IN THE UNITED STATES OF AMERICA

Contents

Introduction

$\mathcal{E}$VER SINCE the 1930's, at least, it has been apparent that festivals should flourish in North America not only because there is so much to celebrate here, but also because of improved transportation, the shorter work week, longer vacations with pay, and labor saving devices on farms and in homes, offices, and factories.

In the late 1960's their prospects for prospering are more promising than ever, because labor saving devices and leisure continue to increase, and the continent is criss-crossed with broad highways and skyways.

The festivals included in this book are all sorts of events to which people go to have fun. They usually reflect the cultural, economic, historical, religious or social aspects of communities.

To dramatize these and other themes many sponsors of festivals throughout North America still rely on the pulling power of parades to attract crowds of spectators. Quite often they are justified in doing so. Nevertheless, fashions in festivals here are changing perceptibly.

The trend is away from milling about in a midway atmosphere, and toward a contemplation of the arts in community cultural centers and on college campuses. So, during the 1960's attention is shifting from allegorical street processions to allegory depicted in the dance, drama, films, music, painting and sculpture.

Evidently this is a tribute to the raising of the educational level, because even at beauty pageants where, quite properly, the emphasis has always been on beauty rather than brains, these days the enthusiasm for higher education is almost equally emphatic. For in addition to receiving the traditional titles and ornamental trophies, today the winners, from Miss America to Miss Teenage America, are also awarded substantial scholarships.

It is hoped that FESTIVALS U.S.A. & CANADA will encourage Americans and Canadians, as well as their thousands of guests from abroad, to get up and go to the festivals which suit their fancy.

May it also serve writers, photographers, researchers in the humanities and allied disciplines, and all others who find festivals a source of inspiration for creative activity as well as fun.

ROBERT MEYER, JR.

New York, New York

Agricultural Festivals

NATURE HAS generously provided Americans and Canadians with myriad opportunities to celebrate her bounty. We have often responded with dancing in the street, yet we could do so even more often than we have. For wherever there are sturdy stands of blossoming fruit trees and other signs of renewal among cultivated crops, there is the promise of the harvest to come. When the crops are ready the promise has been fulfilled. Both occasions are worthy of festivals.

Apple seeds and transplants are supposed to have been brought to the Massachusetts Bay Colony by the British during the first half of the seventeenth century, about 150 years before Jonathan Chapman, who is much better known as Johnny Appleseed, was born in New England in 1774. He is the patron saint of apple lovers because he planted trees wherever he went, and he went as far west as Pennsylvania, Ohio, Indiana, and Illinois. In Pennsylvania he sold or gave apple seeds or saplings to pioneers pushing westward. Then he, too, sailed along the Ohio in canoes filled with bags of appleseeds, and stopped along the way to plant the seeds when he found likely places for orchards. Before he died near Fort Wayne, Ind., in 1847, he had roamed the Midwest for some forty years, tending the trees he had planted and aiding the people who had put in their own orchards. Now during the fourth week in September there is an Apple Festival at Jackson, Ohio, in the territory Johnny Appleseed traversed. Begun in

1937 to celebrate the bumper crop of apples Jackson County had that year, the party was such a success it became an annual event to honor farmers. Traditional attractions are a parade of floats and marching bands, an abundance of apples, and lots of apple cider.

At Burton, Ohio, so many apples are converted into apple butter the community bases a festival on it around the third week in October. On the green before a village museum visitors can buy apple butter, fritters, homemade bread, and apple syrup made on an open fire.

Only six years elapsed between the inauguration of the Michigan Cherry Festival at Traverse City in 1924 and its designation as the National Cherry Festival in 1930. Both the Cherry Festival and its companion, the Cherry Blossom Festival in mid-May, were the dream children of Jay P. Smith, a newspaperman in the Grand Traverse Bay Region, who recognized the importance of the cherry crop to Michigan's economy. Now the Cherry Festival's five-day program each July offers a talent contest, orchard tours, a baking contest, parades, boat races, and a cherry pie eating contest.

Orientals are believed to have cultivated oranges more than 2,000 years before Christ was born, and Columbus is reported to have brought them to America in 1493. Now oranges and other citrus fruits thrive in Arizona, California, Florida, and Texas, despite the fact that groves are being plowed under to make way for houses and industrial plants. While there is still sufficient citrus to see, and the heady perfume from waxy-white blossoms sweetens the night air, March is a good month to visit Arizona, California, and Florida. The first grove of importance in California may have been planted at the San Gabriel Mission around 1804 by Franciscan friars who brought the fruit up from Lower California and Mexico. Some seventy years later a Presbyterian missionary sent several budded orange trees to the country from Bahia, Brazil, and two of them went to Mrs. Eliza Tibbets, in Riverside. From those trees, it is believed, the Washington naval orange indus-

2

try grew. One of the mother trees still flourishes on a site enclosed by an iron fence and designated by a marker. Every year it is seen by thousands of visitors, many of them en route to the National Orange Show at San Bernardino, Calif. Inaugurated in 1911, the show has been staged annually in March, except during war years. Usually visitors gaze at thousands of kumquats, pomelo, grapefruit, oranges, lemons, and limes. Well-known professional entertainers perform, and there are 4-H fairs, queen contests, flower shows, art shows, rodeos, and a fun zone with rides.

The Florida Citrus Exposition, organized in 1924 and still an annual event for a week in mid-March at Winter Haven, Fla., was transformed into the Florida Citrus Showcase in 1965. Its new home is a mammoth domed structure covering four of the site's sixteen acres. Major events, besides the display of choice fruit, are the selection and crowning of a queen.

Date groves are dwindling in Arizona and Southern California, the only region in the United States where dates are grown commercially, because it is more profitable to supplant date palms with houses and industrial plants. However, the National Date Festival inaugurated at Indio, Calif., in 1935, continues to attract more than 200,000 visitors during the third week in February. The attendance record of 253,691 visitors was set in 1963. Total attendance at the 1966 festival was 206,754. Traditional attractions are camel races, an Arabian Nights Pageant, a Babylonian bazaar, displays of dates, citrus fruits, livestock exhibits, a horse show, carnival midway, gem and mineral show, and date-flavored delicacies, such as ice cream, milk shakes, and sweetmeats.

Grapes and wine are symbols of California, and most of the vineyards and wineries there are accessible to motorists. The great desert wine area of the San Joaquin Valley is along US 99, and the six counties in the valley produce a prodigious volume of wine. Other grape and wine districts spread fanwise around San Francisco, the Napa and Sonoma districts to the North, the Alameda-Contra Costa districts to the East, and the Santa Clara-San Benito-Santa Cruz districts down the peninsula to the south. Since California grows more grapes than any other area in North America, it follows that it should celebrate with the most grape festivals. Some of the celebrations, such as those at Lodi and Sonoma in September, and San Anselmo in October, are complete vintage festivals in themselves. Others are staged as part of agricultural fairs. Grapes and wines are prominently displayed at the big California State Fair each September in Sacramento, and some can be tasted by adults. Regular vintage festival features include barbecues, barrel races, folk and general dancing, horse shows, photographic contests, reunions, and rodeos.

The annual Grape Festival and Wedding of the Wine and Cheese at Nauvoo State Park near Nauvoo, Ill., has an intriguing background. In 1839, Joseph Smith, the Mormon prophet, retreated with his followers from Missouri to Illinois and settled in a town named Commerce. They bought several hundred acres of land there and in 1840 renamed the community Nauvoo, which is Hebrew for "beautiful place" or "pleasant land." Orson Spencer, who taught Hebrew in Nauvoo during the Mormon era, may have influenced the prophet to change the name of the community from Commerce to Nauvoo. Originally the place was an Indian village called "Quashquema." Then it was known as Venus before it was named Commerce. In 1846 the Mormons were driven from Illinois, and Nauvoo was deserted for about three years when some French communists moved into the vacant buildings. Their communal colony did not last long either, but some Frenchmen remained. Soon they were joined by Germans who had migrated to Illinois to plant grapes, and this venture succeeded. In the late 1930's, about one-hundred years after the Mormons rechristened the town, an annual Grape Festival was begun there to celebrate the harvest in September. Because Nauvoo also produces cheese a traditional attraction of the fête is the wedding of the wine and

4

cheese. As a rule, the program also includes a pageant, parade, coronation, and displays.

Naples, N. Y., is the center of a prosperous vineyard area, so every year since 1960 the state's century-old grape-growing heritage is celebrated with a parade, coronation ceremonies, a ball, and judging of local grapes. The three-day Grape Festival is timed for about the last week in September to take advantage of the harvest and the flaming foliage which brightens the Finger Lakes area in autumn.

The Welland Ship Canal, which bisects the fruit-growing Niagara Peninsula, just across the Niagara River from New York, to link Lake Erie and Lake Ontario, courses between vineyards thick with grapes. To climax the harvest Canadians and their guests gather at St. Catherines, Ont., during the last week in September for the annual Niagara Grape and Wine Festival. They go to enjoy parades, street dances, selections of a king and queen, barbecues, and wine-tasting parties. A particularly popular event is the Pied Piper Parade in which youngsters wear funny or fancy costumes.

Penticton, in the fertile Okanagan Valley, is the peach capital of British Columbia. It has been celebrating this blessing with a four-day Peach Festival around the first weekend in August since 1948. The highlights are a parade, coronation ceremonies, a regional fair, a rodeo, and square dancing. The square dance is a warm-up for the big separate Square Dance Jamboree which invariably attracts some 5,000 participants to a 25,000-square-foot dance floor outdoors. It has followed on the heels of the Peach Festival since 1954, so many attend both.

Peanut growers from about thirty communities in southeastern Alabama have been gathering in Dothan around the fourth week in October to participate in the National Peanut Festival organized there in 1938. In 1966 the program included a beauty pageant, carnival, fair, Man and Woman of the Year Banquet, parades, and a peanut recipe contest.

A persimmon pudding contest is a high spot of the annual

Persimmon Festival at Mitchell, Ind., during the last week in September. Often more than 200 puddings compete for cash prizes at the celebration inaugurated in 1947. Puddings and fresh persimmons are sold, and there are exhibits.

One of the oldest continuous festivals in the United States is the Pumpkin Show during the fourth week in October at Circleville, Ohio. It began on a small scale in 1903 when a merchant displayed some corn fodder and pumpkins in front of his store for decoration. Others adopted the idea, and within a few years the show was embellished with pie-baking and vegetable-growing contests. Now the schedule includes parades, pie auctions, pie-eating contests, band concerts, and booths where you can buy such pumpkin flavored refreshments as soup, burgers, soft drinks, pie, milk shakes, fudge sundaes, cookies, waffles, doughnuts, and candy.

At Cosby, Tenn., on the fourth Sunday in April since 1953, a Ramp Festival has been dedicated to "the sweetest tasting and vilest smelling plant that grows." The celebration which features food, music and speeches also serves as a homecoming and reunion amid the spectacular scenery of the Great Smoky Mountains.

The Raspberry Festival which has been an annual event at Hopkins, Minn., since 1935, often includes raspberry pancake breakfasts, a barbecue contest, frog-jumping competitions, wrestling matches, a carnival, and a queen contest. It takes place around the third week in July.

The National Raisin Festival at Dinuba, Calif., during the last week in September, is a convincing example of how a community celebration can reinforce a staple of the local economy. The first Raisin Day staged in Dinuba, in 1911, was intended to boost the raisin industry which had fallen on bad times. While some interested parties merely moaned about the sad situation, others whipped up advertising and publicity campaigns to improve it. At first the major Raisin Day celebrations were those in Los Angeles and Fresno, but they withered while the Dinuba edition in the heart of the San

Joaquin Valley raisin belt prospered. Now Dinuba's harvest holiday is one of the largest food festivals in the United States. The highlight is a parade in which local high school bands and floats from nearby communities are featured. There are also a coronation, a barbecue, and a raisin pie-baking contest.

Since 1911 the residents of Walnut Creek, Calif., have been celebrating the local walnut harvest with a festival late in September. Usually there is a queen contest, marathon race, songfest, fashion show, contest for children, a parade, folk dancing, and band concerts.

Rocky Ford watermelons and cantaloupes from Rocky Ford, Colo., in the Arkansas Valley, have enjoyed a fine reputation for flavor at least since the 1880's. Senator George W. Swink, who founded Rocky Ford in 1871, began developing the melons in 1877, and originated Watermelon Day there in 1878 when he gave a watermelon to each passenger and crewman on a Santa Fe train. After that Senator Swink's melons bcame increasingly popular, and Watermelon Day is still the standout attraction on the Saturday of the four-day Arkansas Valley Fair the last week in August. Often the governor of Colorado presents the first watermelon to the oldest surviving member of the late Senator Swink's family. The remaining estimated 100,000 pounds of melons are given to fair visitors.

In 1966 the leader among eleven states in which maple syrup is produced on a commerical scale—Maine, Maryland, Massachusetts, Michigan, Minnesota, New Hampshire, New York, Ohio, Pennsylvania, Vermont, and Wisconsin—was New York. Of the total 1,231,000 gallons of syrup produced by all the states in 1965, and sold for about $7,320,000 in 1966, New York produced some 410,000 gallons of syrup and collected an estimated $2,112,000. To celebrate this sweet fact Schoharie County, N.Y., where there were about two dozen producers and a reported 3,000 persons employed in the industry, staged its first annual Maple Festival on the Village Green, Jefferson, N.Y., on April 30, 1966. The cele-

7

bration started with a pancake breakfast, then there were movies about the maple industry, a display of maple products, tree tapping, an antique show, a pancake-eating contest, a demonstration of taste testing, tree planting, a baked ham lunch, and a crowning of the festival queen.

A folktale attributes the accidental discovery of maple syrup by two American Indians to a family squabble. One day the squaw is supposed to have asked her brave to fill a cooking utensil with water. He demurred, whereupon she placed the pot at the base of a maple tree and returned to her wigwam. Angered because his wife expected him to perform such a menial chore he gouged the tree with his tomahawk and left. The next morning the Indian woman retrieved the pot, found that it contained enough liquid which she mistook for water to cook some venison, cooked the meat in the syrup, and that day became the first squaw in the forest to perform such an exotic culinary experiment. Sometimes the legend of maple syrup is told at appropriate celebrations in Myersdale, Pa.; Chardon, Ohio; Vermontville, Mich.; Aniwa, Wis.; and Monterey, Va. Early in April is the customary time for the Maple Syrup Festival which has been a regular event at Chardon since 1926. The festival was launched to promote the interests of producers of maple products, and now draws considerable crowds. The setting is a public park that has plenty of maple trees. It is converted into a veritable sugar camp during the festival, and several methods of making syrup are demonstrated. There are also exhibits of maple products, a parade, displays of antiques, and free entertainment.

The Maple Syrup Festival in Vermontville, Mich., usually held on the last Saturday in April, was inaugurated in 1940 just to dispose of several hundred gallons of maple syrup in the area. Since the party became an annual event it often offers band concerts, movies, dances, and a meal of pancakes, maple syrup, sausage, and coffee for a bargain price.

Iced carrot sticks for appetizers, a carrot recipe contest, carrot crate races, a drag race, a parade, a beauty competi-

8

tion, and displays are familiar attractions at the Carrot Carnival staged annually in mid-March since 1947 at Holtville, Calif., which calls itself "The Carrot Capital of the World."

Every five years since 1934 on Labor Day Weekend the people of Polish descent who grow large crops of onions in Orange County, N.Y., gather at Pine Island, N.Y., to celebrate with an Old World folk festival. Because most of the farmers are Polish-Americans, Rev. John S. Felczak, a Catholic priest who originated the quinquennial celebration, decided to pattern it after harvest time observances in Poland. There the festival is a feast of thanksgiving at the conclusion of a bountiful harvest. In the old days, at least, harvesters in the Old Country led by a pretty peasant girl presented to the lord and lady of the manor a wreath of flowers entwined with onions and tied with ribbons, a symbol of God's bounty. Then the oldest peasant usually addressed the lord and lady, and asked the priest's blessing upon the harvest and the people. The host greeted the people with bread and honey, and after accepting the gift he would invite everyone to celebrate. At the Orange County Onion Festival it is customary to reenact the tableau and have several hundred celebrants perform the Goralski, a dance of the Carpathian mountaineers, and other Polish folk dances and songs. Shortly after the festival in 1964 a fire in the muckland area near Florida, N.Y. severely damaged the soil surface, but the damage was not considered permanent if onion growers counteracted certain fertility problems which resulted from the fire. In the intervening years since the fire much of the producing land is said to have recovered quite well.

For two days around the third weekend in October, Crowley, La., the rice capital of the nation's major rice belt, is the scene of the International Rice Festival. Inaugurated in 1937, the festival usually features a creole rice cooking contest, a parade, pageant, and sports.

In 1938 the producers of sugar in the bayou country of southwest Louisiana, the nation's sugar bowl, launched a

Sugar Cane Festival. Thousands of Acadians still turn out for it in September to see crop blessing ceremonies, parades, concerts, coronations, and pageants.

The 1965 Green County Cheese Days at Monroe, Wis., was a revival of a festival inaugurated in 1914 in the community which likes to be known as "The Swiss Cheese Capital of the USA." It had been staged only about seven times between its inaugural and 1940 when it was sidetracked by World War II until 1950. It came back strong in 1955, but because it attracted an estimated 100,000 visitors which overwhelmed the community of less than 10,000 population the event was discontinued indefinitely. When the sponsors risked a revival in 1965, attendance was as great as it had been in 1955, but the pressure from overcrowding was reduced because during the preceding decade many motels and restaurants had been erected within comfortable driving distance of Monroe, and the state's highway system had been expanded considerably. In August, 1965, an estimated 130,000 persons attended the celebration which featured Swiss entertainment, a kids' parade, a drum and bugle corps contest, gymnastics, and a Swiss Cheeseland Festival Parade. The festival was not held in 1966, but one was scheduled for September, 1967.

Rural Olympics is an appropriate name for the Antelope Valley Fair and Alfalfa Festival which got going in earnest at Lancaster, Calif., right after World War II. The Rural Olympics on the Saturday of the fair early in September features tractors driven by ranchers and their wives. They drive the vehicles over a mile-and-one-eighth obstacle course, then the winning team and its tractor race a quarter horse. The horse usually wins. There are also three-horse relay races, harness races, a rodeo, hay loading, and truck and trailer backing contests.

Despite the gigantic strides agriculture has made in the twentieth century it has not outdistanced the need for plowing. Down-to-earth Canadians remind us of this each October when they stage the International Plowing Matches somewhere in Ontario Province. Probably the largest outdoor agricultural event of its kind in Canada, its exhibit area covers approximately fifty acres and accommodates an estimated 300 exhibitors. Various types of farm equipment are displayed, and 500 acres of land are usually reserved for plowing competitions, parking and demonstrations. During the four-day event some 600 plowmen compete for prizes worth about $15,000. The matches originated in 1911 when sponsors of local contests founded a Provincial Association. The first international match was run in 1913, and has been held annually since, with the exception of the war years. Sites are selected by county invitation four or five years in advance of the meet. In 1966 the venue was Seaforth, Ont.

When the Threshermen's Reunion of the Western Industrial Development Museum is staged in Saskatoon, Sask., in June or July many of the museum's exhibits come alive. The occasion is called Pion-Era. It revives memories of industrial pioneering in Saskatchewan and other provinces of western Canada by putting into motion once again early model steam threshers; autos with tiller steering, rope drive, and rear entrance; and horse-drawn school vans and hotel busses. Food stalls sell such old-time favorites as bread baked in outdoor ovens.

Arts Festivals

For more than a generation before the vaunted cultural explosion of the 1960's in North America, substantial festivals of the arts were being firmly established there. In 1936, the College Chapel of St. Laurent was the birthplace of the Montreal Festival which has developed into the pièce de resistance of the city that is not only the largest in Canada, but also lays claim to being the cultural as well as the commerical, financial, and industrial center of the Dominion. These days, as a rule, all concerts and other events are held in the Grande

Salle of the Place des Arts, where the Montreal Festivals Society has permanent offices. Typical of the fifteen or more musical events which are presented each year might be a concert version of "Opera d'Aran," by the French composer and singer, Gilvert Becaus, Haydn's "Les Saisons," a concert by pianist Robert Casadesus, classical music by a symphony orchestra, and Count Basie presenting a program of jazz music. Also on the agenda might be a foreign films series, an art exhibition featuring Canadian painters, and a display of cartoons in August.

In November 1942, the University of Texas, at Austin, celebrated the dedication of its new Music Building with the inauguration of a Fine Arts Festival in which soprano Rose Bampton participated. By 1966 the festival had progressed to the point where it filled eight days, Nov. 13th to 20th, with impressive offerings in five cultural categories—architecture, art, concerts, dance, drama, and opera—and interlaced the featured offerings with lectures, forums and films. In architecture an exhibition stressed "The Independence of Environment and Activity," and Paul Rudolph, former Chairman, Department of Architecture, Yale University, talked about "Changing Concepts of Architecture" one evening. Eight pieces of sculpture by Henry Moore were part of the collection of Mr. and Mrs. Ted Weiner in the University Art Museum. Concerts were played by Gary Kerr, string bass, the New York Woodwind Quartet, and the Smetana String Quartet. There were five performances of "The Prodigal Son" and "The Pied Piper," two dance dramas choreographed by Shirlee Dodge, with music by Lothar Klein. The operas were Cimarosa's "Il Maestro di Cappella" and Carlisle Floyd's one-act "Markheim." Composer-director Floyd directed his opera and also lectured on "Problems in Writing Opera."

Among the enduring community arts festivals which have made the most of a novel, time-tested attraction is the annual Festival of Arts and Pageant of the Masters sponsored by the art colony of Laguna Beach, Calif. There visitors see convinc-

12

ing impersonations of characters and scenes from artistic masterpieces posed by men, women, and children of the community. Begun in 1931 as a two-week attraction, and discontinued during World War II, the 31st annual festival was staged from July 8 through August 14, 1966. That season there were twenty-seven tableaux in all, among them The Caryatids from the Porch of the Maidens on the Acropolis, and two contrasting studies of the same subject: Salvador Dali's "The Sacrament of the Last Supper," and the perennial local favorite, da Vinci's "The Last Supper." Also, the 1966 festival displayed the works of numerous ceramists, painters, photographers, sculptors, woodcrafters, and handicrafters, which were offered for sale. Also, there were free-for-all art classes for children, an exhibition of painting by young people, and a puppet show for them.

A Festival of Contemporary Arts was inaugurated on the Urbana Campus of the University of Illinois in 1948. Staged biennially during odd-numbered years, in February, 1965 a major event was the display of contemporary painting and sculpture. Also, there were concerts as well as demonstrations, exhibitions, and lectures in art, architecture, literature, music, and the theatre.

For about 10 days late in July, at Inspiration Point Fine Arts Colony, Eureka Springs, Ark., a Fine Arts Festival started in 1950 climaxes a six-week music theatre camp. Then high school and college students entertain with operas, symphonies, ensembles, dance, and drama.

The White Mountains Festival of the Seven Arts, at Pike, N. H., has presented artists, musicians, novelists, playwrights, poets, professional theatre people, and vocalists for at least two weeks in mid-July since 1950. Winners of the Metropolitan Opera Auditions typify the calibre of artists who have taken part in the festival.

Each year since 1952, art enthusiasts of Brimingham, Ala., have saluted the arts of their home state as well as those of other countries with a week-long springtime Festival of Arts.

13

Between April 22nd and May 1st, 1966, the arts of Alabama, Belgium, Luxembourg, and The Netherlands were honored with an arts parade, displays of architecture and literature, and ballet and drama performances.

An Arts Festival originated in 1955 is now staged at the Museum of Art in Philadelphia, Pa., for three weeks late in May and early in June. Highlights include ballet, music, opera, and theatre in the admission-free Theatre Under the Stars; on the mall at the rear of the museum are an outdoor sculpture show, exhibitions of works of Philadelphia artists under forty-five, and those of distinguished artists of the Greater Philadelphia area over forty-five; a ballet is performed on the great staircase; pertinent displays in several wings of the museum and the presentation of awards are also part of the Festival.

The Nova Scotia Festival of Arts at Tatamagouche, N. S., was established in 1956 as a showcase of Nova Scotia arts and crafts. Usually a four-day festival in mid-August, it presents actors, dancers, musicians, and singers. One year the Canadian performers included pianist John Newmark and Neil Van Allen, humorist Rich Little, and vocalist Diane Davis. Canadian Festivals of Art are staged also at St. Felicien, Quebec, during the second week in May; in Regina, Sask., in mid-May, late June, and early July; and in Moose Jaw, North Battleford, Weyburn, and Yorkton, Sask., in October.

At the Fine Arts Fiesta inaugurated at Wilkes-Barre, Pa., in May, 1956, there are performances by the Wilkes-Barre Philharmonic Orchestra, the music and drama departments of the local public schools and colleges, choral societies, and the ballet guild.

In July, as a rule, three to four weeks are devoted to the vibrant Vancouver Festival, Vancouver, B.C., where it has been an annual cultural event at the Queen Elizabeth Theatre and Playhouse since 1958. There is at least one attraction every day of the limited season. It might be an orchestral concert, a ballet, a musical, or a play. In 1966 the festival paid tribute to youth in British Columbia's Centennial Year. The theme was validated by performances of Humperdinck's opera "Hansel and Gretel," the English musical "Oliver," the North American premiere of a comedy by Henry Livings titled "Big Soft Nellie," and the Bolshoi Ballet. Pianist John Ogden was heard in a concert with the Vancouver Symphony Orchestra and an augmented Vancouver Opera male voice choir. Mireille Lagacé performed an organ concert of music by Bach, and there was an evening of National Film Board productions.

Free concerts, theatre, ballet, art exhibits, and workshops in the arts make up the Fine Arts Festival program which was inaugurated at Fort Wayne, Ind., in 1958, and usually takes place during the last week in May.

The principal attractions at the eighth annual Rhode Island Arts Festival at Providence, R. I., late in May and early in June, 1966, were nationwide open competitions of painting, sculpture, prints, and drawings.

During the second week in April, Savannah, Ga., is the site of the Coastal Empire Arts Festival, inaugurated in 1960. That cultural exposition includes art and photography competitions and architectural displays in a city famous for its architecture. Tours of attractive buildings and special displays recall the eighteenth and nineteenth centuries, and entertainment usually includes ballet, symphonic music, little theatre plays, concerts, and square dancing.

At the Arts Festival inaugurated at Waterbury, Conn., in 1961, and now staged late in July, as a rule, spectators watch ballet and theatrical performances and listen to symphonic chamber music and jazz concerts.

Conductors associated with the Fine Arts Festival, Jackson Hole, Wyo., which was inaugurated in 1962, are all guests well known in the Rocky Mountain area. While symphonic music dominates the festival, which is staged regularly in July and August, an art show, children's concerts, Indian dances, and chamber music also are on the agenda. One of the

15

chamber music sessions might be called a Watermelon Concert because tables are set up in the Auditorium and free watermelon is served before the performance and during the intermission.

The dignity of the title "Congregation of the Arts" is matched by the quality of festival programs presented in Hopkins Center, Dartmouth College, Hanover, N. H., from about the fourth week in June through the third week in August every year since 1963. The honor of opening the music program of the 1966 festival was given to Peter Mennin, composer, who remained as composer-in-residence through July 10th. Two other composers in residence who shared the season with him were Boris Blacher and Witold Lutoslawski. Highlights of that year included the American debut of Gerty Herzog playing two Blacher piano concerti; William Sydeman conducting the world premiere of his viola concerto commissioned by Hopkins Center, with Ralph Hersh as soloist; and Easley Blackwood supervising the world premiere of his oboe concerto, also a Hopkins Center commission, with Alfred Genovese as soloist. There were world premiere performances of works by Carlos Chavez, Milko Keleman, and Lutoslawski, as well as first American performances of works by Lutoslawski and Blacher. In addition to the musical events there was the presentation of four plays by a repertory theatre company, art classes and exhibits, and films.

Four days of festive activities at the Fine Arts Festival, Annapolis, Md., provide a showcase for area talent and help stimulate interest in the performing arts. Inaugurated in 1963, the festival usually takes place during the third week in June. The 1966 program offered art demonstrations, ballet, children's theatre, choral groups, drama, interpretive dance, jazz, literature, and marching bands.

Eventually many colleges and universities in North America and elsewhere will recognize and use the extraordinary

16

opportunities which abound on their campuses to fashion fine festivals. Among the schools which joined the growing list of festival-conscious colleges and universities in 1964 was Stanford University, Stanford, Calif. The Stanford Summer Festival of the Arts was obviously planned with great care to set admirably high standards. By its own admission, "The University senses keenly its obligation within both the local and international communities; i.e., to serve as a fosterer and preserver of the arts, and as the agent through which quality artistic presentations can be made available to an appreciative public at lowest possible costs." To accomplish this it created the festival "to invigorate the summer academic offering of the University, as an international cultural focus for the Western United States, and as wide an audience beyond this as would find interest in an all-encompassing performing arts festival."

In 1964, some seventy events in seven weeks developed the Shakespeare theme. Major participants were Shakespeare companies of the Oregon Shakespearean Festival, Ashland, Ore., and the National Shakespeare Festival, San Diego, Calif.; the Actor's Workshop, San Francisco; the Stanford Players; counter tenor Alfred Deller; balladeer Richard Dyer-Bennet; an exhibit of Treasures from the Plantin-Moretus Museum, of Antwerp, Belgium, and performances by the Institute of Renaissance Music. During eight weeks in 1965 the festival presented "the first major exposition of Mozart in the United States." Outstanding participants included the Stuttgart Chamber Orchestra conducted by Karl Muenchinger, the American debut of the Opera da Camera da Milano, the West Coast debut of the New York City Opera Company, pianist Paul Badura-Skoda, the Amadeus Quartet, the Baroque Comedy Workshop featuring actors from "The Committee," and an exhibit of Bibiener Family theatre designs. The third annual Stanford Summer Festival of the Arts opened on June 22, 1966, with the American debut of Conductor Ernest Ansermet and l'Orchestre de la Suisse Romande. The ten concerts played by the orchestra at the festival between June 22nd

17

and July 5th constituted its only appearance in the United States that year. The theme of the festival was "Twentieth Century Innovations." It was personified by the Swiss Orchestra, pianists Grant Johannesen and Bruno-Leonardo Gelber, violinist Johannes Bruning, soprano Bethany Beardslee, the Lenox String Quartet, the American Conservatory Theater Company, exhibits, a film series, lectures, audience briefings and seminars. The plays performed by the American Conservatory Theater Company were "Charley's Aunt," "Under Milk Wood," "Death of a Salesman," "Six Characters in Search of an Author," "Uncle Vanya," "Misalliance," "Tiny Alice," "Endgame," and "Beyond the Fringe." Retrospective films included "Paris, 1900," "Metropolis," "The Childhood of Maxim Gorky," Greta Garbo in "Camille," Marlene Dietrich in "The Blue Angel," Rene Clair's "Under the Roofs of Paris," and three documentaries, "Song of Ceylon," "Night Mail," and "Listen to Britain."

A Fall Festival of the Arts in 1965 marked the opening of the Owen Fine Arts Center and the beginning of a year-long celebration of the fiftieth anniversary of Southern Methodist University, Dallas, Tex. In October 1966, most of the events at the second annual festival took place in the Center. On the program were the Japanese Noh Theatre, the American premiere of "Leonora," the SMU Chorus-Dallas Symphony presentation of "King David," a concert by pianist Alfred Mouledous, an exhibit of French Art in Texas, four concerts in observance of the Bach Year, and concerts by the University Concert Band, the University Choir, and artists sponsored by the American Guild of Organists.

July 8th, 1966 was the date on which the Saratoga Performing Arts Center began its career as the home of the Saratoga Festival, Saratoga Spa State Park, N. Y. Then, too, it became the summer home-away-from-home for the New York City Ballet and the Philadelphia Orchestra. The ballet company opened the center with a performance of "A Midsummer Night's Dream." The 110-foot-high stage-house and the 5,000-

seat amphitheater are under cover. An additional 7,000 persons can be accommodated on the lawns around the building. The ballet company of sixty-six dancers and fifty-three musicians under the direction of George Balanchine and Lincoln Kirstein entertained during the first four weeks. The Philadelphia Orchestra conducted by Eugene Ormandy held forth during the second four weeks. Guest conductors that year were Seiji Ozawa, Thomas Schippers, and William Steinberg. In addition to ballet, symphony concerts and concert versions of operas, the Saratoga Festival offered chamber music and film masterpieces of the silent and sound eras.

An art contest and exhibition, concerts by the Oscar Peterson Trio and the Marquette University Band and Chorus, lectures by John Browning and W. D. Snodgrass, the Marquette University Players in "The Bald Soprano," the film "Through A Glass Darkly," and showings of Charlie Chaplin and W. C. Fields films comprised the program for the Fine Arts Festival inaugurated in March 1966 at Marquette University, Milwaukee, Wis.

Puerto Rico's first Inter-American Festival of the Arts took place in San Juan, March 24 to April 6, 1966. On the schedule were several evenings of music, films, and ballet, an architectural exhibit at the University of Puerto Rico Museum, and an art display at the Institute of Puerto Rican Culture. The Inter-American Festivals originated in Washington around 1954. They serve as a sounding board for new musical and dramatic works and as a showcase for new works of art.

Beauty Pageants

THE PACEMAKER for beauty competitions throughout the world is the renowned Miss America Pageant staged at Atlantic City, N. J., from Tuesday through Saturday immediately after Labor Day, the first Monday in September. From the very beginning this contest, and others fashioned after it since the inaugural one in 1921, was intended to publicize a locality and even products with which the winners might become identified. For many years the emphasis was on pulchritude, and even though physical attractiveness is still the motivating influence for entering the competitions, since World War II just having a fetching feminine figure is not enough. The girls must also have talent. In four out of five major contests staged in the United States each year the top prizes are scholarships. When the annual bathing beauty show was introduced at Atlantic City less than three years after the end of World War I, what was inside the heads of the lovely ladies was of little or no concern to the sponsors or the spectators.

The first twelve young women who competed for the title of "Miss America" were enrolled because they were bathing beauties. The first to wear the crown was Margaret Gorman, "Miss Washington, D.C." The innkeepers and merchants of Atlantic City cared a lot less about what the contestants thought than what they looked like, because the show was staged to extend summer business at the resort one full week beyond Labor Day. Soon the annual spectacle included a float parade in which the beauties were displayed along the boardwalk, a Miss Personality Contest, and an American Beauty

Ball. Now the contestants are judged for beauty, personality, and talent.

The Miss America Pageant Scholarship Foundation was inaugurated in 1945 when Bess Myerson, who captured the Miss America title, was the recipient of a $5,000 scholarship award. In addition, two scholarships of $1,000 and $750 were donated for the First Runner Up and the Most Talented Non-Finalist in 1945. Since 1946, local and state pageant committees have joined the scholarship awarding program and have distributed a total in excess of $6,000,000 in scholarship monies at their own pageants. Contestants are judged in evening gown, swim suit, and talent, as well as on the basis of personality and intellect. Also, the sincerity, good taste, poise, dignity, personality, and intellect of the contestants are considered during interviews with the judges. Therefore, the sponsors of the Miss America Pageant do not consider it a "beauty contest." Rather, they regard it as "a competition where beauty, talent, personality and intellect are the primary requisites; and educational scholarships are the rewards."

The total estimated value of scholarships distributed annually in the fifty Miss America state preliminaries and the finals is $450,000, of which $250,000 is contributed by the Pepsi-Cola Company and its 550 bottlers. The scholarship awarded Miss America is valued at $10,000. Approximately $40,000 more is distributed among other finalists. Also, the reigning Miss America can expect to earn $75,000 for public appearances. The winner of the scholarship and the prospect of economic security that went with the title Miss America 1966 was "Miss Kansas," Deborah Bryant, who was nineteen years old, five-foot-seven-inches tall, and weighed 115 pounds. A resident of Overland Park, Kansas, she was enrolled at Kansas University, studying to become a pediatrician. Scholarship awards were increased at the national level in 1967. Then every state contestant, regardless of placement in the nationals, was awarded a minimum $500 scholarship. This, coupled with the $1,000 Pepsi-Cola scholarship won at the state level, assures each state winner $1,500 in scholarships to continue her education.

The idea of a Miss Universe Beauty Pageant was dreamed up in 1950, but it did not become a reality until 1952, at Long Beach, Calif. In 1960 the contest was transferred clear across the country to Miami, Fla., where it can usually be seen for about ten days beginning in mid-July. More than seventy-five beauties from as many countries compete. The contestants participate in a Parade of Friendship and ride in convertibles along Flagler St. and up Biscayne Blvd. An exotic event is the presentation of the contestants dressed in the costumes of their native lands. Awards are given for the best native costumes, for Miss Amity, and to Miss Photogenic, who is chosen by the press. The winner of the Miss Universe Pageant receives $10,000, plus a contract valued at $10,000 for personal appearances during her reign, and several valuable prizes.

Perhaps the longest established of the regional beauty contests is the Miss Dixie Contest staged at Daytona Beach, Fla., late in June and early in July. In 1946, exactly twenty-five years after the first nationwide beauty contest in Atlantic City, Floridians adopted the idea. As in Atlantic City, the beauty pageant staged by the Jaycees of Daytona Beach was put on to pep up summer visitor business there. To become eligible for a $1,500 college scholarship and some 30 other prizes, contestants must have placed first or second in another major contest, and must be from Alabama, Arkansas, the District of Columbia, Florida, Georgia, Kentucky, Louisiana, Maryland, Mississippi, Missouri, North Carolina, South Carolina, Tennessee, Texas, Virginia, or West Virginia. To emerge victorious the winner must garner the most points by making impressive showings in the bathing suit, evening gown, talent, I. Q., and personality divisions. Scholarships were introduced the first year when $100 was given to the winner of the event.

During the first twenty years of the Miss Canada Pageant,

which was originated in 1946 and is usually staged around the second week in November, at least half the title winners have claimed Ontario as their home province. Contestants are the twenty-six regional winners from Newfoundland to British Columbia. Gifts, prizes, and cash for each Princess average about $1,000, with Miss Canada receiving as much as $25,000 worth of awards. She also travels an estimated 100,000 miles during the year of her reign. Linda Douma, of Sidney, B.C., Miss Canada 1965, was the first titleholder to travel abroad. She visited Hong Kong and Japan as part of a trade travel mission. In 1963, when emphasis in the competition shifted from grace of face and form to talent and education, a Miss Canada Scholarship Foundation with scholarships worth a total of $5,000 was established as an independent, non-profit organization "to reward deserving candidates and provide a means to further their education and training in areas of their choice. Diane Landry, of St. Boniface, Manitoba, Miss Canada 1966, used her $1,000 scholarship to further her musical studies.

The Miss Dominion of Canada Beauty Pageant inaugurated in 1957 takes place, appropriately enough, on Dominion Day, July 1. It is usually staged in the Grand Ballroom of the Sheraton Brock Hotel, Niagara Falls, Ont. Girls from throughout Canada compete for the title and earn the right to represent Canada in world-wide pageants. Miss Dominion of Canada tours on behalf of civic and commercial projects arranged for her by the pageant. The sponsors do not offer scholarships, nor do they stress talent among the contestants.

America's Junior Miss Pageant at Mobile, Ala., each spring, developed in 1958 as an off-shoot of the annual Azalea Trail Court. The court originally honored only high school seniors from Mobile. Later representatives of southern communities, local and state Junior Chamber of Commerce organizations began sponsoring community and state pageants to select a Junior Miss from each state. The winners go to Mobile for a week-long pageant in mid-March. All the pageants stress the importance of education by offering college scholarships which now are reported to exceed $300,000 annually on the local, state and national levels. Scholarships totaling $10,000 were awarded by the sponsors the first year the pageant was staged. In addition to the $300,000 in scholarships currently being distributed an estimated $90,000 worth of merchandise and grants goes to specific state-supported institutions of higher learning. The judges do not score "pulchritude" at any level. The Junior Misses are rated on "physical fitness, scholastic achievement, poise and appearance, character, ambitions and goals, community service, activity in the church of their choice and awareness of others in relation to themselves." The reigning Junior Miss makes personal appearances during the summer, on weekends, and during vacation periods during the school year, but the schedule is planned to avoid interrupting the continuity of her education. While the appearances are primarily on behalf of the pageant itself, or the national sponsors, America's Junior Miss does occasionally make an appearance for a local civic club for a fee and expenses. The runners-up, as well as state Junior Misses, follow the same procedure within their own states. However, none of the Junior Misses directly endorses any products, even for the national sponsors.

The newest competition among comely misses in the United States is the Miss Teenage America Pageant which originated in Dallas, Tex., in 1961, and moved to Nashville, Tenn., in 1967 when the LIN Broadcasting Corporation of Nashville purchased Teen America Associates, Inc. Since its inception, the pageant has offered some $75,000 in scholarships to contestants. The new owners of the pageant plan to award $17,000 in scholarships to the top four girls. Miss Teenage America will win a $10,000 scholarship, and three runners-up will receive $4,000, $2,000, and $1,000 respectively. The winner of the title is expected to be an above-average student who participates in extracurricular activities, is a leader, and is usually a very attractive young lady. In the competition she is judged equally for intelligence, poise, appearance and talent, the latter quality serving to indicate her abilities in such creative arts as narrator, performer, vocalist, musician, or writer. After winning the 1967 Miss Teenage America contest, Sandy Roberts was scheduled to travel some 350,000 miles to make approximately 105 appearances. All told, the remaining finalists were to cover another 350,000 miles to make 250 appearances.

Community Festivals

THE CELEBRATIONS described in this chapter are called Community Festivals because they were either created to publicize communities or they have become more closely identified with them than with any of the specific subjects to which chapters have been assigned. The Mummers' Parade is a remnant of Philadelphia's English heritage. Mardi Gras is synonymous with New Orleans. The Seafair promotes Seattle's importance as a port and a place for aquatic fun. In this chapter the events are grouped according to the months in which they usually take place, with the older festivals being presented first, as a rule.

JANUARY

The Mummers' Parade, normally staged in Philadelphia, Pa., on Jan. 1st, is one of the oldest community celebrations in America, since its inception has been traced to about 1650. However, the contemporary version dates only to Jan.

1, 1901, when the City Council, recognizing the publicity possibilities inherent in a swarm of gaudily bedecked men parading about town, offered cash prizes for the most elaborate costumes, if the motley crews would team up and stage a well-organized procession. So, now early on New Year's Day, or the following Saturday if bad weather interferes, hundreds of Philadelphians don voluminous silk and satin raiment and towering plumed headpieces to march en masse until nightfall. Annual awards these days are reported to total about $40,-000. Competing for the cash are some 15,000 members who prance to the music of two dozen string bands, which are a world famous fixture of the processions.

FEBRUARY

Happily, midwinter is brightened by Mardi Gras, or Shrove Tuesday. Because the exact date of Mardi Gras is determined by the date of Easter each year, between now and the year 2,000 it will be celebrated as early as Feb. 7th, or as late as March 7th. Such celebrations, which began in North America at Mobile and New Orleans as one-day events around 1830, are proliferating and lengthening. However, New Orleans still reigns as king of the Mardi Gras cities. Throughout the Carnival Season in New Orleans, which begins officially on Twelfth Night, Jan. 6th, there are at least five dozen private masked balls in the Municipal Auditorium. During the final week of Carnival, Orleanians stage a dozen major float parades and don masks for a grand finale. In addition to the long-established festivities in New Orleans, Mobile, Ala., and Biloxi, Miss., Fat Tuesday funfests have sprung up in Boca Raton, Fla.; Lafayette, La.; Brownsville, Tex.; Matamoros, Mex.; on Olvera St., Los Angeles, and in the shadow of the Franciscan Mission Santa Ines, Solvang, Calif. What's more, in Puerto Rico plans are underway to shift the emphasis on carnival capers from the San Bautista Festival around St. John's Day in June to the pre-Lenten period in February or

March, when Christians are supposed to have their final fling before the forty days of penitence.

Pancake races on Shrove Tuesday, the day before Ash Wednesday when Lent begins, are gaining in popularity. Although pancakes are believed to have become Shrove Tuesday fare at least 1,000 years ago, the contemporary practice of flipping pancakes in competition grew out of an incident in Olney, England, around 1445. Then a local woman, late for church, absentmindedly raced to service with a skillet and pancake. Since 1950, women of Liberal, Kansas, have been competing with women of Olney in a 415-yard, pancake-flipping dash. Impressive prizes are awarded the winner of the contest in Kansas.

Young men of Tampa, Fla., became carnival conscious around 1904, and chose the legendary pirate José Gasparilla as their patron. The big day of the week-long Pirate Invasion is the second Monday in February when Ye Mystic Krewe of Gasparilla sails its stately three-masted schooner into Tampa's port amid myriad smaller craft in full dress. Pirates dash ashore, board floats, parade around town, and wind up at the annual Florida State Fair. Their torchlight procession is usually on Thursday night in Ybor City, Tampa's Latin Quarter. The pirate ship departs in a blaze of fireworks on the following Saturday night.

The birthday of America's own bringer of light, Thomas A. Edison, is celebrated during the second week in February with a Pageant of Light at Fort Myers, Fla., where he spent his winters. There are a King and Queen of Edisonia, a Parade of Light, a children's parade, flower shows, turtle races, and an Edison Birthday Party.

Gold Rush Days in Wickenburg, Ariz., are recalled each February with panning for gold in the Hassayampa River, pony express races, a simulated massacre, and a parade.

Kernville, Calif., on the shore of Lake Isabella, celebrates its gold rush period late in February with a community festival called Whiskey Flat Days. It got its name from the practice of

27

bartenders whose bars were flat planks supported by two barrels. Now there are old-time fiddlers' contests, mule races, pet parades, tours of old gold mines, Boot Hill epitaph writing contests, and an authentic 1860 costume competition.

MARCH

Several Florida communities prolong their winter tourist season by staging celebrations in March. Bradenton, near where the Spanish explorer, Hernando De Soto, landed with 600 men on May 30, 1539, has decided that mid-March is the best time to mark the discovery at De Soto National Park. Local men dress up as sixteenth century Spanish grandees, push ashore on shallow draft craft, stage a mock battle with other citizens impersonating Indians, attend sports contests, an art show and dances, and applaud the novelty of orange-colored snow on the courthouse lawn.

At Sarasota, Fla., a community named for the daughter of Hernando De Soto, King Neptune rules his own Frolic during the last week in March. Usually he appears first at a clambake laid on between a water-skiing exhibition and a fireworks display. His week-long fiesta also features a folk festival as well as aquatic events.

Among the more ambitious community celebrations in Florida each spring is the Festival of States, which usually climaxes the winter season in St. Petersburg around the last week in March and the first week in April. At the festival in 1966, spectators were entertained by aerialists in action, bands, concerts, baton twirling, a coronation ball, fencing, festival royalty, Grotto Night, lawn bowling, sailing regattas, a shell show, and senior and junior parades.

APRIL

Several cities in the sun play host at community festivals in April. The Merry Monarch Festival, inaugurated in Hilo,

Hawaii, in 1965, salutes the fun-loving King David Kalakaua, Hawaii's last ruler who reigned from 1874–91. Appropriately, pageantry, parades, dancing, and feasting are on the agenda.

The Tucson Festival, Tucson, Ariz., always staged during the week following Easter because the Easter ceremonial dances performed by the Papago and Yaqui Indians are a major attraction, was launched in 1951 for civic, educational, and philanthropic purposes, and to cultivate and encourage creative activity in various arts and sciences particularly appropriate to the Southwest section of the United States. The sponsors of the festival make the most of their city's proximity to San Xavier del Bac Mission, the "White Dove of the Desert," and dramatize with an admission-free pageant its founding by Franciscan missionaries in the eighteenth century. During an evening under the stars on the Friday after Easter bells toll, Papago and Yaqui Indians dance around mesquite bonfires, torchlight-toting conquistadors on horseback whoop it up as they gallop into the mission yard, a procession of worshippers lights its way with candles while reciting Indian chants and Spanish hymns, and a "Castillo," a large image of the Virgin of Guadalupe outlined with fireworks, is ignited on a nearby hill. Indian and Mexican foods are sold. Back in Tucson at other times during the festival there are a craft fair, children's parade, Mexican street fair, a forum, a pioneer jubilee, art show, flower show, and plays.

In New Orleans, La., during the two-week Spring Fiesta in April or May, young ladies wear capacious costumes of bygone days as they serve as hostesses for a series of tours of antebellum city and country houses. The fiesta's theme capitalizes on distinctive local features, such as a parade and candlelight parties in the French Quarter for "A Night in Old New Orleans," and modern jazz concerts in the midst of contemporary art exhibits in the same neighborhood.

Until recently, what is now the San Antonio Fiesta, in San Antonio, Tex., was the San Jacinto Fiesta, honoring the defeat of General Santa Anna's Mexican troops by General Sam

29

Houston's forces along the San Jacinto River on April 21st, 1836. For some ten days encompassing that anniversary, San Antonio's Alamo, "Cradle of Texas Liberty," is the focal point of probably the most elaborate annual festival in Texas. An impressive Battle of Flowers Parade is staged in daylight. There is a tremendous torchlight parade, and debutante daughters of wealthy Texans splurge on elegant court dresses. The young women take part in extravagant tableaux depicting fanciful themes. Miss Fiesta and her alternates are chosen by popular ballot from Incarnate Word College, Our Lady of the Lake College, and San Antonio College. There are coronation ceremonies and military reviews, but the most distinctive activities, as far as local Latin flavor is concerned, take place at La Villita, the Little Town of the oldest residential section of the city.

Oklahomans have a fond regard for April 22nd, the anniversary of the Land Rush in 1889 when white settlers were permitted to settle in Oklahoma Territory. Guthrie, Okla., marks the occasion with a three-day celebration. In April or May, Guymon salutes the Organic Act of May 2, 1890, when the Oklahoma Panhandle, a No Man's Land, was opened to settlers.

The mayor of Corpus Christi, Tex., inaugurates Buccaneer Days by walking the plank one day in April or May. Then the spring vacation season is enlivened with carnivals, parades, fireworks, sports events, beauty pageants, a coronation, dances, and water sports.

South Carolina sprouted a Spring Festival in Columbia, in April, 1964. An art show, concerts, house and garden pilgrimage, and sports events are staged for seven days when flowers for which the Palmetto State is well known usually are in bloom.

A festive tribute to Valentine Day, Feb. 14, 1912, at St. Thomas, V. I., fostered so many happy memories it served as the inspiration for the annual Carnival inaugurated there in 1952, and still staged the last week in April. The St. Thomas

Carnival features the election and crowning of a king and queen, calypso and steel band competitions, dance exhibitions, parades, and tramps, tramps, tramps, the Virgin Island word for tramping in rhythm behind steel bands.

MAY

As the sun moves northward, festivals which are at their best when the climate is salubrious increase noticeably. In Delaware, the first Saturday in May is dedicated to Dover Day, and the third Saturday is for A Day In Old New Castle. Each community draws on its wealth of well-tended Colonial homes, antiques, heirloom silver, and boxwood gardens. Often period dances are performed on the village greens.

Memphis, Tenn., calls its community festival "The Nation's Party in the Land of Cotton." Staged regularly during the second week in May since 1931, the Cotton Carnival begins in the grand manner when the brightly illuminated royal barge bearing the king and queen and their court ties up by the Monroe St. dock along the Mississippi River. As a rule the governor of Tennessee and other dignitaries are in the welcoming party. During the carnival there are parades, a regatta, tour of homes, one admission-free dance on the ceremonial barge, and balls.

Among the activities which enliven the Capt. Cook Festival on Hawaii's Kona Coast in mid-May are canoe and tiki-carving demonstrations, lei-weaving demonstrations, tapa-making demonstrations, ancient hula recitals, exotic floral arrangements, canoe races, a billfish tournament, an explorers' ball, and a luau for visitors.

JUNE

In June, 1954, New York became the first metropolis in America to cash in each summer on the festive qualities of its existing entertainment facilities. By adding little more than a

31

festival queen, a festival hostess, and a bit of hoopla, the New York Convention and Visitors Bureau began boasting that "New York Is A Summer Festival." The slogan has merit, because numerous long-established open-air concerts, year round professional theatre on and off Broadway, and exhibits at museums, generate more festive fun throughout New York's so-called low season than many cities can whip up at the height of their high season. New York City is so cosmopolitan, to put its visitors from foreign lands at ease, the bureau publishes its visitors' guides in eight languages: English, French, German, Italian, Japanese, Portuguese, Russian, and Spanish.

From mid-June through Labor Day civic leaders of Wash., D.C., strive to put the city's visitors into a jubilant mood by weaving permanent and seasonal attractions into a Summer Jubilee. Reservations are recommended for the Marine Corps Evening Parade on Fridays at nine P.M., Marine Barracks, 8th and I Streets, S.E. Retreat parades are staged monthly at nearby Fort Myer, Va. There are torchlight tattoos, President's Cup aquatic events, and concerts, and drama.

Although kings as political entities are not associated with life in the United States, in Hawaii, June 11th is a public holiday in honor of King Kamehameha who united the islands and ruled Hawaii from 1790–1819. The statue of the revered monarch in Honolulu's Civic Center is draped with twelve-foot plumeria leis. There are parades, luaus, commemorative pageants, and a formal Holoku Ball.

The lure of sun and fun encouraged Myrtle Beach, S. C., in 1952 to title its summer shindig by the sea the Sun Fun Festival. Activities at the celebration in June include a sand castle building tournament, parade, regattas, fishing contests, and aquatic events.

The romantic appeal of Indian lure and Niagara Falls were the inspiration for the Maid of the Mist Festival inaugurated at Niagara Falls, N. Y., in 1956. After staging it in autumn for nine years, and in July for two years, the sponsors have now made the festival the season-opening event each June. In 1966 there were Indian ceremonials, a variety show, street dance, a musical titled "Once Upon a Rainbow," a fashion show, family picnic, parade, ball, and Baby Pocohantas-Hiawatha contest.

Since Pensacola, Fla., is a major U. S. Naval Air Station, it is fitting that the Navy's famous Blue Angels, aerobatic specialists, should zoom across the skies during the city's "Fiesta of Five Flags" in June. The Spanish, French, British, American, and Confederate flags are the five which have flown over Pensacola. On land, during the fiesta, there usually is a treasure hunt; a reenactment of the arrival of Don Tristan de Luna, in 1559, some sixty-one years before the Pilgrims landed at Plymouth Rock; a parade; and fireworks. At sea there are regattas and scuba diving.

Life on the farm is recalled vividly in Rogue River, Ore., on a weekend in June, when the annual Rooster Crowing Contest takes place there. As many as 2,000 spectators have gathered to hear some 150 roosters crow for cash. At the inaugural contest in 1953, within half-an-hour one bantam crowed 109 times, and won $150 for his owner.

Early in this century the people of Nome, Alaska, began celebrating the longest day of the year by staging a Midnight Sun Festival on June 21st. Often the entertainment includes Eskimo dances, athletic contests, blanket tossing, a parade, and raft racing on the Nome River.

JULY

Circuses featuring animal acts, clowns, and trapeze artists in tents are believed to have been introduced in the late eighteenth century, at least a generation before Phineas Taylor Barnum was born in Bethel, Conn., on July 5, 1810. However, Barnum's name became synonymous with the big top when his circus, "The Greatest Show on Earth," which he opened in Brooklyn in 1871 when he was more than sixty

33

years old, became an overwhelming success. Before that, Barnum served as mayor of Bridgeport, Conn., and in the Connecticut Legislature, which are other reasons why since 1949 the people of Bridgeport have been celebrating the anniversary of his birth with a Barnum Festival that lasts from about June 25th to July 5th, as a rule. A ringmaster sets the pace for a "Jenny Lind" contest, a circus parade on July 4th, a Wing Ding for youngsters, antique auto competitions, and a Ballyho Show of Stars.

On July 4th, 1963, what might be termed a second gigantic community Barnum birthday celebration, along with the one at Bridgeport, Conn., was inaugurated in Milwaukee, Wis. The title of the citywide celebration is "Old Milwaukee Days," and its theme is pure late nineteenth century circus. Its rolling stock and props come from the authentic Circus World Museum in Baraboo, Wis., where Ringling Bros. Circus had its winter quarters for thirty-four years. The main attraction is the parade with 170 purebred Percherons, Belgians, and Clydesdales; three dozen historic circus parade wagons; five dozen clowns; and two dozen bands. Now "Old Milwaukee Days" lasts five days, or longer. The circus train arrives the first day, and the gaudy red, gold, and silver wagons and circus souvenirs are displayed at the show grounds for the duration. The Schlitz Brewery sponsors the festival.

Maine ballyhoos its estimated $78 million annual poultry industry income with a Broiler Festival at Belfast for two days in mid-July. A public barbecue, Maine chicken cooking championship, sheep shearing, and wool spinning are featured at this community event which dates to 1948.

The legendary Indians, Hiawatha and Minnehaha, immortalized in Longfellow's epic poem, "The Song of Hiawatha," are enshrined in Minnehaha Park, hard by the laughing waters for which the maiden was named, in Minneapolis, Minn. Other laughing waters in almost two dozen lakes in the city's public parks system inspired the creation of an annual Aquatennial in 1940. Appropriately, one of the first events on the ten-day program in July is a three-day canoe race in which

34

Indians paddle on the Rum River from Fort Mille Lacs to Minneapolis, thus connecting the state's fabled 10,000 lakes with the city. Also on the program are parades and personal appearances by entertainers such as Bob Hope and Gene Autry. The number of individual community activities scheduled at the Aquatennial would be a challenge to any community festival.

At Henderson, Minn., Sauerkraut Days has been an annual event since 1930. At the celebration during the latter part of July the townsfolk and their guests join in a kraut eating contest, select a queen, watch parades, and dance in the street.

During Days of '47, the Mormons' annual tribute to the cross-country trek their forebears made in 1847, period fashions in clothing and transportation are displayed in the big Pioneer Parade on the streets of Salt Lake City. Other communities in Utah also remember that it was on July 24, 1847, that approximately 150 Mormons led by Brigham Young found the place for which they had been searching. The cities and towns stage rodeos, concerts, and religious meetings.

The blessings of Puget Sound which affect the economy and recreation of Seattle, Wash., are hailed during the city's annual ten-day Seafair late in July and early in August. The festival created by Greater Seattle, Inc., in 1950 features impressive parades, an aqua show, a Japanese Bon Odori party, Scottish Highland Games, a Scandinavian Frolic, and a Fiesta Filipina. However, the activity which attracts attention around the world is the unlimited hydroplane race at Lake Washington which brings the festival to an exciting climax.

Among the off-beat community celebrations is the International Brick and Rolling Pin Throwing Contest on the third Saturday in July, at Stroud, Okla. It is an international event because on the same day citizens of three other communities named Stroud—in Gloucestershire, England; Ontario, Canada, and New South Wales, Australia—stage similar contests. Men throw five-pound solid patio bricks furnished to all

35

contestants here and abroad by Stroud, Okla. Women throw two-pound hardwood rolling pins made of Brush Boxwood, and manufactured in New South Wales from trees in a vast hardwood forest, and supplied to all contestants by Australia. There are also "Champions of Champions" events in all categories. In Stroud, Okla., there is also a Miss Bricktop Contest to select the most beautiful Oklahoma redhead, age 17–22. The international contest was inaugurated in 1960.

AUGUST

Baby parades have been standard events in New Jersey each August since the first one was presented in Ocean City in 1906, and another began in Wildwood in 1910. Youngsters competing for prizes ride on miniature floats, push doll carriages, or pull wagons with animals in costumes. In 1966 there were Baby Parades at Avalon, Ocean City, Sea Isle City, Stone Harbor, and Wildwood.

One of America's more famous resort cities by the sea, Atlantic City, N. J., calls attention to the personnel of local hotels and restaurants by staging a Skills Day Derby in August. Waiters move faster than ever as they juggle food-laden trays in a race on the boardwalk, maids compete in bed-making contests, chefs carve turkeys, display ice sculpture, prepare fancy cake decorations, and even turn out pastel pizzas for pizza pie twirling contests.

Food often affords inspiration for community festivals. The people of Sheboygan, Wis., on the shore of Lake Michigan, have built a celebration around the bratwurst, a sausage of German origin, which has become a local specialty. For one day in August, usually the first Saturday, while the aroma of barbecued bratwurst permeates the air, the celebrants listen to music, watch regattas, a parade, and a queen contest.

At Grand Haven, Mich., on the eastern shore of Lake Michigan, during a three-day Coast Guard Festival staged to salute the birthday of the U. S. Coast Guard on Aug. 4th, ships of this fleet are open to visitors, there are parades on land and on Lake Michigan, a water thrill show, and a kite flying contest.

To publicize the little known fact that their community has in the nearby Highland Lakes an abundance of water for recreational purposes, in 1962 the people of Austin, Tex., put together a lively Aqua Festival. Staged annually for ten days in mid-August when water sports have great appeal, the Aqua Festival offers on the lakes a canoe race, Aquacade and Water Follies, spearfishing contests, open water swimming meet, an illuminated water parade, stock boat races, and a sailing regatta. On land there are sheepdog trials, beauty contests, a parade, model and sports car contests, a Dixieland Jubilee, dances, a golf tournament, and a gospel sing song.

A festival to glorify Chicago's Lakefront is usually held during the third week in August. On the program are parades on land and on Lake Michigan, the crowning of Miss Chicago, the arrival of Neptune, swimming races, a regatta, music in Soldier Field, pipe bands, and drum and bugle corps championships.

Corn-on-the-Curb Days were inaugurated at LeSueur, Minn., in 1959. In 1966 an estimated 20,000 festival goers consumed twelve tons of corn and several hundred pounds of butter. Some twenty persons participated in a corn-eating contest, the winner of which ate nine ears of corn in three minutes. There were also parades, a queen contest, and drum and bugle demonstrations.

Gold Discovery Days at Custer, S. D., late in August, gives the whites and the Indians of the area an opportunity to recall the period when the town sprang up soon after gold was discovered there in the 1870's.

SEPTEMBER

The pedigree of the three-day Santa Fe Fiesta over Labor Day weekend in Sante Fe, N. M., dates to 1712 when the

Marques de la Penuela, Governor and Captain General of the Province of New Mexico, decreed that the Elevation of the Holy Cross and the bloodless reconquest of the city of Santa Fe by General Don Diego de Vargas in 1692 be fittingly observed. His proclamation bound all successors to follow suit. It is traditional for the celebration to begin with the burning of Zozobra, "Old Man Gloom." During the rest of the festival Indians perform tribal ceremonials, there is much Mexican music, a solemn march to the cross of the Franciscan friars martyred in the Indian rebellion of 1680, a pageant in which De Vargas rides again into the city to plant the cross and the royal banner of Spain once more in the plaza before the Palace of the Governors. The fiesta usually ends with a parade caricaturing prominent persons and events.

Box Car Days at Tracy, Minn., on Labor Day, was inaugurated in 1927 when box cars were the primary means of transporting food and other commodities across the nation. That is why civic leaders of the community, mindful that the town's railroad yards were crowded with trains loaded with grain, decided to honor the vehicle that performed such noble service. As a rule the festivities include a parade, horse show, a coronation, and free entertainment.

OCTOBER

A study in contrasts among community festivities during October emphasizes the diversity of themes in the United States and Canada. For while New England, the Maritime Provinces, and other regions along the Canadian-U. S. border are bright with flaming fall foliage, on Pacific islands studded with coconut palms and pineapples, Hawaiians weave a festival around their favorite word, "Aloha," a friendly welcome. Aloha Weeks are scheduled on all the islands, with the principal celebrations taking place around Honolulu and Waikiki Beach, on Oahu Island, about the third week in October. The other islands are Hawaii, Kauai, Maui, and Molokai. Pageants depict Hawaii's royal past, and on Oahu there is a Hawaiian songfest, street dancing by costumed Polynesian, oriental, and western entertainers, a flower parade, an outrigger canoe race from Molokai to Waikiki, an exhibition of poi-pounding, tapa-making, lei-stringing, hala-weaving at a recreated Hawaiian grass-thatched village in Ala Moana Park, a formal Monarchy Ball, and an informal Barefoot Ball.

As Hawaiians display their birthrights in the 50th state, the people of Alaska celebrate the birthday of the 49th state. Ceremonies marking the transfer of the recently purchased Alaska from Russia to the United States took place at Sitka on Oct. 18, 1867. A reenactment of the Changing of the Colors —lowering of the Czarist Russian flag and raising of the Stars and Stripes—is a traditional happening. The program might also include an historical pageant, "In This Place," parades, reviews, a memorial service at Sitka National Cemetery, native dancing, song recitals by the Russian Orthodox Cathedral Choir, and the Castle Ball at which residents wear costumes of 1867. The site of Old Sitka, where the Russian Baranof established a city later razed by Indian Massacre, is a Registered National Historic Landmark. So is Castle Hill, with its old Russian cannon still pointing toward the island-dotted Pacific Ocean.

A ball is one of two major events of the two-night Veiled Prophet festivities in St. Louis, Mo. It is primarily a formal, private affair reminiscent of the old-line New Orleans Mardi Gras balls. The similarity between the two celebrations is enhanced by the typical Mardi Gras float parade the second night. In fact, civic and social leaders took their cue from the New Orleans festival back in 1878 when they sought ideas for a community celebration which would counteract the negative influence of post-Civil War despondency and a yellow fever epidemic which had plagued the Mississippi Valley. The Veiled Prophet, a mythical character from a make-believe Kingdom of Khorassan, became the personification of merriment, and adopted as his motto, "Laughter keeps step with progress."

Although there are antique sales galore throughout Canada

and the United States, the one staged annually in October at Millerburg, Ohio, is probably the only one around which a festival has been built. Known officially as the Holmes County Antique Festival, it features a fireman's parade, queen contest, a procession of antique cars and marching bands against a backdrop of store windows stocked with items of ancient vintage. October is also fall foliage time in Ohio.

Converting tobacco leaves into smokable products is the leading industry in Richmond, Va., the self-styled "Tobacco Capital of the World." So, each October the city is a logical place for the annual week-long National Tobacco Festival which was inaugurated in 1949. The party begins with a grand ball, then adds a fashion show, tours of tobacco factories and James River plantations, lunches and receptions, a Tobacco Spectacular, band concert, illuminated parade, Tobacco Bowl football game, and the Tobacco Ball.

NOVEMBER

Just because they felt that their community needed a festival some citizens of Charlotte, N. C., dreamed up one in 1947, christened it Carolinas' Carrousel, and have been promoting it around Thanksgiving ever since. Major activities are a coronation ball and a Thanksgiving Day parade.

DECEMBER

Colonial Williamsburg, Va., is one community which was literally resurrected to sell itself. A pet project of the late John D. Rockefeller, Jr., it was his aim to restore the once opulent capital to its original attractiveness so that it would provide a convincing demonstration of eighteenth century gracefulness and graciousness in America. He spent millions of dollars to realize that ambition. Now throughout the year there are several pertinent seasonal events at Williamsburg, one of which is the old English Christmas. It was inaugurated in

1934, the first year of a formally "open" Williamsburg, and the outdoor decorations were colored lights on eight evergreen trees. The next year candles in the windows supplanted the electric lights on the trees, which eventually created the "white lighting" for which the town has become known. Some 2,000 candles brighten the way to the Christmas open house, musical events, tagging the tree, firing of Christmas guns, a yule log ceremony, and a torchlight parade through the community to Merchants' Square where cookies and cider are served.

Crafts Festivals

ALTHOUGH THE noblest accomplishments of craftsmen's fairs are the convincing demonstrations of pride in workmanship and the rescuing of vanishing arts from oblivion, they can also add to the festive life of communities by presenting entertainment and food long identified with the area. The prevailing interest in crafts fairs can be traced to the depression years of the 1930's. Representative of the undertakings in this field which took root in that bleak era and continued to grow in better times is the League of New Hampshire Arts and Crafts. Created in 1931 with the enrollment of a few craftsmen, the League is reported to have increased its membership to approximately 3,100. It entertains and instructs about ten times that many people who visit its five-day fair at Mt. Sunapee State Park during the first week in August, because demonstrations and lectures supplement displays of the winter's efforts. Products on display range from minor gift items to major pieces of furniture, silverware, hand-printed and handwoven fabrics, rugs, and jewelry. All articles made for sale are first judged for excellence of technique and design. In 1966, the thirty-third annual fair featured demonstrations

41

in rug hooking, pottery, wood carving, silk screen printing, crewel embroidery, and displays of Early American decoration, as well as a concert by the string Ensemble of the New Hampshire Music Festival Orchestra.

The York State Craft Fair, Ithaca, N. Y., is staged during the first week in August. Inaugurated in 1959, its sponsors emphasize its educational aspects and morning workshops in at least four crafts. They like to draw on the talents of experts such as Fong Chow, the Assistant Curator of the Far East Wing of the Metropolitan Museum, who demonstrated ceramics at the fair for two years and was also honored as a featured craftsman.

Craftsmen of nine Southern highland States have been gathering in Asheville, N. C., for five days in mid-July each year since 1948 to display their skills and creations. Folk dancing and music enliven the event which includes work on stained glass, enameling, pottery, wood carving, basket weaving, jewelry making, block printing, pewter smithing, marquetry, knotting and fringing, weaving, and crafting dulcimers of cherry, butternut, sassafras, chestnut, and maple.

Southern Highlands craftsmen from Virginia to Georgia have been showing off their wares at Gatlinburg, Tenn., annually since 1948. Now during the third week in October they also show how it is done, making baskets, brooms, and chairs, creating thread from flax or fleece, handlooming, using iron dye pots and vegetable dyes, blowing glass, woodworking, and using out-of-the-ordinary native materials for decoration. Folk dances and music of the region also are presented.

Folk singing and dancing in costume have been daily features of the Arts and Crafts Festival at Fairhope, Ala., in March since it was started in 1953. There are demonstrations of pine needle crafts, ceramics, net-making, pottery-on-wheel, polishing rocks and semi-precious stones, and shell craft. Added attractions include crowning of the Dogwood Queen, since the festival is staged when dogwood is in bloom, and a home and garden pilgrimage, horseman's show, and a play.

For several days during the last week in October, when fall foliage is particularly attractive in the Ozark Mountains, craftsmen from Arkansas, Missouri, and Oklahoma, gather in War Eagle, Ark., to stage the Ozarks Arts and Crafts Fair, inaugurated in 1954. There are demonstrations of doll-making, leather tanning, and wood carving. Barbecued chicken is served.

The Old Town Plaza, Albuquerque, N. M., has been the site of a four-day Arts and Crafts Fair the last week in June since 1962. Indian and Spanish motifs are featured, and there are also performances of Indian and Spanish dances. Troubadours roam the area, Indian bread and traditional Spanish foods are sold, and there are pinata parties and fast draw contests.

The Missouri Festival of Ozarks Craftsmen established in Branson, Mo., in 1963, is a mid-October event. Among the native arts and crafts demonstrated there by specialists are candle-making, gunsmithing, ironworking, log hewing, meat smoking, shingle splitting, soap-making and sorghum production. Coon meat and persimmon might be on the menu.

At the second annual Bond's Alley Arts and Crafts Show, Hillsboro, Tex., during the last week in June, 1966, there were an open air show of handicrafts and paintings from Central Texas, jazz concerts, and a book stall. The display of books was a logical adjunct to this annual exhibition because it was organized by the Hill County Library, which also realizes any profit from the undertaking.

In Newfoundland, there usually are Homecrafts Exhibitions at Harbour Grace in September and at St. John's in October.

Dance Festivals

Modern dance became firmly established in New England when Ted Shawn began presenting weekly concerts during the summer of 1933 at Jacob's Pillow, near East Lee, in Massachusetts' Berkshire Mountains. However, the current Jacob's Pillow Dance Festival, featuring pantomime, modern and ethnological ballet, was launched nine years later, in 1942. The ten-week season lasts from late June until the end of August. In 1966 it offered the East Coast debut of the San Diego Ballet, Edward Villella and Company, Glen Tetley and Company, the First Chamber Dance Quartet, Murray Louise and Company, Maria Alba Spanish Dance Company, Myra Kinch and Company, Jean Leon Déstinée and Company, and the Jacob's Pillow Dancers.

New England's position in the field of modern dance has been enhanced by the annual American Dance Festival, which was staged for the first time in August, 1948, at Palmer Auditorium, Connecticut College, New London, Conn. The festival was inaugurated by the N. Y. U.–Connecticut College School of the Dance to give students and visitors an opportunity to see contemporary works performed by their creators. An adjunct of the School of Dance, it has sponsored the premieres of quite a few contemporary classics. In the festival's first nineteen years its sponsors either commissioned or gave premiere performances to some ninety new dance works. Among them were Martha Graham's "Diversion of Angels" and "Secular Games," Doris Humphrey's "Night Spell" and "Fantasy and Fugue," Jose Limon's "The Moor's Pavane" and "The Traitor," Merce Cunningham's "Antic Meet," and Paul Taylor's "Aureole."

44

Representative of the type of performances at the annual World Dance Festival inaugurated at Columbia University, New York City, in 1955 and usually presented early in March are the American Negro Folk Group, El Grupo Folklorico de Costa Rica, the East Indian dancer Larry Landau, Suzushi Hanayagi of Japan, and the Ukrainian Dancers of Astoria.

Since 1956 when the first Southeastern Regional Ballet Festival was staged in Atlanta, Ga., three other regional dance festivals have begun. The Northeast Regional Ballet Festival was co-sponsored for the first time in 1959 by the Ballet Guilds of Scranton and Wilkes-Barre, Pa. The Southwestern Regional Dance Festival got started in Austin, Tex., in 1963, and the Pacific Western Regional Ballet Festival began at Sacramento, Calif., in 1966. The Gala Program is only one part of any festival. It is just the icing on the cake for the dancers, teachers, directors, and board members of all the regional ballet companies concerned. Panel discussions, board meetings, dance classes conducted by famous teachers, and showings of dance films help make the festivals very important for everyone who belongs to a Regional Ballet Festival Association.

Cities of the Southeastern Region in which festivals have been staged since the first one in Atlanta in 1956, include Miami, Fla., 1957; Birmingham, Ala., 1958; Miami, Fla., 1959; Atlanta, Ga., 1960; Louisville, Ky., 1961; Orlando, Fla., 1962; Jacksonville, Fla., 1963; Nashville, Tenn., 1964; Memphis, Tenn., 1965, and Orlando, Fla., 1966. Ballet companies that performed at the 1966 festival were Constance Hardinge's Concert Ballet, of Bristol, Va.-Tenn.; the Nashville Ballet Society; Miami Ballet; Southern Ballet, of Atlanta; Ruth Mitchell Dance Company, of Atlanta; Atlanta Civic Ballet; Ballet Royal; and the Birmingham Civic Ballet. Cities of the Northeast Region in which festivals were staged during 1960–66, include Erie, Pa., 1960; Dayton, Ohio, 1961; Schenectady, N. Y., 1962; Detroit, 1963; There was no festival in 1964; Ottawa, Canada, 1965, and Washington, D. C.,

1966. Ballet companies that participated in the 1966 festival included the Regional Ballet of Washington, Wabash Valley Junior Ballet, Schenectady Civic Ballet, McLean Ballet, Ballet Guild of Cleveland, Dayton Civic Ballet, Detroit City Ballet, Erie Civic Ballet, Ballet Trianon of Philadelphia, Orange County Ballet Theatre of Newburgh, N. Y., and the Ballet Imperial of Canada.

After its inaugural performance at Austin, Tex., in 1963, the Southwestern Regional Dance Festival took place in Houston in 1964, in Dallas in 1965, and at Fort Worth, Tex., in 1966. On the list of ballet companies that performed at the 1966 festival were the Austin Ballet Society, Dallas Metropolitan Ballet, Ballet Joyeux of Lake Charles, La., the Wichita Falls Ballet Theatre, the Dallas Civic Ballet, the Allegro Ballet of Houston, and the Fort Worth Ballet Association.

Ballet companies performing at the 1966 Pacific Western Regional Ballet Festival in Sacramento, Calif., were the Laguna Beach Civic Ballet, Cairns Dance Group of Tacoma, Wash., the Peninsular Ballet of San Mateo, Calif., the Dorothy Fisher Concert Dancers of Seattle, Wash., the Sacramento Civic Ballet, and the Concert Ballet of Tacoma, Wash. All the regional festivals take place between the end of March and mid-May. All correspondence and inquiries regarding any festival, or matters pertaining to civic ballet in general, should be addressed to Mrs. Deane Crockett, Secretary, National Regional Ballet Association, 3839 H St., Sacramento, Calif., 95816.

A Dance Festival has been an annual offering of the University Musical Society, University of Michigan, Ann Arbor, Mich., each October since 1962. At the first Chamber Dance Festival the program included the José Molina Bailes Españoles, Kovach and Robovsky Dance Company, and the Phakavali Dancers from Thailand. In 1966 the terpsichoreans were members of the Fiesta Mexicana, the Hosho Noh Troupe from Japan, and the Robert Joffrey Ballet.

Since 1962 the New York Shakespeare Festival has closed its

annual summer season of plays at the 2,300-seat outdoor Delacorte Theater in Central Park by presenting the admission-free Rebekah Harkness Foundation Dance Festival for at least a week late in August and early in September. Programs of classical, modern, and ethnic dance have been performed by companies from the United States and abroad. Individuals and companies that participated in the 1966 festival were Al Guang, Carmen de Lavallade, Carole Luppescu and Robert Rodham, Claire Sombert and Michel Bruel, Glen Tetley Dance Company, Haryou Dancers, Lotte Goslar and Company, Nala Najan; New Choreographers: Gus Solomons, Jr. and Judith Willis, Patricia McBride and Edward Villella, Reyes/Soler Ballet Español, Tony Lander and Bruce Marks, and Scott Douglas and Sallie Wilson/Veronika Mlakar.

At least two evenings of dance are included in the ten evenings of cultural entertainment on weekends in July and August at the Long Island Arts Center Festival in the C. W. Post College Theatre Tent, Brookville, N. Y. It began in 1963.

The second annual Harper Theater Dance Festival in Chicago, Ill., during November, 1966, gave each participating company a full week of performances. The companies, in order of appearance, were the Murray Louis Dance Company, the Boston Ballet, Lotte Gosler's Pantomime Circus sharing the bill with Daniel Nagrin, Paul Taylor and Company, Glen Tetley and Company, and the three-year-old Pennsylvania Ballet. Paul Taylor and Glen Tetley produced works having their North American premieres, and the Pennsylvania Ballet gave a completely new work, "Villon," about the French vagabond poet François Villon, by Robert Butler, with music by Robert Starer, and setting and costumes by Rouben Ter-Arutunian. Also presented were John Butler's "Carmina Burana," set to popular music; Robert Rodham's "Trio," John Taras's "Design with Strings," and "Aurora's Wedding."

Titles of Ballets presented in August 1966, at the Stephens

College/Perry-Mansfield School of Theatre and Dance Festival, Steamboat Springs, Colo., were "Papillons," with music by Robert Schumann and choreography by Rita Charisse; "Minoan Suite," music by Kenneth Klaus and choreography by Harriette Ann Gray; and "East Indian Suite."

The dance state of the United States could easily be New Mexico, because there several thousand Indians commemorate with special dances various religious events throughout the year. They begin with the Buffalo or Deer Dance to welcome the New Year on January 1st, and by December 31st they have danced their way through some three dozen ceremonial occasions.

The exact date of the Hopi Snake Dances, held in Arizona the latter part of August, is not revealed until ten days prior to the event. The organization that receives first word of the date is the Winslow Chamber of Commerce, P. O. Box 621, Winslow, Ariz.

To express enthusiasm for their native dances Hawaiians often stage a Hula Festival on the first two Sundays in August, at Honolulu, the capital of Hawaii. Hula classes sponsored by the Honolulu Board of Parks and Recreation, students at professional hula schools, and individual performers dance both ancient and modern versions.

An annual event specializing in folk dancing is the two-part Mountain Folk Festival sponsored by Berea College, Berea, Ky. The first part usually takes place on the college campus in April. The second part, or adult section, is staged in Levi Jackson State Park, London, Ky., during the last week in September.

Between early April and late October at least six nine-day Square Dance Festivals are staged at Fontana Village, N.C.

The Royal Winnipeg Ballet, directed by Arnold Spohr, danced the world premiere of "Rose Latulippe" as the featured attraction of the customary ballet portion of the Stratford Festival, Stratford, Ont., in August, 1966. The choreography was by Brian Macdonald, and the music by Harry Freedman.

Familiar settings for three dance festivals in Canada each summer are Cardston, Alta., often the locale for the Blood Indian Sundance Festival during the first half of August; Penticton, B. C., site of a mammoth Square Dance Festival around the second week in August, and Lethridge, Alta., where another Square Dance Festival takes place about the fourth week in August. The dance at Penticton is titled the British Columbia Square Dance Jamboree. Inaugurated in 1954, it is reputed to be the most popular event of its kind in Canada. Normally it attracts thousands of participants from near and far.

Drama Festivals

MORE SHAKESPEAREAN festivals are staged regularly in the United States than in any other nation. In 1964 when the 400th anniversary of William Shakespeare's birth was observed in many places throughout the world the United States and Canada were preeminent among the nations which have a fine tradition of annual Shakespearean festivals. The current vogue for Shakespearean festivals in North America began at Southern Oregon College, Ashland, Ore., when Angus L. Bowmer, a young English instructor, persuaded a group of businessmen to underwrite a festival in an abandoned Chautauqua Hall in 1935. The businessmen agreed to do so, provided Bowmer permitted "Twelfth Night" and "Merchant of Venice" to share the program with a boxing match, to forestall a deficit at the box office. However, the boxing match is said to have lost money, but the plays earned enough to cover both undertakings. Bowmer is still producing director. The season at Ashland has grown from performances on two days in 1935 to a fifty-one-day full-fledged Oregon Shakespearean Festival offering fifty-one night performances and eight matinees. The repertoire in 1966 included "A Midsummer Night's Dream," "Othello," "Two Gentlemen of Verona," and "Henry VI, Part 3." John Gay's "The Beggar's Opera" was the Festival's Music and Dance Department's offering at eight matinees in the Varsity Theatre, downtown Ashland. An hour before the nighttime performances there was a Tudor Fair with strolling musicians, singers, and dancers-on-the-green. As usual, performances were given on a full scale Elizabethan stage fashioned after London's late sixteenth century Fortune Theatre. The educational division of the festival is the Institute of Renaissance Studies. When its 1966 season closed, the festival had once again broken all its preceding records. Total attendance at the five productions was 63,106. That was 2,166 above the previous record set in 1964. Both "A Midsummer Night's Dream" and "Othello" were sold out for the entire season. Also, there were forty standing-room-only nights in 1966 compared with the previous high of thirty-seven in 1964.

The National Shakespearean Festival in Balboa Park, San Diego, Calif., traces its beginning to the California Pacific International Exposition in 1935–36, although the current annual series did not begin until 1949. That year "Twelfth Night" played twenty-two performances to fewer than 6,000 spectators. In 1966, between June 14th and Sept. 1st, the troupe of professional and semi-professional actors played 111 performances of thirty-six productions, which were seen by an estimated 37,000 viewers. That brought the total to 1,130 performances of forty-six productions, which were witnessed by 401,788 persons in a 400-seat replica of Shakespeare's original Globe Playhouse in London. On the greensward in front of the theatre for half-an-hour before each play begins there is a program of Elizabethan music and dances. In 1966 the period prologue preceded the presentations of "Romeo and Juliet," "Two Gentlemen of Verona," and "The Tempest." If a conviction of many Shakespearean specialists is correct, "The Tempest" has the distinction of being the only play the master set in the Western Hemisphere. The drama is believed to have been based on the shipwreck which led Sir George Somers and his crew of potential Virginia settlers to discover Bermuda in 1609. Accepted as evidence is the fact that the playwright had close connections with several of the Bermuda adventurers. He might even have been acquainted with the ship *Sea Venture* which piled onto the reefs that are now called "Sea Venture Flats" and are in full view of Bermuda's Fort St. Catherine. Inspiration for "The Tempest" also could have come from reading Sylvester Jourdan's "A Discovery of the Bermudas," published in 1610, or a perusal of the Bermuda wreck written by William Strachey, who was aboard the *Sea Venture* when she met disaster. Shakespeare is believed to have written "The Tempest" between the years 1609 through 1613.

Canada's Stratford-on-Avon, Ont., is the site of that country's outstanding Shakespearean Festival. The plays were first presented under a tent in 1953, and got off to a splendid start with Alec Guinness as "Richard III." Subsequently the starring roles of other plays were performed by such celebrated actors and actresses as Eileen Herlie, James Mason, Siobhan McKenna, and Christopher Plummer. The four-month season, which lasts from early June to early October, is no longer presented in a tent, but in a permanent round theatre designed by Robert Fairfield. Its unique stage was designed by Tanya Moiseiwitsch and Sir Tyrone Guthrie. Plays performed on the extraordinary stage in 1966 were "Henry V," "Henry VI," and "Twelfth Night."

At the nearby Avon Theatre audiences saw Strindberg's "The Dance of Death," Mozart's "Don Giovanni," in English;

"Nicholas Romanov," William Kinsolving's new play about the last czar of Russia; and the world premiere of the ballet "Rose Latulippe," with choreography by Brian Macdonald and music by Harry Freeman. Since its inception in 1953 the Stratford Festival of Canada has presented forty-five plays which drew a total attendance of 2,633,558. Another 494,373 persons attended musical and ballet performances. In the spring of 1967, three plays by Shakespeare and Gogol's "The Government Inspector," which were in the repertory of the Stratford Festival that year, were discussed at four evening lectures scheduled by the University of Toronto Division of Extension in Toronto.

The American Shakespeare Festival on the banks of the Housatonic River at Stratford, Conn., has been in business since July, 1955, when it opened with "Julius Caesar." Ten years and some thirty plays later the sponsors report that approximately 150,000 persons attend festival performances each year. In addition, more than 100,000 high school and college students usually attend a 9-week Student Audience program, which might be called the festival's first of two seasons each year, beginning around the end of March. The second season in 1966, June 19th to Sept. 12th, featured "Falstaff," "Henry IV, Part II," "Julius Caesar," and "Twelfth Night." Lawrence Langer was the founder of the American Shakespeare Festival. His twin goals were the establishment of a permanent home for Shakespeare's plays in the United States, and a training academy for professionals, young actors and students who could develop their talents. The repertory company takes to the road from time to time, and in 1961 performed at the White House. The theatre boasts one of the major collections of paintings, sculpture, and Shakespearean memorabilia in the nation. There is also a costume museum which depicts costume styles and periods of various Shakespearean plays.

While all Shakespearean festivals in the United States and Canada enjoy the status of nonprofit cultural organizations, in

52

order to defray expenses most of them charge admissions and sponsor associations to which members subscribe. A notable exception to this rule, however, is the New York Shakespeare Festival. Its twelve-week season of nightly performances in the 2,263-seat Delacorte Theatre in New York City's Central Park is admission free. Reserved seat tickets are distributed from the box office each evening at 6:15 P.M. for the eight P.M. show. Persons who voluntarily contribute ten dollars or more per season may reserve seats by mail. In 1966 audiences saw "All's Well That Ends Well," "Measure for Measure," "Richard III," and "Macbeth." The latter play was performed in both English and Spanish. "Potluck," a show for youngsters, was also in the repertoire. The guiding spirit of this successful top-quality undertaking is Joseph Papp. In 1954 he gathered together a group of actors who were willing to perform Shakespeare's plays for nothing. Their first performance took place in the Emmanuel Presbyterian Church on Manhattan's lower East Side. Two years later the City of New York granted the troupe the use of the East River Amphitheater, and in 1957 it moved to Central Park and used a temporary stage until the Delacorte Theatre was ready in 1962. Each June, July, and August for ten seasons, 1957–66 inclusively, an estimated 2,300,000 spectators attended 938 performances of 44 productions. Also, an estimated 75,000 students attend the shows during the company's touring season.

Just fifteen performances of a single play is the extent of the annual Shakespeare Festival inaugurated at Susquehanna University, Selinsgrove, Pa., in April, 1950. In 1966 the play was "Romeo and Juliet." Sometimes a lecture on Shakespeare is given during the festival.

The Champlain Shakespeare Festival, which the University of Vermont created in 1959 as part of the 350th anniversary of Champlain's explorations in the Northeast, has prospered so well it became an Actor's Equity Company in 1965. During the five-week season which concluded at the end of August,

1966, the new Equity members performed "Hamlet," "Henry VI, Part I," and "The Comedy of Errors" in the Arena Theatre of the Fleming Museum on the University of Vermont campus in Burlington, Vt. The 8-season score totaled 252 performances of twenty-five productions for approximately 53,500 spectators.

Drama students at the University of Miami, Coral Gables, Fla., have been credited with originating the school's Southern Shakespeare Repertory Theatre in 1961. Graduate student actors support professional actors and technicians, and the entire company helps construct sets, props, and costumes to learn their craft. Through most of July, 1966, the collegians presented in nightly rotation at Beaumont Hall on the campus "A Midsummer Night's Dream," "Coriolanus," "Macbeth," and "The Winter's Tale." The troupe averaged 4 plays per season for 6 seasons, and presented 144 performances for about 32,700 spectators.

Since the summer of 1958 a Shakespeare Festival has been an integral part of the Creative Arts Festival inaugurated at the University of Colorado, Boulder, Colo., in 1948. For their eighth Shakespeare Festival in 1966 the students staged "Coriolanus," "The Merchant of Venice," and "The Merry Wives of Windsor." Tragedy, history, and comedy have been the balanced fare offered at the outdoor Mary Rippon Theatre on the university campus during the first two weeks in August. From 1958 through 1966 almost 100,000 spectators attended 136 performances of twenty-seven productions.

In the 500-capacity open-air amphitheater of the Marin Art and Garden Center on a converted ten-acre estate at Ross, Calif., the only annual Shakespeare Festival in the Redwood Empire has been staged regularly since 1961 from about mid-July to around Labor Day. The three-play series in 1966 consisted of "Julius Caesar," "The Merchant of Venice," and "Richard III." The Center at Ross is approximately a half-hour's drive over the Golden Gate Bridge from San Francisco.

The College of Southern Utah, Cedar City, Utah, has been the site of a Shakespearean Drama Festival around the last three weeks in July since 1962. It combines professional, collegiate, and local talent to present three productions on a replica of the Fortune Theatre Tiring House stage in an outdoor theatre seating 500 persons. In 1966, the three plays presented under the stars nightly in rotation were "Julius Caesar," "Taming of the Shrew," and "Two Gentlemen of Verona." In five seasons some 22,300 spectators witnessed eighty-one performances of fifteen plays. Cedar City, in southwest Utah, is near Cedar Breaks National Monument, and not very far away from Zion National Park.

Two parts Shakespeare, one part contemporary author, is the formula for the New Jersey Shakespeare Festival, Cape May, N. J. Inaugurated in 1963, in July, 1966 the repertoire included Shakespeare's "Macbeth" and "A Comedy of Errors" and John Whiting's "The Devils," based on Aldous Huxley's novel, "The Devils of Loudun."

The three plays selected for the inaugural season of the Catskill Mountain Shakespeare Festival in Woodridge, N.Y., during April and May, 1966, were "Hamlet," "Macbeth," and "A Midsummer Night's Dream."

Someday there may be a friendly annual competition to determine the best community and college theatre groups in the United States and Canada. This could be an ideal extension of the Dominion Drama Festival which began officially in October, 1932, when His Excellency, the Right Honourable Earl of Bessborough, Governor General of Canada, gave the undertaking his blessing. The first festival was staged at Ottawa, Ont., in April, 1933, and, except during the war years, has been a springtime event ever since. To select the outstanding amateur theatrical troupe in Canada the country's fourteen regions were grouped into eight zones in 1959. In 1960 the Canadian Association of Broadcasters became the festival's major sponsor. Canadians adjudicate the regional festivals and select the winning play of each zone. Winning casts participate in the finals staged each year in a different city. In 1966, Victoria, B. C., was the host city. There the performance of Ann Jellicoe's "The Knack" won for the Theatre Society, Calgary, Alta., the coveted D. D. F. Final Festival Trophy and cash prize of $1,000 donated by the Canadian Association of Broadcasters, for the best presentation of a full-length play in either English or French, at the Final Festival. The first prize challenge trophy executed by Miss Florence Wyle, R.C.A., of Toronto, Ont., represents a symbolic figure of the Grecian contribution to the theatre. It and the other fourteen regional trophies created by Miss Syle, Miss Francis Loring, R.C.A., also of Toronto, and Miss Sylvia Daoust, R.C.A., of Montreal, form a collection which is regarded as a fine contribution to Canadian sculpture and art, and worthy of representing the top honors of the festival.

The remaining six theatre groups and the plays they performed at Victoria, B. C. in 1966 were: Vancouver Little Theatre Association, Strindberg's "The Father"; University of New Brunswick Drama Society, Fredericton, N.B., Arthur Miller's "Death of A Salesman"; Le Mouvement Contemporain, Montreal, Jean Genet's "Les Bonnes"; Lakeside Theatre Productions, Ottawa, Tennessee Williams' "The Glass Menagerie"; the London Little Theatre, London, Ont., Bertolt Brecht's "Mother Courage and Her Children"; and the Questors, Toronto, "A Stranger Unto My Brethren." These awards were presented also: The Festival Plaque, for the best presentation in English, excluding the winner of the D.D.F. Final Festival Trophy. The Martha Allan Challenge Trophy, for the best designer of the Final Festival. The Louis Jouvet Trophy, for the best director at the Final Festival. The Massey Award, for the best Canadian playwright at the Final Festival. The Henry Osborne Challenge Trophy, for the best performance given by a man, and the Nella Jefferis Challenge Trophy, for best performance by a woman at the Final Festival. The French Language Radio and Television Association Trophies, for best supporting male role and best supporting female role at the Final Festival. The Sir Barry Jackson Trophy, for the best presentation of a full length play written by a Canadian. A scholarship of $3,000 for studies either in Canada or abroad offered by the Government of Quebec to the most promising actor or actress, director or set designer, whose mother tongue is French. A prize of $200 offered by La Fondation Les Amis de l'Art to the best actor or actress twenty-five years of age or under. Four baby mirror spots for the best stage lighting. The Bessborough Trophy for outstanding achievement in the presentation of classical plays in each of the zones of the Dominion Drama Festival. Six scholarships awarded to talented students who participated in the D.D.F. Regional Festivals and usable at the Banff School of Fine Arts summer session.

The 1964 Perry-Mansfield Drama and Dance Festival in Steamboat Springs, Colo., was the first of several dozen drama and dance festivals originated by Charlotte Perry and Portia Mansfield to be presented under an arrangement with Stephens College, Columbia, Mo. The misses Perry and Mansfield transferred the School of the Theatre to Stephens as a gift in 1963. In July and August, 1966, the Theatre Festival offered "The Other Heart" and "Dark of the Moon," as well as a children's theatre production. The dance concert of 1966 included the premiere performance of "Minoan Suite," "East Indian Suite," and the ballets "Papillons" and "X Nea Xepa," or "The Young Widow," suggested by *Zorba the Greek*.

A theatre festival has been a regular attraction each August in Central City, Colo. since 1932, when the prime movers and shapers of the cultural event were the late Anne Evans and the late Ida Kruse McFarlane. In August, 1966, the gilt and plush Opera House, which dates to 1878, featured "The Odd Couple."

In 1932, during the worldwide depression, Robert Porterfield started the Barter Theatre in Abingdon, Va., and accepted farm produce in lieu of cash from patrons of the Barter

Drama Festival. The title remains, and the dates of the festival are still late July through mid-August, but the box office has long since adopted a policy of cash only. Among the offerings in 1966 were "Twelfth Night," "The Bat," "The Importance of Being Earnest," and "Marat Sade."

The Yale Festival of Undergraduate Drama, referred to more succinctly as the Yale Drama Festival, was inaugurated in 1957. It is produced by the Yale University Dramatic Association founded in 1900 over strong faculty opposition. The conflict led to its being chartered as a non-profit corporation legally independent of the University. This independence has been retained, and the Dramat, as it is popularly known, pays all production and annual expenses, except its director's salary, from box-office revenue. Michael O'Neal, Chairman of the Festival, reports that the first few Festivals were very much Ivy League. However, in 1960 Rollins and Ohio State participated, and in 1964 the troupe that traveled the greatest distance to New Haven, Conn., came from Occidental College, Los Angeles, Calif. Schools affiliated with the Canadian University Drama League have produced at Yale every year since 1963. That year, too, guest lecturers were introduced in an attempt to correlate developments in commercial and educational theatre with what undergraduates themselves were doing. Discussions have proved popular and valuable, and attempts to fit more expression of opinion into the tight Festival schedule are being made. Summer stock company interviews have been introduced, and a design exhibit is being expanded. The opportunity which the Festival presents for the production and discussion of original plays by student playwrights has proved one of its major strengths, according to O'Neal, and subject to the availability of adequate scripts, originals will continue to appear in considerable numbers. It is believed that such works offer perhaps the best insight into all aspects of undergraduate experience.

No particular theme governs selection of shows for the Festival. The Festival Committee solicits scripts and production plans in November from interested schools, and in February invites twelve schools—sometimes including Yale, O'Neal points out—to produce in March. The producers strive to present the best shows possible in themselves, to bring together a representative sampling of what is being done in undergraduate theatre, and to choose bills which demonstrate different solutions to similar dramatic problems. Visiting critics lead discussions following each bill, but there is no adjudication, because it is felt that the giving of awards would present insuperable problems and detract from the primary purpose of establishing communication and learning from each others' work. The Yale Festival is normally attended by about 600 students and assorted instructors from some forty schools. Recently emphasis has been placed on the presentation of good original works by student playwrights, subject to the limitations of the material submitted. Twelve plays and the schools which presented them at the 1967 Festival were: "Electra," by Hugo von Hofmannsthal, Wheaton College. "Escurial," by Michel de Ghelderode, Broome Technical Community College. "Home Free!," by Lanford Wilson, Syracuse University. "I, Myself, and Me," by Robert Clymire, Wabash College. "Cuckold," by Ellen Gautschi, Sir George Williams University. "Postscript," by Merritt Abrash, Rensselaer Polytechnic Institute. "Donner," by Robert Murray, Emerson College. "The Brig," by Kenneth H. Brown, Ohio State University. "Oh, What a Lovely War!," by Joan Littlewood, Rollins College. "Apollo of Bellac," by Jean Giraudoux, University of Maryland. "The Tiger," by Murray Schisgal, Rutgers University. "I'm Going to Pin My Medal on the Girl I Left Behind," by John Palmer, Carleton University.

Performances of plays in Spanish, and dances by the Ballet de San Juan, are standard fare at the Puerto Rican Theatre Festival which runs for about six weeks in April and May at the venerable Tapia Theatre in Old San Juan. Inaugurated in 1958, the festival is sponsored by the Institute of Puerto Rican

Culture. Titles of plays presented in 1966 were: "Los Soles Truncos," by René Marques; "Mi Senoria," by Luis Rechani Agrait; "Vejigantes," by Francisco Arrivi; and "Bienvenido, Don Goyito," by Manuel Mendez Baleste. The ballet that year was "Los Renegados," with choreography by Juan Anduze, music by Carlos Surinach, and the story by Ricardo E. Alegria. In February, 1966, the Institute of Puerto Rican Culture inaugurated the International Theatre Festival. Its object is to have local theatre groups interpret plays from other nations.

The Shaw Festival at Niagara-on-the-Lake, Ont., was founded by Brian Doherty in 1962. He and his colleagues adopted Shaw as their hero not only because after Shakespeare he was the only major English playwright to write more than forty full-length plays, but also because his wit and wisdom is pertinent and pert. The first year of the festival "Candida" and the Hell Scene from "Man and Superman" were featured. By 1966 the program was expanded to three full plays—"Man and Superman," "Misalliance," and "The Apple Cart,"—and the season ran nine weeks, through July and August. A Shaw seminar and a concert also were offered. In May, 1967, four evening lectures were scheduled by the University of Toronto Division of Extension, Toronto, to introduce the plays in the Shaw Festival that year.

The site in Tuscumbia, Ala., where Helen Keller was born in 1880, became in 1962 the setting for the staging of William Gibson's memorable play, "The Miracle Worker," in July and August. Miss Keller was blind and deaf from the age of two. At age seven she was put under the charge of Anne Sullivan, who taught her to speak, and remained her teacher and companion for almost fifty years. This compelling play dramatizes the early years of Miss Keller, and the heroic efforts of Miss Sullivan in an all but hopeless situation.

Florida's official state theatre is the Asolo Theatre, a 200-seat Venetian theatre, built in Italy in 1798 and moved to Sarasota to become part of the Ringling Museum. During

60

July and August a Theatre Festival devoted mainly to Baroque and Renaissance plays is sponsored there by the Museum and Florida State University. Productions given in rotation nightly in 1966 were Shakespeare's "Much Ado About Nothing," Molière's "The Miser," Robert Bolt's "A Man For All Seasons," Sophocles' "Oedipus the King," and Ionesco's "The Bald Soprano."

The outdoor drama which is undoubtedly enjoying the longest run of all is the Ramona outdoor play which was staged for the first time by residents of Hemet and San Jacinto, Calif., in the shadow of snowcapped Mt. San Jacinto, in 1923. The drama was inspired by Helen Hunt Jackson's novel about the Indian girl Ramona and her love for the Indian brave Alessandro. Each year the performances are staged in a natural amphitheater during afternoons on the last weekends of April and the first weekend in May, as a rule. A permanent, authentic hacienda was built about 100 feet from the audience, and the nearby hills are part of the gigantic set on which as many as 250 actors cavort.

Outdoor dramas have become such an important segment of summertime recreation activities in the United States an Institute of Outdoor Drama was founded in January, 1963, by the Chancellor of the University of North Carolina at Chapel Hill, under the sponsorship of the Department of Dramatics Art and The Carolina Playmakers. Its basic purpose is three-fold: to serve equally as a source of stimulation, advice, and information. North Carolina seems like a logical choice for the headquarters of this organization because the Tarheel State has become the fountainhead of contemporary outdoor dramas. Since 1937, Paul Green's "The Lost Colony," which dramatizes Sir Walter Raleigh's ill-fated expedition to the area in 1587, has been firmly established at Manteo, on Roanoke Island. "Unto These Hills," about the Cherokee Indians who were forced to walk the Trail of Tears to Oklahoma, has been performed annually at Cherokee, N. C., in the Great Smokies since 1950, and "Horn In The West," which depicts some of

61

Daniel Boone's exploits in the territory he roamed, has been staged regularly at Boone, in the Blue Ridge Mountains, since 1952.

In 1938, the people of New Glarus, Wis., began staging in a meadow on the edge of town the story of William Tell, the Swiss folk hero who refused to pay homage to Gessler, a tyrannical Austrian bailiff. They did that when the independence of many European nations was threatened, just to remind the world of the successful fight the Swiss waged against oppressive Austrian dictators more than 600 years before. Through the years the play has become so popular its annual presentation was increased from two to three afternoons during the Labor Day weekend. Normally the play is performed in English on Saturday and Monday, and in German on Sunday. Also in New Glarus, an annual Volksfest is staged to commemorate the birthday of the Swiss nation on Aug. 1st.

The 25th revival since 1939 of the perennial symbol of nineteenth century melodrama, "The Old Homestead," was staged in the Potash Bowl, Swanzey, N. H., as usual during the weekend nearest the full moon in July, 1966. The original old homestead about which the play was written is near the bowl, which was named Potash because it is on a site where wood ashes once were processed in a huge iron bowl to produce potash for soap and other uses.

During July and August, Kentuckians honor the memory of Stephen Foster with a musical drama at Bardstown, Ky. "The Stephen Foster Story," in the back yard of My Old Kentucky Home which inspired the song of that title, is a potpourri of many of the composer's well-known melodies. Among them are "Old Folks At Home," "Oh, Susanna," "Jeanie With the Light Brown Hair," "Beautiful Dreamer," and "My Old Kentucky Home." The show opened in 1959.

The annual Shaker Festival and Pageant, "Shakertown Revisited," has been regaling visitors to Auburn, Ky., in July, since 1962. The original Shakertown Colony operated at nearby South Union, 1807–1922.

"The Legend of Daniel Boone," billed as "Kentucky's living monument to a great American," had its first season June 17 to Sept. 4, 1966, in the Fort Harrod Amphitheater at Old Fort Harrod, near Harrodsburg, Ky.

Fairs, Livestock Shows

ALTHOUGH THE United States and Canada are in the vanguard of agricultural nations, heavy industry also greatly influences the economy of both countries. That fact is obvious these days at state and provincial fairs where farm produce and homemade products which once dominated the exhibit space must now share a high percentage of it with durable goods and mass-produced articles. Of course, by using modern mechanized equipment and some of the improved chemical fertilizers displayed at the fairs, farmers have increased their yields and stepped up their efficiency with even less manpower. Also, there is much to be said in favor of labor-saving devices for the home. Every year some 2,000 farm fairs are staged in the United States, and another 150 are put on in Canada. The seeds for the bumper crops of fairs in the two countries were planted first in Canada where prizes for exhibits of cattle, hogs, horses, sheep, butter, cheese, grain, and homespun cloth were awarded in 1765 at Fort Edward Hill. In 1811 the Berkshire County Fair was inaugurated at Pittsfield, Mass. Contemporary Canadians like to refer to their Canadian National Exhibition in Toronto, Ont., as "the world's largest annual fair." Its size can challenge all comers, since the 350-acre park-like area includes fifty-four permanent buildings valued at $50 million, some 2.25 million square feet of display space, a 25,000-capacity grandstand centered around a revolving stage, and an estimated annual attendance of almost 3 million during two-and-a-half-weeks before Labor Day, the first Monday in September. Usually on that workman's holiday a three-mile procession of labor representatives, floats, and bands goes marching through the Dufferin Gates. When the CNE was incorporated in 1879 one building called the Crystal Palace housed all the exhibits. Today it is the nation's greatest agricultural fair. Preferred produce is displayed proudly. Cattle and other livestock pass in review as they compete for prizes. Housewives hover about exhibits in the multi-million dollar Better Living Center which contains a model home and many things needed to run it. Aquatic events, such as swimming, sailing, and tugboat races can be viewed from stands on the shore of Lake Erie. World-renowned entertainers perform in the grandstand, and a fireworks display climaxes the night's activities. The CNE is truly an amusement and educational city within a city.

Elsewhere in Canada major exhibitions include the following two dozen. Agricultural and Homecrafts Exhibition, Harbour Grace, Newfoundland, Sept. Lobster Festival and Exhibition, Summerside, P.E.I., July. Old Home Week and Provincial Exhibition, Charlottetown, P.E.I., August. Provincial Exhibition, Truro, N.S. Sept. Nova Scotia Fisheries Exhibition, Lunenburg. N.S. Sept. Hants County Exhibition, the oldest in Canada since it dates to 1765, Windsor, N.S., Sept. Atlantic National Exhibition, Saint John, N.B., Sept. Exhibition and Livestock Show, Fredericton, N.B., Sept. Provincial Exhibition, Quebec, Que., Sept. Royal Winter Fair, Toronto, November. Red River Exhibition, Winnipeg, Man., June. Provincial Exhibition and Western Canada Trade Fair, Brandon, Man., June. Provincial Exhibition, Regina, Sask., July. Exhibition, Moose Jaw, Sask., July. Horticultural Show, Saskatoon, Sask., Aug. Klondike Days Exhibition, Edmonton, Alta., July. Exhibition, Stampede, Calgary, Alta., July. Exhibition, Fair, Lethbridge, Alta., July. Horticultural Show, Red Deer, Alta., Aug. Industrial, Agricultural Exhibition Victoria, B.C., May. Pacific National Exhibition, Vancouver,

B.C., August to Sept. Interior Provincial Exhibition, Armstrong, B.C., Sept.

The biggest cooperative fair in the United States is the Eastern States Exposition, established in West Springfield, Mass., in 1914. It is the official state fair for Connecticut, Maine, Massachusetts, New Hampshire, Rhode Island, and Vermont. Each state has its own building. There are additional buildings for livestock and industrial art, and emphasis is placed on the education of children as tomorrow's producers and consumers. As a rule each September the mammoth Exposition is launched with Governor's Day. That special occasion is customarily followed by All New England Day, Maine Day, Vermont Day, Connecticut Day, Massachusetts Day, New Hampshire Day, Rhode Island Day, and even New York Day, because so many New Yorkers visit it. Children's Day is an official school holiday in the region. There are contests and a music festival for children, plus three outdoor stages with free attractions daily. The poultry show has had as many as 1,323 entries representing more than 135 breeds. A scholarship worth at least $750 is awarded a young lady chosen Exposition College Queen. In 1966 attendance exceeded 563,000. That year the roster of entertainers included the Andrews Sisters, Arthur Godfrey, Barry Sadler, Frank Fountaine, George Kirby, Hurricane Hell Drivers, Kelton Pony Circus, Lone Ranger, and Mike Douglas. A rodeo and daily parades also were on the program.

Millions of people who never set foot in Iowa are acquainted with the Iowa State Fair staged in Des Moines during August because they read Philip Strong's novel "State Fair," or saw one or more of the three motion pictures the book inspired. The Iowa State Fair, which dates to 1854, is one of the truly great agricultural expositions in the country. However, even in that stronghold of the tall corn, in 1962 for the first time industrial exhibits slightly outnumbered agricultural displays. At least half-a-million visitors are said to attend the Iowa State Fair every year, amusing and enlightening themselves at the demonstrations of family living, baby health contests, and competitions among future farmers, the young people. In the livestock division cattle, hogs, and other farm animals compete for at least $100,000 in premiums. The 200-acre fair grounds also have a fish and game show, art and photographic salon, public school exhibits, a Hall of Science, harness and saddle horse shows, auto races, three-ring circuses, fireworks, farm animal teams' pulling contests, old fiddlers' competitions, and cash prizes for the best practical inventions by farmers to help make life easier down on the farm.

Gatekeepers reported that 2,919,416 persons attended the 16-day Texas State Fair at Dallas in October, 1966. The daily average was about 182,465, and on Saturday, October 15th, a total of 354,469 clicks of the turnstiles set a new single day's record at the fairgrounds. Dating to 1886, it is one of the major state fairs in the nation. That might be expected since Texas is one of America's principal agricultural states. Texas has the greatest number of farms of any state. Its chief products are cotton, sorghum, oats, rice, wheat, livestock, wool, mohair, spinach, tomatoes, potatoes, cabbage, pecans, peaches, apples, pears, figs, and berries. Two events emphasize young people. They are Rural Young Day, when an estimated 75,000 future farmers and farmerettes are guests of honor, and a Music Festival Day, which is dedicated to top-ranking public school bands, orchestras, and choruses from all parts of the state. The trade mark of the exhibition is the 52-foot-tall Big Tex, a grinning cowboy whose grimace is a yard wide. He dominates the 200-acre area, about 2 miles from downtown Dallas, which embraces exhibition and recreational facilities valued at approximately $40 million. Principal permanent buildings which are used the year round include the Cotton Bowl, State Fair Auditorium, and the Museums of Fine Arts and Natural History. Among the special events announced for the 1966 fair were a Czech-American Festival, Golden Age Day, Mexico Day, German Day, and the perennially popular Pan American Livestock Exposition. "Fiddler On The Roof" was the Broadway musical of the year.

The California State Fair and Exposition, inaugurated in San Francisco in 1853 and subsequently moved to Sacramento, traditionally runs twelve days each year, beginning on the Wednesday before Labor Day. Attendance at the 208-acre plant in 1966 was almost 952,000. There is parking space for more than 5,000 automobiles. This is an important fair because California is the primary agricultural state in the Union. When 1965 reports from throughout the nation were tabulated it emerged as the most productive. It was first in almonds, apricots, avocados, boysenberries, cantaloupes, dates, figs, grapes, honeydews, peaches, Persian melons, naval oranges, nectarines, pears, persimmons, plums, pomegranates, prunes, sweet cherries, strawberries, walnuts, artichokes, beeswax, asparagus, broccoli, Brussels sprouts, carrots, cauliflower, celery, garlic, green lima beans, lettuce, olives, peppers, spinach, sugar beets, and tomatoes. Many major stars have entertained there. The rodeo, which runs the full twelve days of the fair, is probably the longest sustaining RCA approved show in the world. In 1966, during the 10-day program of Thoroughbred, Quarter Horse and Harness Horse racing, visitors wagered approximately $6.130 million. The fair's annual Art Show is a showcase for artists and photographers throughout the world. The perennial favorite at the fair is the huge cupola-topped Counties Building which houses exhibits from almost all fifty-eight California counties. The midway, or carnival, is so large that three of the major operators in the West combine their facilities to stage the show. There is nearly a million square feet of exhibit space. Featured, too, are floriculture, home economics, the largest livestock show in the West, and entertainment. Officials expect to erect a new state fair by 1970 on an 1,100-acre site along the American River adjoining the City of Sacramento. The new plant is expected to cost more than $100 million.

While forty-four states sponsor state fairs in their own

bailiwicks, the New England States team up to stage the six-sided Eastern States Exposition at West Springfield, Mass. Most states have a single state fair, but Idaho divides the honor between eastern and western parts of the state, and Washington has central, southeast, and southwest fairs. Here are places and months in which state fairs usually begin their runs: Birmingham, Ala., Oct.; Palmer, Alaska, Sept.; Phoenix, Ariz., Nov.; Little Rock, Ark., Oct.; Sacramento, Calif., Sept.; Pueblo, Colo., Aug.; Harrington, Del., July; Tampa, Fla., Feb.; Macon, Ga., Oct.; Honolulu, Hawaii, July; Eastern Idaho Fair, Blackfoot, Idaho, Sept.; Western Idaho Fair, Boise, Idaho, Sept.; Springfield, Ill., Aug.; Indianapolis, Ind., Aug.; Des Moines, Iowa, Aug.; Hutchinson, Kansas, Sept.; Louisville, Ky., Aug.; Shreveport, La., Oct.; Timonium, Md., Aug.; Eastern States Exposition, West Springfield, Mass., Sept.; Detroit, Mich., Aug.; St. Paul, Minn., Aug.; Jackson, Miss., Oct.; Sedalia, Mo., Aug.; Great Falls, Mont., July; Lincoln, Neb., Sept; Nevada Fair of Industry, Ely, Nev., Aug.; Trenton, N. J., Sept.; Albuquerque, N. M., Sept.; Syracuse, N. Y., Sept.; Raleigh, N. C., Oct.; Minot, N. D., July; Columbus, Ohio, Sept.; Oklahoma City, Okla., Sept.; Salem, Ore., Aug.; Pennsylvania Farm Show, Harrisburg, Pa., Jan.; Columbia, S. C., Oct.; Huron, S. D., Sept.; Nashville, Tenn., Sept.; Dallas, Texas, Oct.; Salt Lake City, Utah, Sept.; Richmond, Va., Sept.; Southwest Washington Fair, Chehalis, Wash., Aug.; Southeastern Washington Fair, Walla Walla, Wash., Sept.; Central Washington Fair, Yakima, Wash., Sept.; Lewisburg, W. Va., Aug.; Milwaukee, Wis., Aug.; Douglas, Wyo., Aug.

The festive feeling of a country fair usually pervades livestock shows which have multiplied considerably since the first one, the American Fat Stock Show, was inaugurated in Chicago, Ill., in 1877. It was discontinued in 1893 when hard times overcame livestock producers. The oldest continuous livestock show is the Southwestern Exposition and Fat Stock Show, which was staged for the first time at Fort Worth, Tex., in 1896. The original one-day event, which came about as the result of a conversation between two stockmen, has developed into a ten-day exposition. The initial show was held under a group of shade trees along Marine Creek, not far from the Fort Worth Stockyards. By 1908 the burgeoning exposition moved into the newly completed North Side Coliseum. That site was requisitioned by a war industry in 1942, so the stock show moved to its present location, the Will Rogers Memorial Building, in time for the 1944 event. Back in 1896 prizes were such things as western hats, saddles, spurs, bridles, cowboy boots, and small jewelry donated by local storekeepers. Now late in January and early in February, as a rule, more than 10,000 entries in cattle, horse, pigeon, poultry, rabbit, sheep, and swine divisions vie for some $115,000 in premiums, with approximately $35,000 in additional entry fees and premiums at stake in the horse show events. Among the Southwestern's claims to fame are the introduction of specialty acts in a rodeo, cutting horse contests, and the commingling of horse show and rodeo activities. Also, in 1917, it produced the world's first indoor rodeo. Entertainment features in the 6,200-capacity Will Rogers Memorial Colosseum include comic and spectacular specialty acts, riding clubs in costume, and standard rodeo events.

A Livestock Show and Rodeo Exposition has been a going concern at Houston, Tex., since 1932. Normally these days it attracts several hundred thousand visitors to eighteen performances during twelve days in January and February. Big events include a rodeo, calf scrambling, dairy milking races, and auctions of grand champion steers.

During the livestock show season in Texas, between mid-January and mid-March, expositions might be staged also at Abilene, Amarillo, Austin, Bay City, Coleman, Donna, Eastland, El Paso, Fort Worth, Gatesville, Hereford, Hondo, Jacksboro, Kerrville, Lamesa, Levelland, Lyford, Mercedes, Plainview, Rusk, San Angelo, San Antonio, San Saba, Sequin, Van Horn, and Vernon.

The second oldest continuous livestock and horse show in the United States is the Great American Royal at Kansas City, Mo. It takes place for nine days during the third and fourth weeks in October. Back in 1899 the first show in the current series was staged in a small circus tent. Cattle were tied along a rope because there were no stalls, and herdsmen slept with their cattle on straw beds. Prior to 1899 the shows and sales were held sporadically, usually when the spirit moved the cattlemen, or the need for something of the kind arose. That was before motor trucks were commonplace, so animals were shipped by rail from state fair to state fair, and they climaxed their journeys at Chicago. These days it is not unusual for livestock, pedigreed and otherwise, to fly through the air with the greatest of ease aboard cargo planes. The 1899 show was a Hereford cattle exposition and sale, known as the National Hereford Cattle Show. An estimated 500 head of Herefords are reported to have been entered, and approximately 300 of them were sold after the show for more than $65,000. Shorthorn breeders joined the exposition in 1900. Their animals shared space with Herefords in a horse barn of the Kansas City Stock Yards Co. Galloway cattle were added in 1901. The Aberdeen Angus species came into the lineup in 1902, and purebred swine, lodged in a big tent, became a part of the exhibition in 1903. Anyone thinking about American livestock shows is not apt to associate them with their British counterparts. Yet the American Royal derived its regal title from the prestigious British Royal Livestock Show. On June 1, 1901, the *Drovers Telegram,* a trade paper, suggested naming the midwestern exhibition for Britain's foremost cattle competition. For almost twenty years the American Royal outgrew one building after another. Then, in 1922, the Shorthorn and Hereford Breeders Assn., and the Kansas City Chamber of Commerce, dedicated new quarters valued at $100,000. These days the indoor arena covers an estimated ten acres, and some five acres are devoted to parking. On the entertainment level there are an elaborate coronation ceremony on

70

opening night and a long-established, top-quality horse show twice a day throughout the run of the exhibition. The American Royal, of course, also attempts to meet its obligation to educate. The Junior Department has been a part of the American Royal since 1922, and for quite some time it has been the educational extension department of the Kansas City market and the Kansas City Stock Yards Co. There each year outstanding breeding animals from all parts of the country are shown by vocational agriculture students and 4-H members. The best in carload stock, both finished and unfinished, are judged by teams from agricultural colleges and other pertinent organizations, then auctioned. The youth groups are supported by Congressional appropriations authorized under the Smith-Lever and Smith-Hughes Acts. Kansas City is the National Headquarters of the Vocational Agricultural Students Organization.

Establishing livestock shows which proved to be hearty perennials seems to have been a fad around the turn of the century. The third oldest continuous show in the nation is the International Livestock Exposition which opened at the Chicago Stockyards in 1900. Now in late November and early December it attracts approximately 10,000 entries and upwards of 300,000 spectators. The spectators might have supposed that the big show came about because there were so many fine specimens of cattle, hogs, sheep, and horses in the Middle West, but the sponsors of the Exposition are quick to contradict that supposition. They insist that the show came first, and improvement of the breeds followed. The records reveal how styles in livestock have changed since 1900. Then scrawny, tallow-laden steers between three and five years old were a familiar sight. Now the yards are crowded with yearlings and two-year-olds yielding cuts of handy weight size, and carrying a better proportion of lean to fat. Lard-laden 500-pound butcher hogs have been displaced. Lamb has superseded less profitable mutton sheep. These are some of the changes which might be traceable to the incentives and educational opportunities provided by the Exposition. Agricultural schools and state and federal Departments of Agriculture have also contributed much to the progress in this field. At any rate, the growth of American purebred livestock has been prodigious. Purebred livestock record associations are reported to have approximately 2 million head of pedigreed cattle, swine, and horses on their rolls. What's more, experts contend that artificial insemination, particularly in dairy cattle, makes it possible for one purebred sire to father as many as 1,000 to 2,000 pedigrees a year.

The Grand National Livestock Exposition, inaugurated in 1941, usually takes place late in October and early in November at the Cow Palace, San Francisco, Calif. The sobriquet "Cow Palace" was bestowed on the exhibition hall during the depression-plagued 1930's when a local newspaper editorial writer criticized the city administration for failing to provide adequate low-cost housing for people, although it spent thousands of dollars on building a palace for cows. Now civic boosters are agitating for a bigger and better Cow Palace. As many as 3,500 entries compete for prizes and participate in the Grand Champion auction sale at the Grand National. There are milking contests, as well as demonstrations of carcass judging and modern cutting methods. At the rodeo high point, champion cowboys from some two dozen states compete on Brahma bulls and bucking broncs. There are also a Grand National Horse Show and a Livestock Queen contest. Mexican charros often perform trick riding and roping feats, and the feminine chinas execute intricate Mexican dances.

Civic leaders in Birmingham, Ala., launched a stock show in 1946 to dramatize the importance of agriculture and livestock in their state. Early in May visitors watch the judging of calves, see a parade of championship cattle, and attend a Wild West Roundup.

The Arkansas Livestock Show, which was started in Little Rock in 1938, and is usually staged the first or second week in October, has the status of a state fair since it is the only statewide exposition.

A multi-million dollar display of steaks and chops on the hoof highlights the Great Western Exposition and Livestock Show at the Great Western Exhibit Center, Los Angeles, Calif., about the third week in November. First staged in 1926, one of the entertainment features is a calf scramble in which 4-H and FFA youngsters catch and halter calves.

As long ago as 1906 the National Western Stock Show was begun in Denver, Colo., and it is usually staged during the third week in January. Visitors who throng the auditorium look at prize cattle, hogs, horses, rabbits, and sheep, and see Livestock's Man of the Year receive an award.

The crowning of a rodeo queen is a feature of the two-day Kissimmee Valley Livestock Show, Kissimmee, Fla., during the third week in February.

Champion bulls, cows, heifers, the presentation of championship awards, community singing, pony hitches, horsemanship contests, and circus acts are the main attractions at the National Dairy Cattle Congress, Waterloo, Iowa, during the first week in October.

March is a major livestock show month in Oklahoma. Among the communities in which competitions are staged are Alva, Anadarko, Antlers, Cherokee, Chickasha, Clinton, Duncan, Edmond, El Reno, Enid, Guthrie, Hobart, Madill, McAlester, Muskogee, Oklahoma City, Vinita, Weatherford, and Woodward.

An indoor rodeo and horse show enliven proceedings at the Pacific International Livestock Exposition in Portland, Ore., during the second week in October. Angora goats, beef and dairy cattle, and prize poultry have been the chief exhibits each year since 1911.

The Golden Spike National Livestock Show, considered to be one of the outstanding shows in the West, has been an annual attraction at Ogden, Utah, during the second week in November, since 1920. There are exhibits, contests, horse shows, judging events, sales, and entertainment.

One of Canada's livestock shows is at Summerside, P.E.I., in conjunction with the annual Lobster Festival in mid-July, and another is linked with the Fredericton Exhibition, Fredericton, N. B., during the second week in September.

Film Festivals

THERE WERE quite a few attempts to establish film festivals in North America during the first fifty years of the American-born movie industry. However, it was not until the San Francisco International Film Festival created by Irving M. Levin in 1957 proved its validity and stability that the United States could claim an annual competition which might approach the stature of the venerable Venice Film Festival, nurtured during peacetime in Italy since 1932, the one inaugurated in Cannes in 1948, and the Berlin Festival begun in 1951. A historian of the San Francisco Festival reports that the idea for such an annual event in the California city was conceived early in the 1950's. Theatre people there made some ineffectual gestures to organize a festival, but it was Levin who made the first effective experiment in 1956 when he limited the entries to five new Italian films. Then, in September, 1957, Levin and Mayor George Christopher jointly issued the first formal invitation to the film producers of countries with consulates in San Francisco "to take part in an international film exhibition." Sixteen features from twelve nations were entered, including "Il Grido," Italy; "Pather Panchali," the first part of Satyajit Ray's classic Indian trilogy; "Kanal," Poland; "Throne of Blood," Japan; and "Uncle Vanya," a Hollywood film directed by John Goetz and Franchot Tone. Tone was master of ceremonies at the festival. The jury was composed of drama critics of the Bay Area's five leading newspapers.

Again in 1958 there were sixteen feature films. On the list

were "Aparajito," the second part of Ray's Indian trilogy; "White Nights," Italy; "The Rickshaw Man," Japan; and "Eve Wants to Sleep," Poland. In addition, fifty-eight short films were shown in competition, including Poland's popular "Two Men and a Wardrobe." The jury was composed of critics Arthur Knight and Albert Johnson, and the dean of Bay Area film exhibitors, Irving Ackerman. Interest on the international level was increased in 1959 when nineteen nations sent twenty-four features, four of which were out of competition, and fifty-two short films. The City of San Francisco boosted its financial contribution, and the social lustre surrounding the festival also increased as more visitors from outside the United States attended. They saw such films as "Black Orpheum," Brazil; "General Della Revere," Italy; "The Hidden Fortress," Japan; "Nude in the White Car," France; "The Mouse That Roared," England; "World of Apu," the final entry in Ray's Indian trilogy, and "Crime and Punishment," United States. On the jury were Barnaby Conrad, writer; Edward Dmytryk, Hollywood director; and John McCarten, film critic.

Some twenty features and forty-three short films on various interesting subjects from nineteen countries were shown in 1960. Russia participated for the first time with "Ballad of a Soldier." France sent "The Love Game"; the popular U.S. entry was "Shadows"; and from Czechoslovakia came "Romeo, Juliet and Darkness." An innovation was the Film As Communication, soon referred to as FAC, a competition for sixteen mm. nontheatrical films. At a symposium on the role of films in international culture, speakers included directors Jean Renoir, of France; Grigori Tchukhrai, of Russia; and Edward Dmytryk, of Hollywood. On the jury were Alexander Karagonov, a Russian film critic; Herman Weinberg, film translator; and Darius Milhaud, composer. The festival's historian noted that by the time the fifth annual San Francisco International Film Festival was ready in 1961, the event "had grown into a major international cultural event, as well as one of the major social events of the year for many San

Franciscans." That year twenty-two features from nineteen countries were screened, and so many short films were entered that a special day was set aside for their showing. FAC welcomed 250 countries. Popular feature films included "Summerskin," Argentina; "Animas Trujano," Mexico; "Antigone," Greece; "Ghosts in Rome," Italy; "Viridiana," Spain, and "The Clear Sky," Russia. The jury of five included John Malas, British producer-director; Arthur May, of the United States; and Kira Paramanova, of Russia, both critics; and Tapan Sinha, of India, and Joseph von Sternberg, United States, directors. When the entries for the sixth annual festival were totalled in 1962 there were twenty-three features, sixty-two short films, 300 FAC entries, and nineteen entries in the newly inaugurated Newsreel Competition. Features included "David and Lisa," United States; "Disorder," Italy; "America the Unexpected," France; "Keeper of Promises," Brazil; "Ivan's Childhood," Russia; "Baron Munchhausen," Czechoslovakia; and "Hamlet," Germany. The jury consisted of Mrs. Kashiko Kawakita, Japanese film authority; Lewis Milestone, American film director; Jiri Weiss, Czechoslovakian director; Leopoldo Torre-Nilsson, Argentine director, and Darius Milhaud, French composer. The seventh festival in 1963 offered 21 feature films, fifty-three short subjects, eight newsreels, and 340 entries divided among FAC and Film as Art. Features included "Paula Cautiva," Argentina; "The Boxer," Czechoslovakia; "Weekend," Denmark; "My Enemy, the Sea," Japan; "Paper Man," Mexico; "How to be Loved," Poland; "Optimistic Tragedy," Russia; and the American film, "The Victors." Although "The Victors" was shown out of competition, it marked a milestone for the festival. For the first time a major Hollywood distributor, Columbia, not only supplied the film, but sent the director and a group of stars, and was also reported to have underwritten the expenses of a rather sizable press corps from out of town. That grand gesture was followed by an announcement by Arthur Freed, president of the Academy of Motion Picture Arts and Sciences and production head of MGM, that the American movie industry would henceforth support the San Francisco Festival, without any strings attached. That marked the end of a six-year boycott of the Festival by Hollywood studios. It also was a major triumph for Irving M. Levin, the founder of the festival, who had worked diligently to obtain significant cooperation and endorsement from the American movie moguls. The two-week-long eighth annual San Francisco International Film Festival, Oct. 14–27, 1964, offered "Lemonade Joe," Czechoslovakia; "Epilogue," Denmark; " The Winner," France; "Encounter in Salzburg," Germany; "Between Tears and Smiles," Hong Kong; "Yes," Hungary; "Sallah," Israel; "The Naked Hours," Italy; "All Mixed Up," Japan; "The Well," Mexico; "The Human Dutch," Netherlands; "Yesterday in Fact," Poland; "The Happy Sixties," Spain; "There Is Such A Guy" and "At Your Doorstep," Russia; "The Luck of Ginger Coffey," United States-Canada; and "Wild Growth," Yugoslavia. Appropriate to the locale, the prizes for the first achievements in each catagory are known as Golden Gate Awards. The categories are feature film, director, actor, actress, supporting actor and actress and screenplay, short thirty-five mm. films, Film as Communication and Film as Art.

In March, 1965, the San Francisco Chamber of Commerce assumed, as a one-year experiment, "all responsibility for the 1965 film festival," as well as "full and complete authority for operation, control, management, and financing" of the event. Until then the festival functioned under the sponsorship of the San Francisco Art Commission, headed by Harold Zellerbach, who also was president of the festival's directors. Irving Levin, who founded the festival and had served as its director for eight years, became an advisor. In the programs of the 1965 festival the new management published this announcement: "In its ninth year the San Francisco International Film Festival has come under the jurisdiction of the San Francisco Chamber of Commerce in an effort to broaden the pase of participation by both citizens and the motion picture industry—in America and abroad. It has as its purpose to demonstrate through the exhibition of the finest in motion pictures, the development of cinematic art in different countries, to contribute to knowledge of film history, and to reveal styles and trends in film making. It has the objective of presenting a broad spectrum of the film maker's art and of promoting film as a medium of artistry and expression. The most significant change in this year's event is the abolition of competition between theatrical films. This step was made to establish the festival as a cultural event of the highest order. It has allowed the widest possible choice in programming from the world's artistic film productions. The step was taken after close consultation with the International Federation of Film Producers Associations, which strongly urged such a course. In this program book, you will find highlights of the major facets of our ninth festival. We are able to present this vast array of events because of the generous support and energies of many citizens, in addition to a devoted staff. Extensive volunteer hours, contributed goods and professional services, have generated an operation far beyond its budgeted capacity. The community owes a debt of appreciation to all those who gave so generously. To those in our festival audiences we extend greetings and hope that you enjoy sharing the experience of international cinema."

Bows were made in the direction of distinguished established film directors, and to new directors whose initial efforts indicate that they are major talents, with showings of ten old and ten new films in addition to the twenty-one feature films which received top billing.

The featured films at the 1965 festival in San Francisco included: "Rapture," United States-France; "Two People," Denmark; "A Shop On Main Street," Czechoslovakia; "The Camp Followers," Italy; "Italiano Brava Gente," Italy; "Dry Summer," Turkey; "Passages from Finnegan's Wake," Ireland; "The Leather Boys," Great Britain; "The Saragossa Manuscript," Poland; "Samyong, the Mute," Korea; "The

Royal Track," Sweden; "Young Aphrodites," Greece; "The House in Karp Alley," Germany; "The Crazy Quilt," United States; "Yoyo," France; "Shadows of Forgotten Ancestors," Russia; "A Soldier's Father," Russia; "Simeon of the Desert," Mexico; "The Assassination," Czechoslovakia; "Charulata," India; and "Tokyo Olympiad," Japan. The tenth San Francisco International Film Festival at the Masonic Auditorium, Oct. 20–30, 1966, featured films from thirty-one countries in four categories: theatrical features and shorts, film as communication, film as art and television programs, in cooperation with the International Federation of Film Producers Associations, the Motion Picture Association of America, and Independent Film Importers and Distributors of America.

The thirty-one countries represented in 1966 were Argentina, Australia, Brazil, Canada, Czechoslovakia, Denmark, France, Germany, Great Britain, Greece, India, Ireland, Israel, Italy, Japan, Mexico, Netherlands, New Zealand, Poland, Portugal, Puerto Rico, Romania, Scotland, South Africa, Spain, Sweden, Switzerland, Thailand, United States, U.S.S.R., and Yugoslavia. The twenty-one noncompetitive films from some of those countries were "A Funny Thing Happened on the Way to the Forum," United States; "Long Live the Republic," Czechoslovakia; "Young Torless," Germany; "Mamma Roma," Italy; "A Man Is Not A Bird," Yugoslavia; "Hunger," Denmark; "Night Games," Sweden; "The Hunt," Spain; "The Face of Another," Japan; "The Dance of the Heron," The Netherlands; "Fists in the Pocket," Italy; "The Great City," India; "Incubus," United States; "Captive's Island," Japan; "The Shameless Old Lady," France; "Black Wind," Mexico; "Pharaoh," Poland; "The Power Game," Switzerland; " '17'," Denmark; "The Nameless Star," Romania; "Mata Hari," France. Attendance for the tenth annual San Francisco Film Festival was reported to have increased twenty-three percent over the previous year. A total of 55,270 persons attended 41 separate events. The theatre was filled to eighty-seven percent of capacity, and four programs were sellouts. They were "A Funny Thing Happened on the Way to the Forum," "Hunger," " '17'," and "Night Games." "The Shameless Old Lady" was almost a sellout.

New York's first major International Film Festival which was held concurrently at the 2,600-seat Philharmonic Hall in Lincoln Center for the Performing Arts and at the Museum of Modern Art, Sept. 10–19, 1963, was patterned after the London Film Festival established in 1956. The British festival differs from those in Berlin, Cannes, and Venice in that it has no judges, no juries, no starlets, no prizes. Its primary concern is the showing of the best of the year's best films, selected from other film festivals. Thus, its alter ego in New York offers American audiences an opportunity to see in their original versions a sampling of the world's fine films. The opportunity is presented in association with the British Film Institute, and in cooperation with the Independent Film Importers and Distributors of America, Inc., and the Motion Picture Association of America. In this vein the inaugural New York Film Festival opened with Luis Bunuel's "The Exterminating Angel," and also included "In the Midst of Life," "Knife in the Water," "Love in the Suburbs," "Harakiri," "An Autumn Afternoon," "The Terrace," "Elektra at Epidaurus," "Hallelujah the Hills," "All the Way Home," "The Sky," "Trial of Joan of Arc," "The Fiances," "Rogopag," "The Servant," "The Sea," "Magnet of Doom," "Le Joli Mai," "Muriel," "Barravento," "Sweet and Sour." The 26 films selected for the second New York Film Festival at Lincoln Center in September, 1964, included a Russian film of "Hamlet," "The Inheritance," "Fail Safe," "Nobody Waved Good-Bye," "Woman in the Dunes," "Hands Over the City," "Salvatore Giuliano," "A Woman Is A Woman," "Band of Outsiders," "Nothing But A Man," "Lilith," "The Taira Clan," "The Brig," "Passenger," "L'Age d'Or," "Diary of a Chambermaid," "Enjo," "To Love," "Alone on the Pacific," "King and Country," "Inside Out," "Before the Revolution," "She and

He," "Cyrano and d'Artagnan," "Ça Ira," "The Great City."
A series of approximately a dozen special panel events
entitled Film '65 in the 212-seat auditorium of the new
Library and Museum of the Performing Arts in Lincoln
Center was a highlight of the third New York Film Festival,
Sept. 7–18, 1965. The role of criticism was also discussed.
That year the list of twenty-five films included "Alphaville,"
"Knave of Hearts," "Mickey One," "Ravens End," "The Shop
On Main Street," "Camille Without Camellias," "Charulata,"
"The Wedding March," "Black Peter," "Thomas The Impos-
tor," "Identification Marks: None," "Walkover," "Shake-
speare Wallah," "Les Vampires," "Buster and Beckett,"
"Tribute to Bette Davis—Of Human Bondage," "Caressed,"
"Six in Paris," "Le Petit Soldat," "Gertrud," "Between Two
Worlds," "The Koumiko Mystery," "Unreconciled," "Red
Beard," and "Sandra." By the autumn of 1966 when the
fourth annual New York Film Festival was presented at Lincoln Center, September 12–22, it had increased in stature. In
addition to a solid series of new and retrospective films and
cinematic vignettes its admission-free special events program
in the 212-seat auditorium of the Library covered various
aspects of contemporary independent film-making. Devoted
primarily to the independent American cinema, from new
"underground" films to social documentaries, television films,
and intermedia presentations, there were also lectures and
discussions with film-makers, screenings of new works and
works-in-progress, and open interviews with visiting directors
from abroad. The new feature films chosen by the program
committee which covered most major festivals and production
centers and was reported to have seen approximately 600
features and 800 shorts before making its final choices, included "Loves of a Blonde," "The War Game," "Wholly
Communion," "Hunger," "The Grim Reaper," "The Eaves-
dropper," "Balthazar," "The Creatures," "The Hawks and the
Sparrows," "Accattone," "Do You Keep a Lion At Home?,"
"Meet Marlon Brando," "Troublemakers," "Notes for a Film

on Jazz," "The Burmese Harp," "A Woman of Affairs," "The Cheat," "The Shameless Old Lady," "Intimate Lighting," "Three," "The Roundup," "Masculine Feminine," "The Hunt," "Shadows of Our Forgotten Ancestors," "Pearls On The Ground," "The Man With the Shaven Head," "La Chienne," "Pierrot Le Fou," "Almost a Man," and "The War Is Over."

To honor the artistry and skill of student film-makers, the sponsors of the New York Film Festival inaugurated the National Student Film Awards in 1966 with the presentation of specially selected films at Philharmonic Hall in November, 1966. Awards were given in four categories: dramatic, documentary, animated, and experimental. Students in all accredited colleges and universities could enter their films. The showing of award-winning films in 1966 was preceded by four public screenings of several dozen finalists at the Hunter College Playhouse. A West Coast Program featuring the award-winning films was developed by the sponsors in cooperation with the Theatre Arts Department at the University of California at Los Angeles.

The Chicago International Film Festival was inaugurated at the Carnegie Theatre in November, 1965. The second annual festival, presented at the Playboy Theatre in 1966, included Harold Lloyd's "Funny Side of Life," United States; "Not Loved," Poland; "Bride of the Andes," Japan; "Yul 871," Canada; "Brother Gabrielsen," Norway; "Bushido," Japan; "Sabina and Her Men," Israel; "The Uprising," Roumania; "The Rivals," Greece; "The Boy Across the Street," Israel; and "The Hunt," Spain.

In Southern California on two consecutive evenings in February, 1966, two-and-one-half-hour programs of underwater film documentaries were shown at the ninth annual International Underwater Film Festival. The theatre was the Civic Auditorium, Santa Monica, just a few miles from Hollywood.

The showing of award winning films from the National Film Board of Canada list has become a regular feature of the

82

Vancouver Festival, inaugurated at Vancouver, B.C., in 1958. On July 25, 1966, during the ninth Vancouver Festival, these films were considered for showing: "Corral," the breaking of a wild pony; "City of Gold," nostalgic recollections of the Yukon gold rush; "The Shepherd," a pastoral tableau; "City Out of Time," a portrait of Venice and its art; "Roughnecks," a story of oil drillers; "60 Cycles," cinemaverite set in Montreal; and a series of featurettes by Norman McLaren.

The week-long Montreal International Film Festival, which has been a fixture at Montreal, Canada, since 1960, is intended to promote the distribution of foreign films in Canada. It is credited with bringing about agreements between Canada and the major film producing countries, and encouraging Canadians to appreciate short films more deeply. The seventh Montreal International Film Festival at Loew's Theatre, July 29–August 4, 1966, stressed the importance and value of new cinema by programming nine North American premieres of promising young film-makers. The noble nine were "The Green Hearts," by Edouard Luntz, of France, winner of the Hyères Grand Prix 1966; "Intimate Lighting," Ivan Passer, Czechoslovakia; "A Man Is Not A Bird," Dusan Makavejev, Yugoslavia; "Unreconciled," by Jean-Marie Straub of Germany, winner of the New Cinema Grand Prix '66 Pesaro; "The Shooting," Monte Hellman, United States; "The Dead Woman," by Leon Hirszman of Brazil, winner of a special jury award '65, Rio de Janeiro; "Tale of a Lonely Child," by Leonardo Favio of Argentina, winner of the International Critics' Award '65 at Mar Del Plata; "Between His Parents," Dimiter Petrov, Bulgaria; and "Katia and the Crocodile," Vera Plivova-Simkova, Czechoslovakia.

An International Documentary Film Festival held at Yorkton, Sask., biennially since 1950, has the Golden Sheaf trophy as its principal prize. This is appropriate because the province produces great quantities of grain. Films must be sixteen mm., either black and white, or in color, normal vision, and not exceeding thirty minutes in length. During the celebration in October, 1964, the coveted award was given to "The Edge of the Barrens," produced by the National Film Board. The festival due in 1966 was postponed until 1967 to be a part of Canada's Centennial celebration.

Canada's National Film Board, Ottawa, Ont., has assembled a veritable treasure house full of cinematic gems. One of its latest creations is a Canadian Center for Films on Art, which in turn encourages the staging of Canadian festivals devoted to films on art. The first fete took place May 23–25, 1963, in Ottawa, when the Canadian National Commission for Unesco sponsored the 1963 Unesco Festival and Seminar on Films on Art. The festival provides a splendid opportunity "to see and enjoy films which interest and inform, reveal the diversity of man's art heritage, and quicken interest in periods of cultures other than our own." It also enables participants to discuss the principles and methods of production, acquisition, distribution, and programming of films on art, as well as the new possibilities offered by television. That sparked annual festivals in Toronto, London, and Kingston, Ont., and Regina, Sask.

Fish Festivals

Most fish festivals feature one of the strangest rituals known to polite society. The very fish that inspire the celebration, and in whose honor the parties are staged, invariably wind up as the pièce de resistance of the feast. This certainly is true at lobster festivals. In Rockland, Me., where the Maine Seafood Festival has been an annual event on the first weekend in August since 1947, the townsfolk point with pride to "the world's largest lobster boiler." It is 24-feet long and 14-feet wide, and has two 1,000-gallon tanks supported by a steel frame encased in cement. The tanks have four hatches and are fired by a two million BTU gas generator. As much as 800 pounds of lobster can be put into each hatch at one time. It takes about fifteen minutes to load the eight hatches, then it is time to start unloading them. In 1966 as much as 5,000 pounds of lobster were cooked in one hour. That year, too, more than 6,400 seafood dinners were served. The complete plate consisted of a salad, potato chips, a nine-ounce cod fillet, a lobster weighing between one and two pounds, melted butter, and coffee.

The price of the seafood dinner varies from year to year since it is the intent of the Festival Corporation's Board of Directors to price the meal at cost. In 1966 the break-even price was $2.75 per plate. The serving of food usually starts about noon on Friday in a 1,000-capacity candy-striped tent on the green between the Maine Fishermen's Memorial Pier and the harbor seawall. The sponsors are the Maine Department of Sea and Shore Fisheries, the fishing industry, and some seventeen clubs in the city. They stage a parade Saturday morning, arrange exhibits of coastal arts and crafts and Maine industries, sanction a midway, and provide square dancing and fireworks.

Canada's east coast is so well supplied with lobster each summer there are lobster festivals at Summerside, Prince Edward Island, and Shediac, New Brunswick. At Summerside, lobsters share the honors with cattle, but the livestock can walk away when the party is over. The annual Lobster Carnival was introduced in 1955 and a Livestock Exhibition was added in 1960. The event has become one of the island's major summer attractions for about a week in mid-July. A parade of floats customarily starts the festival on Monday, and judging livestock begins on Wednesday. The feature of the celebration, of course, is fresh boiled lobster served from four to eight P.M. in Civic Stadium. However, diners have a choice of lobster or barbecued chicken, as a rule. There are daily displays of cooking, fancy work, handicrafts, quilts, and rugs as well as demonstrations of pottery-making and wood-crafting. A program of baby contests, concerts, sports events, harness racing, and dancing is climaxed with the crowning of Miss Prince Edward Island and a parade.

Two parades, plays in French and English, a national open sports-car rally, folk singing and dancing, water skiing, an Air Force fly past, Army displays, antiques exhibits, and variety entertainment are the added attractions at the Lobster Festival in Shediac, N. B., where lobster is king and the king must die, around the third week in August. Magnetic Hill, where vehicles seem to roll up a steep grade, is about twenty miles from Shediac, and New Brunswick's Fundy National Park is approximately an hour away by car.

On July 1st, Dominion Day in Canada, there is a Gathering of the Clans and a Fisherman's Regatta, at Pugwash, N. S. Lobster-canning factories along the shore of the River Philip identify a major economic activity of the area, and the inspiration for its fishing festivity. This particular festival is brightened by the tartans worn by Frasers, MacDonalds, MacDougalls, and Stewarts.

The harvest of the sea has been the theme of the Fisheries Exhibition and Fishermen's Reunion at Lunenburg, N. S., since it began in 1916 as a one-day picnic and sports meet. It is now a five-day event around the third week in September, at which time draggers, longliners, schooners, and trawlers break out their flags to add a splash of gaiety. Lunenburg is one of the old-time Canadian shipbuilding and fishing communities. The historic Bluenose, racing champion of the Atlantic, was built there, and before World War I as many as 135 fishing vessels carrying an estimated 3,000 men to handle the catch used to sail from Lunenburg to the Grand Banks off New-foundland. A Memorial Chamber is dedicated to the memory of more than 100 Lunenburg vessels lost at sea, some forty of them with all hands on board. Even so, the competitive spirit is still upon the seafaring men of Lunenburg. After the Grand

Parade Day, which launches the Reunion, junior and senior dory races, outboard, sailing, trawl-baiting, and hauling contests and swimming are featured on Water Sports Day. The main event, though, is usually the Double Dory Race open to all Canadian fishermen. The winner of that contest competes on the following day in an international race between Canada and the United States. Many of the Americans are from the historic fishing community of Gloucester, Mass. Out of this annual contest was created the two-part International Double Dory Race for Americans and Canadians. The first part is staged at Gloucester in June, and the second part at Lunenburg during the Reunion. In the race two-men teams row double dories a mile in any kind of water or weather. Another popular contest is devoted to fish-filleting in which an expert can fillet as much as 100 pounds of cod in six minutes. At the exhibition American and English manufacturers vie with Canadian firms in displaying wares for fishermen and their industry. The winner of the inevitable beauty contest is crowned the Queen of the Sea.

Fishing through holes chopped in the ice that covers lakes and ponds in the winter has become a popular pastime, particularly at winter carnivals. At La Perade, Quebec, on the Sainte-Anne River, just east of Trois-Rivières, though, it is the raison d'être of the Tommycod Fishing Festival which lasts from Christmas Day till Feb. 15th. The French-Canadians of La Perade call the tommycod le petit poisson, the little fishes. Peradiens trundle their *cabanes,* or wooden huts, to holes in the ice. As many as 1,500 heated huts make up the impromptu fishing village. The fishermen sing their own theme song written to the tune of "Jingle Bells." The melody enlivens the festival which fans out around a toboggan slide and a gigantic ice sculpture. The ice is usually thick enough for cars and trucks to drive over. Streets are laid out, and signs advertise huts for rent or fish for sale. Although tommycod is premiere in this *poisson* parade, other species that bite the bait and jingle the telltale matchsticks on lines strung up inside the

87

huts, are carp, perch, pike, smelts, speckled trout, and walleyes.

Fish in northern Manitoba waters around Flin Flon are so hefty the average size of lake trout that have captured first prize since the Flin Flon Trout Festival began in 1951 is around thirty-five pounds. Although the festival encompasses the independence days of both Canada and the United States, July 1st–4th, the trout derby usually begins during the third week in June and continues until sunset, July 3rd. All other fishing events usually begin during the fourth week in June, and also end on July 3rd. The cash prize for catching the biggest trout can be as much as $1,000, in addition to other prizes. Besides fishing for cash and fun visitors to the festival can participate in an amateur canoe race, the Gold Rush Canoe Derby for professionals, water skiing, diving, and boat races. Indians stage wrestling matches and pack flour in feats of strength. To salute the visitors who travel great distances to take part in the fishing derbies there is a special class for the best fish caught by the visitor farthest from home. The town's symbol is a twenty-four-foot statue of Joshiah Flintabbety Flonatin, mythical hero of a book written in 1905, who inadvertently gave the town its name.

Livingston, Mont., has been staging a National Fresh Water Trout Derby in August since 1941, to attract attention to the fine fishing possibilities in the nearby Yellowstone River. One trout can be worth as much as $1,000 if it is the largest fish caught. River police inspect and tag catches as soon as possible after they are landed in a designated area at least twenty miles long.

Within the space of a few weeks late in spring and early in summer, Gloucester, Mass., usually has two fish festivals. One is sponsored by local Portuguese, and the other by Italian fishermen. Blessing of the respective fleets is standard practice at the celebrations. The Portuguese-Americans who stage the first one attend the Church of Our Lady of Good Voyage and schedule the festival to coincide with the Feast of Corpus

Christi, in May or June, sixty days after Easter. They march through the narrow streets to the waterfront where open air ceremonies have been staged regularly since 1944. The Italians venerate St. Peter, the patron saint of all fishermen, before a big outdoor altar on his feast day, June 29th. The celebration, which lasts three days, dates to 1931. The first half of the Gloucester-Lunenburg double dory race is rowed, and there are swimming races and fireworks displays. St. Peter's Day celebrations also are staged in Provincetown, Mass., and in other communities which have sizable populations of Italian fishermen.

Fisher-folk in San Francisco, Calif., prefer to stage their fish festival coincident with the Feast of St. Francis on Oct. 4th.

Practically all the shrimp festivals in the United States are staged in communities adjacent to the Gulf of Mexico, from Florida to Texas. The shrimp boats go first to the Island Shrimp Festival at Fort Myers, Fla., during the last week in February. There are turtle races, a street dance, and a blessing of the fleet. The traditional blessing of the fishing fleet is the big event of the Biloxi, Miss., Shrimp Festival on the first Sunday in June. Louisianians stage two shrimp festivals in the bayou area of the state. The first is the Louisiana Shrimp Festival at Morgan City, over the Labor Day weekend, and the other is the Shrimp Festival and Fair at Delcambre, around the third week in October. Shrimp festivals in Texas are at Aransas Pass, the second week in June, then at Brownsville-Port Isabel, in mid-June and again the first week in July.

The fish festival with an abundance of local color and spontaneity is the Crayfish Festival staged during the fourth week in April, during even-numbered years, at Breaux Bridge, La., in the heart of the romantic Evangeline Country. French-Acadian folk music, songs, and dances enliven the two-day event, and sometimes there are trips to the farms where the succulent crayfish are cultivated. Steamed crayfish, a festival specialty, is just one of the culinary delights. Before, during and after the biennial celebration restaurants in the area serve tasty crayfish stews, bisque, and salads at reasonable prices.

Several species of crab are plentiful along the shores of North America. Two that are edible, the blue crab of the Atlantic Coast and the king crab from Alaskan waters, are probably the only ones that have inspired festivals. The older of the two celebrations is the National Hard Crab Derby, inaugurated in 1948, at Crisfield, Md. It has become a popular tourist attraction over Labor Day weekend. Standard features are a crab feed, fishing contests, a beauty pageant, and a crab race. The king crab, a gigantic crustacean with several pairs of legs averaging at least three feet in length, is a mainstay of the economy of Kodiak, Alaska. A plan to publicize this fact was proposed to the Kodiak Chamber of Commerce by a quartet of civic leaders in 1956, but nothing was done about it until May 2nd and 3rd, 1958, when the inaugural King Crab Festival featured a huge crab feed, a crab recipe contest, the judging of crabs for size and weight, street games such as a tug o' war, and two dances. Buoyed by success, the people of Kodiak proclaimed their city the King Crab Capital of the World. There were only about ten entries in the size and weight contest because prospective sponsors learned that the most formidable entry had a leg span of about 60 inches and weighed more than twenty-one pounds. Recently other events, including a parachute jump, deep sea and scuba diving, an arts and crafts exhibit, and boat tours have been added. The festival had been expanded to three days over the first weekend in May when the catastrophic earthquake of March 27, 1964, damaged Kodiak so badly festivities were curtailed. The festival during the first week in May, 1966, offered crab races, skin diving, a carnival midway, an arts and crafts exhibition, dances, and plays.

"Fly Me to the Moon" was the theme of the twenty-first annual Clam Festival at Pismo Beach, Calif., in mid-November, 1966. Highlights included a parade, flower and art shows, a horse show, sports car races, a clam dig, a free clam chowder feed, a torchlight parade, and a statewide surfing contest.

In Hawaii a fishing festival is a hukilau. Huki means pull, and lau is the leaf of a plant which festoons the huge fish nets. According to tradition, every hukilau guest is supposed to help pull in the net, otherwise he is not entitled to share in the catch. Dates and places of the hukilaus vary. When they are staged at Laie Bay, on Oahu Island, Samoans and Hawaiians who live there recreate old island customs, and perform ancient skills and dances. They weave baskets and hats for visitors, pound poi, and display tapas, seed, and shell ornaments. Sometimes a pig sheathed in leaves is baked in a pit for the feast.

Whaling is no longer the way of life it used to be, but the memory of its heyday a century or more ago lives on in at least two locales under the American flag, several thousand miles apart. At Lahaina, Maui, Hawaii, where an estimated 500 whaling ships and 1,500 whalers clustered in the mid-eighteenth century, a Whaling Festival has been staged on the first weekend in November since 1962. It opens with a waterfront parade on Friday. There are a ukulele contest, fireworks, and Hawaiian entertainment on Saturday, and several outrigger canoe races on Sunday.

At least 7,000 miles northeast of Hawaii, at Sag Harbor, L. I., N. Y., the Age of the Whale has been simulated during a three-day Old Whalers Festival about the second weekend in June since 1963. Huge facsimile whales made of wood, burlap, and canvas float offshore, and dozens of men pile into round-bottom boats and paddle seaward to harpoon the mock mammals. Ashore there might be debates between descendants of mariners from Massachusetts and Long Island about the old days of whaling and going down to the sea in Ships, a queen contest, concerts, folk songs, and fireworks.

Celebrating a successful whaling season for real is still done in Alaska at Barrow, Point Hope, and Wainwright, early in

June, and at Kotzebue, in July. However, festivals take place only when there has been a successful season. If so, then that is the time to dance by the light of the midnight sun and enjoy Eskimo games, blanket-tossing, Miss Arctic Beauty Queen and Arctic Baby Contests, muktuk-eating competitions, Eskimo high-kicking contests, Eskimo dances, kayak and motorboat races, and the awarding of prizes to the Eskimo hunter who brought in the biggest beluga whale since winter icebreakup.

Floral Festivals

Blossom time, for many of the most eagerly awaited period of the year, is the most evanescent. Yet even a fleeting glimpse of pale pink or white blossoms is a welcome signal to bid adieu to winter and hail the approach of spring. To present that tangible sign each year Nature labors longer than most men realize. In temperate regions she forms the buds of blossoms which appear between March and May as early as the previous July. For performing this labor she reserves the right to decide when the blossoms shall appear, even though the ensuing uncertainty can create frustration among sponsors of major blossom festivals who must perfect many of their plans as far ahead of time as the preceding summer. In Southern California, where there still are many fruit orchards, A is for the Almond Blossom Festival at Quartz Hill. When it is staged during the second week of March it anticipates the formal arrival of spring by more than a week. Partisans point out that the festival, an annual event since 1950, takes place near "the world's biggest almond grove," which covers six square miles of the Antelope Valley. The fete features a carnival, pet and western parades, and tours of the area to preferred vantage points of the orchards.

In the nine-county Redwood Empire of Northern California and Southern Oregon, spring and prune blossoms often arrive simultaneously during the fourth week of March in the vicinity of Healdsburg, so tours to the orchards are timely. A forty-four-mile posted Apple Blossom Tour fans out of Sebastopol and meanders among the orchards of the fertile Russian River Valley each April. With luck, the peak of bloom occurs when the Apple Industry Show is on at Sebastopol.

The most ambitious of all the apple blossom festivals is the Washington State Apple Blossom Festival at Wenatchee, Wash. It invariably begins three days prior to the first Sunday in May, blossoms or no blossoms. However, specialists have figured that this is the time when billows of low-hanging, sweet-scented clouds of blossoms should be hovering over the Wenatchee Valley. They are the harbingers of a 100 million dollar apple crop that matures between June and October, and enables Wenatchee to claim the title "Apple Capital of the World." The local festival grew out of a simple songfest larded with speeches praising Wenatchee, its blossoms and its fruit, on the Court House lawn in 1920. The following year an apple blossom queen was selected, and during the ensuing forty-five years the royal court was expanded to include several dozen princesses from communities in Washington and western Canada. There are also a grand parade which is witnessed by tens of thousands of spectators, a state art exhibition, a carnival, school parade, horse show, stage play, gem and mineral show, antique autorama, outdoor pancake breakfast, motorcycle hill climb, hydroplane races, a girls' drill team conclave, Canadian tattoo, coronation, and ball.

Virginians have been celebrating apple blossom time in the Shenandoah Valley with a festival at Winchester since 1924. It is timed to begin about three days before the first Sunday in May. Then visitors might view blossoming orchards in the entourage of the reigning Queen Shenandoah, see the results of an apple pie-baking contest, a majorette contest, queen's coronation, talent and beauty contest, grand parade, square dancing, and dances to honor the queen.

93

An estimated 700,000, trees on 18,000 acres of fruit orchards near Gettysburg, in Adams County, Pa., normally bear apple, cherry, or peach blossoms the last week in April and the first week in May. So, the local Fruitgrowers Association posts signs along the road to guide motorists and publicize the first Sunday in May as Apple Blossom Festival time. Blossom hosts steer visitors through orchards and answer questions about planting and cultivating, while wives and daughters of growers serve free apple juice at roadside booths and information centers. At South Mountain Fair Grounds, nine miles south of Gettysburg, various apple dishes enrich a Sunday dinner from eleven to five. The queen is crowned about two P.M., and there is a band concert.

Orchard owners in the Monadnock Region of New Hampshire welcome tourists who follow the apple blossom trail designated each spring by the Monadnock Region Association, Peterborough, on or about May 10th. Usually arrows point the way from Milford through valleys and over hills to Greenville, Lyndeborough, Mason, Peterborough, Temple, and Wilton.

Since the 1930's, Canadians and Americans have been trekking to the Kentville-Grand Pré Area of Nova Scotia, around the last week in May to enjoy the Annapolis Valley Blossom Festival. About that time of year the delicately scented blossoms of an estimated one million apple trees provide a festive backdrop for the queen's coronation, a parade, barbecue, and dances. Grand Pré was the home of the Acadians whom Longfellow immortalized in his poem "Evangeline."

About April 5th, 1966, billows of single flowering cherry blossoms encircled the Tidal Basin in Washington, D. C. That was a few days before the start of the annual National Cherry Blossom Festival staged to celebrate their appearance, but the blossoms did reach their peak of bloom during the festivities. In other years the single blossoms which customarily furnish the background for the festival have bloomed as early as

94

March 20th, or as late as April 15th. The date of Easter is the major consideration for setting the date of the Cherry Blossom Festival. However, the sponsors also aim for the first or second week of April because the first blossoms are apt to come out then. Whenever they arrive the blooms are always lovely to behold, while they last. For the single strain is so short-lived most of the blossoms vanish within a few days. After they disappear there is usually a lull for about ten days to two weeks, then trees in East Potomac Park sport their hearty double blossoms. This species enjoys a longer life than the single blossoms do, usually holding on for about ten days.

Cherry blossoms as the symbol of the nation's capital is an increasingly popular conception. The U.S. Travel Service reports that they are high on the list of things visitors from abroad hope to see when they come to the United States. Some people believe, mistakenly, that the blossoms are in season throughout the year, and often express disappointment when they learn that the trees flower only in April, as a rule, and that they do not bear fruit. Soon there will be more cherry trees in the District, because the Washington Convention and Visitors Bureau has given Mrs. Lyndon B. Johnson 200 specimens to help beautify the city as she sees fit. What's more, Ambassador Takeuchi, of Japan, has announced that his country will give many more cherry trees to America for planting in Washington. Although Japan is the land of cherry blossoms, its people have probably never staged a festival like the one in Washington, D. C. The Capital's tourist attraction stems from a generous gesture by the Japanese in 1909. That year the first shipment of cherry trees sent to Washington as a gift from the people of Tokyo reached the United States, but it had to be burned on arrival because it was infected with insect pests and fungus diseases. The Ikitsu Imperial Horticultural Station then grafted cultural plants with wild roots and nursed them for two years before shipping. They arrived in Washington early in 1912, and the first tree was planted by Mrs. William Howard Taft, the wife of the President.

Thousands of people from miles around Traverse City, Mich., drive to the nearby cherry orchards when they are in bloom, usually during the first two weeks in May. The exact period of blossoming, of course, is determined by the weather. From time to time, since 1924, there has been a solemn blessing of the blossoms on the first or second Sunday in May, at Bowers Harbor, some seven miles from Traverse City. Local clergymen and school choirs participate.

Each spring since 1938 motorists as well as flying farmers from Colorado and surrounding states have converged on Canon City, Colo., to savor the sight of lilacs, tulips, and several thousand acres of cherry trees in bloom. Among the entertainment features in recent years have been barbecues, concerts, parades, coronations, drills, and marching exhibitions, as well as tours of orchards and even the Royal Gorge. In 1966, the Blossom Festival was staged May 5th and 6th.

Because cherry trees do not prosper in Hawaii's tropical climate Americans of Oriental descent who live there fashion reams of pink paper into decorative artificial blooms for the Cherry Blossom Festival which has been an annual event in Honolulu, during March and April since 1953. The imitation flowers and real lanterns are used to decorate floats in a parade that rolls along Kalakaua Ave. to Kapiolani Park by the sea. The floats are peopled with costumed Japanese fairytale characters, a Shinto shrine is carried by men in kimonas, and kimona-clad school children carrying lighted lanterns bring up the rear. After the parade there are Bon dances, traditional Buddhist folk rites honoring ancestral spirits. Occidental visitors often join the dancers as they circle lantern-lit towers to the beat of a gigantic drum. During the Cherry Blossom Festival there are also operettas, a Lion Dance, fashion show, queen contest, popular entertainment, a coronation ball, and a cultural show at which elaborate formal and informal kimona and kokeshi dolls are displayed.

Since potatoes are important to Maine's economy, the state whoops things up in behalf of its spuds when a green and white carpet of potato blossoms is spread across farmlands in the Pine Tree State. The current series of Maine Potato Blossom Festivals began at Fort Fairfield in 1935. Immediately after World War II, Caribou, Houlton, and Van Buren played host to the festival. In 1949 it returned to Fort Fairfield, and has been an annual event there around the third weekend in July ever since. Familiar attractions include a beauty queen contest, art and farm machinery displays, sports contests, a parade, coronation, and a Potato Blossom Festival Ball.

Blossoms and wildflowers are so popular that requests for information about the best times and places to see them are high on the list of questions its members ask the Auto Club of Southern California. The club usually charts the progress of spring flowers in California and Nevada from late in February until late May, and when members make inquiries they are invariably cautioned about the unpredictability of the flowering due to changes in conditions. The spring show of desert flowers in the Anza-Borrego Desert State Park of eastern San Diego County often begins in February, reaches a peak late in March, and fades away in May.

Some citizens of Julian, Calif., believe their community stages the "premier Wildflower Show in America." Blooms from the desert, wild lilies, flowers from high mountain ranges, and myriad wildflowers are collected by the women of Julian and exhibited in the Town Hall, usually during the second and third weeks in May.

Botanists and just plain garden variety flower-lovers converge on Gatlinburg, Tenn., late in April to take part in the annual Wildflower Pilgrimage there. They hike through the Great Smoky Mountains and listen to lectures by naturalists. At night in the Auditorium at Gatlinburg they watch motion pictures of wildflowers in the area.

Azaleas, camellias, dogwood, roses, tulips, and wildflowers brighten North Carolina in the spring, but the state's largest seasonal festival features azaleas, around the first week in April. Inaugurated in 1948 as the Wilmington Azalea Festival, by 1959 it was deemed so representative of the state the title was changed to North Carolina Azalea Festival at Wilmington. The festival queen is usually someone prominent in the entertainment field. Reigning performers have been stars of stage, screen, and television. On the festival program are garden tours, variety shows, fireworks, a hootenanny, a teenage royal court, outdoor art show, two coronation performances, band concerts, sailboat races, and a parade.

Norfolk, Va., began staging an International Azalea Festival in 1954. It derives its international flavor from the presence of the Atlantic Command Headquarters of the North Atlantic Treaty Organization in Norfolk. So, the festival's queen and princesses represent the fifteen NATO nations. The program includes much military participation as a salute to the member countries, and princesses are designated by their respective embassies. In 1965, Luci Baines Johnson, daughter of President and Mrs. Lyndon B. Johnson, was Queen of Azaleas, and escorts for the queen and her court were midshipmen from the U. S. Naval Academy. Staged for about five days around the last weekend in April, as a rule, the highlights of the festival include concerts under the stars, an azalea parade, coronation ceremony, military demonstrations, a civic ballet, and fireworks. The foremost social event is the Junior League Azalea Ball.

The Junior Chamber of Commerce of Palatka, Fla., helps the city stage an Azalea Festival around the first week in March each year. Festivities presented against a background of an estimated 100,000 azalea bushes in the eighty-five-acre city-owned Ravine Gardens include a talent contest, parade, ball, and beauty pageant.

Azaleas in bloom along a cultivated thirty-five-mile Azalea Trail that winds through Mobile, Ala., and the flowering of other large and small azalea plants and camellias, provide the floral decorations for the annual America's Junior Miss Pageant in that city, usually during the last week in March.

The first camellias brought to Sacramento, Calif., are believed to have been taken there by L. L. F. Warren, a nursery-man from Boston, Mass., on February 7, 1852, just two years before Sacramento was chosen to be the state capital in 1854. Because the flower flourished in the mild Sacramento climate, two dozen camellia plants of six varieties were planted in the garden around the capitol when it was finished in 1869. Almost forty years later, in 1908, Sacramento is believed to have been referred to for the first time as the Camellia Capital when a play glorifying the flower was presented there. The camellia has since become the official flower of both the City and County of Sacramento, and is represented in the extensive Capitol Park alone by more than 2,800 plants covering some 800 varieties. Since 1924 Sacramento has had an anuual Camellia Show early in March, and it staged its first Camellia Festival in 1955. The ten-day event takes place during the first and second weeks in March. Major events of the twelfth annual Camellia Festival in March, 1966, included the twenty-first annual meeting of the American Camellia Society, which was the Society's second visit to Sacramento. Also, there was the admission-free forty-second annual Camellia Show, a camellia ball and queen's coronation, Babies' Day when camellia plants were given to all babies born in Sacramento County on that day, a fashion show luncheon honoring past Camellia Queens, a performance of the Camellia City Ballet at, appropriately, Luther Burbank High School, and the Camellia Cup Regatta on Folsom Lake.

A camellia nursery center in Temple City, Calif., was the inspiration for the three-day Camellia Festival which has been an annual event there since 1945. To celebrate the peak of the camellia-blossoming season around Temple City, a camellia court is chosen from among youngsters in first grade, and some 5,000 school children pull four by six-foot flower floats of their own design in an annual parade on Friday of the last weekend in February.

A golden carpet of daffodils spreads out across Washington's Puyallup Valley at the base of majestic, snowcapped Mt.

Rainier, late in March and early in April. To capitalize on the beauty of that carpet during the first and second weeks in April, civic leaders of Puyallup, Sumner, and Tacoma have been sponsoring a Daffodil festival since 1934. Often motorists from many states and Canada tour the valley past the flowering fields. They examine several hundred varieties of bulbs, and watch a floral float parade that usually visits the three participating towns. They also ride a special train through the daffodil fields between Tacoma and Orting, visit a Daffodil Flower Show, watch a regatta on Tacoma's Commencement Bay, and attend the Queen's coronation ceremonies and grand ball.

Dogwood grows in such profusion in the foothills of the Great Smoky Mountains around Knoxville, Tenn., during April, that a ten-day Dogwood Arts Festival has become an annual event there since 1961. It offers music, dancing, singing, arts and crafts, drama, and historical tours of homes and gardens. There are also several trails of flowering pink and white dogwood trees, a regional high school band competition, a water parade, sports-car races, golf tournament, and an opening ceremony preceded by a parade which might include as many as thirty-five bands.

The people of Atlanta, Ga., began to make merry when the dogwood comes in bloom around mid-April by staging a Dogwood Festival for the first time in 1964. They dance atop 800-foot Stone Mountain, and stage tours along the dogwood trail and to private homes and gardens.

Dogwood trails fan out from Palestine, Tex., so in mid-April activities saluting the blossoms often include an art show, beauty pageant, and square dancing.

Hydrangeas, the official flower of Atlantic City, N. J., flourish in July, which was the logical reason for inaugurating an annual Hydrangea Festival there in July, 1942. Usually a Hydrangea Queen leads a procession along the Hydrangea Trail which beautifies the residential district of the resort.

One of Virginia's heartiest perennials is the statewide Historic Garden Week inaugurated in the Old Dominion in 1929, and staged regularly during the last week in April. The idea for the revenue-producing garden tour developed when the Garden Club of Virginia was asked to help restore the grounds and gardens of the Betty Washington Lewis Home, "Kenmore," at Fredericksburg. Proceeds from the first tour were donated to the Kenmore Association. Now late in April thousands of people stroll through dozens of gardens, and the coffers of restoration projects in Virginia are enriched. Most of the gardens are usually closed to visitors.

The gardens and architecture of Colonial Williamsburg, Va., are the subject of study by those who attend the Colonial Home and Garden Symposiums which have been a standard attraction at Williamsburg in March since 1947. Discussions are led by specialists.

The annual Maryland House and Garden Pilgrimage sponsored by the Federated Garden Clubs of Maryland has been a successful venture since it was started in 1936. As many as two hundred of Maryland's finest houses and gardens are open late in April and early in May, as a rule. Proceeds from ticket sales help maintain such fine examples of late Colonial architecture as Hammond-Harwood House in Annapolis. Built in 1760, it has been called "the most beautiful example of Georgian architecture in America."

The golden age of Natchez, Miss., was during the half century before the Civil War began in 1861. Many elegant plantation homes were built then, and moonlight and magnolias figured prominently in romantic conceptions of the town in that era. Since 1932 the garden clubs of the community have been doing their bit to perpetuate that dream by sponsoring conducted tours of the antebellum homes and gardens during the month of March.

From around mid-April until early in May flower fanciers join a pilgrimage to various handsome homes and gardens in southeastern Tennessee, between Nashville and Knoxville. The pilgrimage was inaugurated in 1951.

In the spring of 1931, Mrs. Annie Walker Burns persuaded the people of Pineville, Ky., to make the most of their abundance of laurel by making it the theme of an annual festival. Since then the Kentucky Mountain Laurel Festival has been staged regularly around the last weekend in May. The celebration, staged in a natural amphitheater at Laurel Cove, Pine Mountain State Park, is ruled by a queen chosen from among college students wearing white evening dresses and carrying bouquets of laurel. Customarily the queen is crowned by the Governor of Kentucky, and attractions include an art exhibit, band concert, receptions, fireworks, a parade, coronation, a grand ball, queen's breakfast, style show, and ball.

May 1st, traditionally flower day throughout the northern hemisphere, has special significance in Hawaii, where May Day is Lei Day. That is the only festival dedicated to the handmade necklace of flowers, the traditional symbol of Hawaiian friendship and aloha spirit. On Lei Day everyone wears the vari-colored garlands. Prizes are given for the best of those placed in competition, and entertainment includes dancing, singing, chanting, hulas, and pageants. The major Lei Day party takes place at Waikiki Beach Park. Often the favorite entries at the official state lei exhibition in Queen Kapiolani Park by the sea are leis made of the seldom seen golden ilima, once reserved for Hawaiian royalty, and those strung from the blue-green jade vine blossoms.

Spokane, Wash., began flirting with a Lilac Festival in 1938. That year the local Associated Garden Clubs staged a lilac show and a small parade. In 1940 a lilac queen contest was added and high schools joined the parade. Now there are three parades—a torchlight procession at night and a Junior Parade and an Armed Forces Grand Parade in the daytime—during the second week in May. There are also band concerts, baton-twirling contests, a rodeo, and flower show.

Orange blossoms, the familiar bridal symbol, began to be identified with Florida near the close of the nineteenth century after Mrs. Julia Tuttle, of Lemon City, Fla., now a section of

Miami, used them to persuade Henry M. Flagler, who had built the Florida East Coast Railroad as far south as Palm Beach, to extend the tracks another seventy-five miles southward to Miami. Mrs. Tuttle, who subsequently became known affectionately as "the Mother of Miami," in the winter of 1894–95 while frost was on the ground elsewhere, shipped some sprigs from an orange tree in her back yard and sent them to Flagler to bolster her letter-writing campaign to the tycoon. The orange blossoms were credited with convincing him that Miami did indeed have mild weather in winter. He not only extended the F.E.C. to the small settlement at the mouth of the Miami River, he also built the imposing Royal Palm Hotel at the end of the track. On July 28, 1896, three months after Flagler's first "Florida Special" reached Miami from New York, Miami was incorporated by 343 voters. Now housing developments and industrial plants are usurping much of the land once occupied by grapefruit, lemon, and orange groves in Florida, Texas, Arizona, and Southern California, the leading producers of citrus fruits in the United States, so the heady aroma of blossoms in these states has been greatly reduced. However, the atmosphere is perfumed enough in February and March to make a visit worth the effort.

Southern Florida is one of the few places in the United States where the flamboyant poinciana grows, so the people who live in and near Miami have been celebrating the novelty with a Royal Poinciana Fiesta around the second week in June since 1935. As a rule, at that time of year the graceful trees with lacelike foliage resemble big red umbrellas when their blossoms are in full flower. Fiesta festivities include a coronation, art exhibits, a concert, fashion show, and dinner. Often there are tours to see the trees in bloom, and even the distribution of poinciana sprigs, since the original purpose of the festival was to encourage propagation of the tree.

Roan Mountain, in the Great Smoky Mountains shared by North Carolina and Tennessee, is the one place where two states stage separate festivals at the same site to salute the same flower, the rhododendron. Between 1947 and 1957 citizens of the Tar Heel and Volunteer States cooperated in staging the celebration. In 1958 they accepted a recommendation of the Forest Service that there be two events, one sponsored by each state. They would alternate between the third and fourth weekends in June. So, in 1966, North Carolina played host June 15th to 18th, and Tennessee the next week. The North Carolina Rhododendron Festival is sponsored by the Lions Club of Bakersville. Their big promotion is a queen contest and pageant, because the queen travels to promote the festival and the state. The main attraction is the floral display in 600 acres of flame red or deep purple rhododendron, about twelve miles from Bakersville. Paved highways lead to gardens atop the 6,327-foot mountain from Bakersville, and also from Roan Mountain, Tenn.

The most famous floral parade in the world now has at least sixty flower-bedecked floats in its line of march beginning at nine o'clock New Year's morning. It is the stately Tournament of Roses Parade which has been rolling along Colorado Street in Pasadena, Calif., regularly since 1886. Now that city of approximately 120,000 people is crowded with hundreds of thousands of visitors, many of whom wrap themselves in blankets and huddle on curbstones through the night awaiting the spectacle. It was Charles Frederick Holder, a naturalist and author, who persuaded fellow members of the Valley Hunt Club to celebrate the ripening of oranges in Southern California by decorating their carriages with natural flowers and parading them through the town on New Year's Day.

From the very beginning the delicacy and natural beauty of fresh flowers prevailed. The carriages which made up the first few parades were garlanded with homegrown blossoms. Now fresh flowers are flown in from across the sea to augment the domestic supply. Ten of the sixty floats may be sponsored by commercial firms whose sales messages must be discretely sheathed in fresh blooms, while the remaining fifty flower festooned floats publicize communities, states, and nations.

104

The theme of the 75th annual Tournament of Roses Parade in 1964 was "Symbols of Freedom." Former President Dwight D. Eisenhower served as the Grand Marshall, and in the procession was the first Negro float ever to participate. Titled "Freedom Bursts Forth," it commemorated the 100th anniversary of the Emancipation Proclamation. "It's a Small World" was the theme of the sixty fresh flower floats in the 77th parade on January 1, 1966. Cups, trays, merchandise awards, and enlarged photos of the floats have been given as prizes. After the parade the floats are exhibited at the Tournament's post parade area, where visitors usually are welcome to linger and look at the entries until ten P.M. on January 1st, and from ten to ten the next day.

For a community that has very few commercial flower growers and nothing extraordinary about its residential gardens, Portland, Ore., has nevertheless successfully used its annual Rose Festival and one of the nation's approximately two dozen international rose test gardens to inflate its reputation as a City of Roses. The celebration launched in 1907 grew out of an annual Rose Show inaugurated in 1889. Since 1930 the queen has been a high school senior selected from a court of princesses nominated by high school student bodies. Because each princess receives a college scholarship from the Rose Festival Association, more than $150,000 worth of scholarships has been distributed. In 1936 the sponsors of a junior rose festival were invited to have their parade become an official part of the festival. It is usually staged the day before the Grand Floral Parade, which normally takes place on the second or third Saturday in June. The fifty impressive floats bedecked with fresh flowers depicting a theme are convincing prototypes of those in the granddaddy of all rose parades, the Tournament of Roses Parade at Pasadena, Calif., on New Year's Day.

Tyler, Tex., home of the Texas Rose Festival, boasts that it is the center of Smith County's best-known enterprise, its rose industry. At least 600 carloads, averaging 15,000 plants to the

105

car, are shipped north and east from Tyler each year. The shipment of rose blooms by air express is a growing activity. In 1933 nurserymen of Tyler began to celebrate their prowess with a festival during the fourth week in October. Floats adorned with roses are featured in a parade which often extends two miles. There are tours of fields from which an estimated fifteen million rose bushes are sold annually, a rose show, and a coronation. One of two dozen rose test gardens in the United States is at Tyler.

Thomasville, Ga., widely known as a city of flowers, climaxes its blossom time each spring with a Rose Festival in mid-April. The festival developed gracefully from a rose show first staged in 1922. That year there were a few entries of tea and hybrid tea roses and decorated tables. Now there are hundreds of entries, new varieties of roses, and artistic arrangements. Thomasville also has one of about two dozen rose test gardens in the United States. During Rose Festival Week there in April, 1966, in addition to an impressive rose show and visits to areas of natural loveliness in and near Thomasville, there was an air show, a beauty pageant, folk music, a golf tournament, horse show, a parade, and tours of plantations.

Since the rose is the official flower of New York, and various species thrive in open gardens and hot houses there, a few more rose festivals would be welcome in the Empire State. One that has been well received since it was inaugurated in 1930 takes place in a 17-acre garden that has an estimated 35,000 plants bright with blooms in early summer, at Newark, N. Y. At the Rose Festival staged during the fourth week in June a high point is the debut of new roses. Among the newcomers have been Polynesian Sunset, the 1966 All-America floribunda Apricot Nectar, and two hybrid tea roses: the pure white John F. Kennedy, and the fragrant red Hallmark rose. The festival is believed to sponsor the only national flower arranging competition, and offers specially arranged gardens of color for inspection. On the site is one of the two dozen rose test gardens in the United States.

An annual event of special interest to tropical flower lovers and professional and amateur gardeners is the Tropical Flower Festival which has been taking place in February and March since 1961 at the Agricultural Experiment Station of the University of Puerto Rico, Rio Piedras, P. R. The grounds are usually filled with varied and colorful displays of orchids, hibiscus, ornamental plants, and medicinal herbs contributed by island garden clubs, commercial nurseries, civic groups, and the station itself. Among the novelties at the festival have been a twenty-foot clock and a huge calendar, both decorated with flowers and plants, and both in working order.

As its name suggests, Holland, Mich., is in a part of the Wolverine State settled by the Dutch. Also, at least in the northeastern United States, the community's fame as a tulip center is par excellence. Since 1929, when civic leaders decided to decorate the city with 100,000 plantings to publicize the local tulip nurseries, Tulip Time in Holland, Mich., has been an annual four-day festival beginning on the Wednesday nearest May 15th. During the fete visitors are entertained in the heart of town by klompen dancers, a volks parade, sidewalk and street scrubbing, soccer, a symphony concert, barbershop quartets, a baton twirling contest, and square dancing. To add a touch of Old World authenticity early in the series a wooden shoe carver was brought over from the Netherlands. Annually now, the wooden shoe factory in Holland reportedly produces about 20,000 pairs of wooden shoes made of poplar logs.

Dutch descendants in Orange City, Iowa, began saluting their heritage in 1936 with a Tulip Festival on the second weekend in May. Residents in traditional Dutch costumes mingle with visitors at the tulip exhibit and flower show, street scrubbing, a parade of floats, coronation ceremonies, drill demonstrations, and a Dutch street dance.

107

Far-sighted is an appropriate description of the several hundred immigrants from The Netherlands who settled in 1847 in what is now Pella, Iowa. They decided on the name of their new home a year before they even had enough funds to sail to America. Pella means City of Refuge. In May, 1936, they began giving a sentimental salute to their Dutch ancestry with a three-day Tulip Festival. Authentic Dutch costumes are worn, streets usually lined with tulips are scrubbed in a public ceremony, there are folk games, dances, a parade, pageant, and coronation.

Albany, N. Y., where the Dutch settled more than 300 years ago, recalls its ethnic origin in May with a Tulip Festival that offers a display of Holland tulips in Washington Park, a flower show at the Albany Institute of History and Art, scrubbing of State St. by Dutch-costumed women, a coronation, pageant, concerts, and a children's carnival.

During World War II, Princess Juliana of the Netherlands, who subsequently became Queen Juliana, lived in Ottawa, Ont., with her children. After she returned to Holland at the end of the war, she presented 100,000 Dutch tulip bulbs to Ottawa as a token of her affection for the Canadian capital. To the Queen's gift bulb growers of Holland added 60,000 bulbs, and promised that each year enough new stock would be added to keep up the supply. Now during the last half of May the gardens around Parliament are bright with tulips of various hues for the Canadian Tulip Festival. Visitors see a tulip show, square dancing, a war canoe derby, and fireworks, and hear choral music. In the last week of the festival, as a rule, floral exhibits are flown in from countries around the world, and dignitaries from some thirty embassies take part in an International Flower Festival enlivened by national songs and dances.

Folk Festivals

To NORTH Americans the customs of other lands from which their antecedents came frequently serve as inspiration for folk festivals. Sometimes the celebrations salute a single ethnic group, but quite often several nationalities are represented at a single party. A Festival of Nations has been staged regularly in St. Paul, Minn., since 1932, as a part of the usual work of the St. Paul International Institute. The significant thing about this festival, and others of its genre, is the absence of commercialism. The spontaneity and enthusiasm of volunteers invariably engenders a wholesome atmosphere of dedicated nonprofessionalism. The emphasis is not upon achievement of perfection, but upon the process of people living and working together in peace and mutual appreciation of each others' contributions. There is informal folk dancing in which all can participate, as they might in any old-time village square abroad. There are exhibits of folk arts and crafts, as well as little houses in which national foods are served. The houses are remindful of those in the countries from which the people who play host in them trace their ancestry. Now staged triennially, during May, as a rule, in 1964 a Latin American house was added to the collection to welcome the newcomers from the Caribbean, Mexico, Central and South America to the St. Paul area. That year, too, some three dozen nationality groups participated, and gastronomic specialities from at least twenty-eight countries were served.

The costumes of many nationalities are in evidence whenever the International Folk Festival which was inaugurated in 1948 is staged at Duluth, Minn. One day late in July or early in August foods and handicrafts from abroad are displayed.

Also, there is a program of music and dances in which hundreds of people in folk costumes participate.

In Wisconsin a veritable Trail of Nations completely encircles the Badger State. The jewels on this necklace are folk festivals which identify the areas where various other nationals from Europe dug in during the years of the great migrations in the nineteenth century. From Milwaukee the trail leads northward to the Holland Festival, Cedar Grove; Fyr Bal Fest, Ephraim; Scandinavian Festival, Washington Island; Polish Festival, Pulaski; Sas Keekah, Keshena; National Finnish American Festival, Hurley; French Bazaar, Somerset; Syttende Mai, Woodville and Chippewa Falls; International Festival, Eau Claire; Oktoberfest, La Crosse; Founders' Day, Mineral Point; a Swiss Fun Weekend, Holiday in Heidiland and Wilhelm Tell Festival, New Glarus; Syttende Mai, Stoughton; International Folk Festival, A Pageant of Our People, Madison; Gymanfa Ganus, Cambria, Dalton, and Pickett, and several pow-wows by the first Americans, the Indians, at Lac du Flambeau, Hayward, Prairie La Crosse, and Wisconsin Dells.

The International Institute of Milwaukee County and thirty-five nationality groups in Milwaukee, Wis., have been sponsoring a Holiday Folk Fair there each November since 1944. At the inaugural one there was a costume parade around the hall, a Croation orchestra playing intermittently on a small stage, a singing Mexican guitarist, and Polish accordionists. Since then a folk pageant enlisting several dozen volunteer dancers, singers, and actors has been added, and visitors can sample foods of many nations, old and new, such as Arabia, Armenia, Bavaria, Cuba, Czechoslovakia, Denmark, Finland, France, Germany, Greece, Italy, Latin America, Latvia, Norway, the Philippines, Poland, Serbia, Slovakia, Sweden, Switzerland, and the Ukraine.

One World Day, inaugurated at Cultural Gardens in Rockefeller Park, Cleveland, Ohio, in 1944, has become an annual

110

event about the second Sunday in September. In 1966 a program of folk dancing and singing by representatives of 18 nationalities at the 23rd annual celebration also saluted the 50th anniversary of the gardens which typify landscaping and sculpture of several nations.

Around the last weekend each January since 1946 several thousand devotees of folk songs and dances have gathered at the Music Hall in Cleveland, Ohio, for the annual Folk Festival there. Entertainers play bagpipes and perform the dances of Scotland, the Ukraine, Russia, Poland, Lithuania, Japan, Sweden, Germany, and Israel.

The Festival of Nations customarily staged in Red Lodge, Mont., during the third week in August, began in 1951. It is a bona fide non-profit venture in friendship, "dedicated to the close relationship and enjoyment of people of many nationalities, and to the presentation of the customs, foods, music, arts and crafts of the old world and those of Montana." Residents of the area still donate their talents, time and money to support the admission-free festival. It was mining and lumbering that attracted many emigrants mainly from northern Europe to Red Lodge in the nineteenth century. Mining has been passé around Red Lodge for years, but the descendants of the early settlers there have developed other skills. Predominant ethnic groups that cooperate to stage the annual Festival of Nations include the English, Germans, Irish, Italians, Scandinavians, Scots, and Yugoslavs. Each nationality has its day, with one notable exception. In Red Lodge the English and the Irish get along so well together they usually share the same day. Each day is dedicated to distinctive activities of the host nationality. That includes copper enameling, lace-making, oil painting, pottery-throwing, spinning, wood carving, and the serving of foods prepared by old-timers. In the high school gym, stories, songs, and dances recall entertainment that flourished in Europe, particularly before World War I.

111

Some fifty booths for food and displays of handicrafts produced by at least twenty nationalities are a feature of the International Folk Festival inaugurated at Pittsburgh, Pa., in 1957, and usually staged there annually during the second week in June. The festival sponsored by Morris Junior College also offers dances and music by groups representing Bulgaria, China, Croatia, England, Germany, Greece, Hungary, India, Ireland, Israel, Italy, Latvia, Lebanon, Lithuania, Philippines, Russia, Scandinavia, Scotland, Serbia, Slovenia, and the United States.

Every autumn since 1961 many ethnic groups in Chicago have taken part in the annual Holiday Folk Fair during mid-October on Navy Pier.

Regional folk singing in the style of a century ago has been presented regularly since 1958 by nonprofessional singers about the second week in August in Newcastle, N.B., on the banks of the Miramichi River. Their showcase is the Miramichi Folksong Festival, their fare the songs and ballads from lumber camps, Acadian French, Arabic, and German music, and tunes well played by local fiddlers. Performances are judged by folklorists.

Many bilingual natives of southwestern Nova Scotia trace their French heritage to Brittany and Normandy. To mark the 200th anniversary of the expulsion of the French Acadians by the British in 1755, the people of Clare County staged an Acadian Festival at Church Point, in 1955. Ever since then the week-long celebration has been timed to end on Assumption Day, Aug. 15th. Gabriel and Evangeline, the protagonists of Longfellow's romantic poem "Evangeline," are chosen from among the young people of the community. After they are annointed in public ceremonies they preside over a flower show, handicraft displays, games, songfests, dances, a huge bonfire, a chicken barbecue, and a banquet. During the festival eighteenth century Acadian costumes are de rigueur.

The largest colony of Basques in the United States is in Idaho. They migrated to the United States from a small area in the Pyrenees Mountains which their ancestors staked out centuries ago between France and Spain. The greatest influx began in 1949 when the U.S. Government relaxed Basque immigration quotas because they are excellent sheepherders and we needed their skill to bolster our sheep industry. Devout Catholics, the Basques of Boise usually celebrate the feast of their patron saint, St. Ignacius of Loyola, on July 31st, with a picnic where sports contests include weight lifting and wood-chopping. They also celebrate at Christmastime with a dance that crowds the ballroom of the building in Boise owned by the Euzkaldunak, a social organization. Old-timers dance such lightning fast steps as la jota, porrosolda, and arreska to music of accordions, guitars, and tambourines. Younger Basque-Americans dance to contemporary tunes played by an orchestra.

The most cheerful New Year's salutations among Chinese is "Gung hay fa choy," Cantonese for good luck and prosperity, and "Kung hsi fa tsai," Mandarin for "Best wishes for good fortune." Since Canton is a large city in southeast China a high percentage of Chinese who migrated to North America came from there. The largest Chinese neighborhoods under the American and Canadian flags are in Hawaii, Los Angeles, New York, and San Francisco, in the United States, and in Vancouver, B. C. The most densely populated of all the Chinese neighborhoods on the mainland is at San Francisco, where an estimated 55,000 Chinese-Americans hail the lunar New Year with gongs, a parade, fireworks, roving lion dancers, a "Miss Chinatown USA" contest, a coronation ball, Chinese drama, opera, judo, jujitsu, and a grand parade. Because the date of the Chinese New Year is regulated by the lunar calendar it might occur as early as Jan. 21st, or as late as Feb. 21st. On Jan. 1st, 1912, the Chinese government discarded the lunar calendar and supplanted it with the solar calendar to be in tune with western practices. Nevertheless, the tradition of the New Year's celebration is so firmly rooted in Chinese tradition the government officials had to retain the

113

holiday. They saved face by referring to the new festivities as the Spring Festival. In North America the celebration which begins with the new moon after Jan. 19th and ends with the Feast of Lanterns two weeks later when the moon is full, is still called Chinese New Year. To the Chinese the New Year is a time of hope; also it is the birthday of every Chinese. Traditionally, a Chinese is considered to be one year old the day he is born. The following New Year's Day he adds another year. Therefore, anyone who is born on New Year's Eve automatically becomes two years old the following day. Because the Chinese prefer the intimacy and conviviality of family gatherings during the actual holiday period, the public celebration is staged a few days later. In 1966, Chinatown streets were bedecked with red and green decorations to greet the Year of the Horse. It was the year 4664 by the Chinese lunar calendar. When organizing this calendar in 2697 B.C., Huang Ti perfected a system of sixty-year or sexagenary cycles.

The present cycle started in 1924. It is the third in the 26th group, so we are in the 78th cycle, since three times twenty-six equals seventy-eight. The 26th group began in 1804 and will continue to 1983. The twelve-part cycle of years is dedicated to eight animals, a fowl, two reptiles, and a rodent, in this order: the Rat, Ox, Tiger, Hare, Dragon, Serpent, Horse, Sheep, Monkey, Rooster, Dog, and Boar. Although westerners attribute flattering and unflattering influences to the various animals for which the years are named, modern Chinese disown the practice. However, at the public celebrations the appearance of one cavorting animal, a Buddhist lion, invariably means fun for the spectators and pay-up for businessmen. As the lion dances through the crowd it roars and grimaces menacingly until it is appeased with coins from shopkeepers. The dance is so popular at the Chinese New Year celebration in New York's Chinatown it is often staged every day during the festival.

An estimated 10,000 visitors stroll Pender St., in the heart of Chinatown in Vancouver, B.C., during the Chinese New

Year celebration. They fill the restaurants to eat abalone, crab, lobster, roast duck, and suckling pig, and then return to the lantern-festooned street to watch the lion dances and chase away evil spirits by exploding fireworks.

A Narcissus Festival is the favorite way to usher in a New Year among Chinese in Hawaii. There the rampaging lion roams streets decorated with the fragrant flowers, and there are beauty contests, dances, dinners, art, fashion, and garden shows, and the traditional tea ceremony.

The distinctive food, costumes, music and dances of Czechoslovakia are spotlighted during the annual Czech Days inaugurated at Tabor, S.D., in 1949, and now a regular event there in mid-June.

At the Danish Days Festival in Solvang, Calif., for about three days in mid-September, in the vicinity of Copenhagen Square visitors might sample an aebleskive breakfast, Danish open-face sandwiches for lunch, and Danish meat balls for dinner. Often a torchlight parade, folk dancing, and singing are on the program in this community north of Santa Barbara modeled after their homeland by its Danish founders. Old-world customs are still cherished and maintained by second generation Danish-Americans.

The largest Danish community in Canada is New Denmark, N. B., east of Grand Falls. To celebrate the arrival of their forefathers in the mid-nineteenth century the Danish Canadians don old-country costumes and perform the traditional dances, about the third week in June.

The 105th consecutive Stiftungsfest was celebrated in Young America, Minn., as usual on the last Friday, Saturday, and Sunday in August, 1966. The folkfest got started around a German songfest in 1862. Since about 1956, some changes in and additions to the traditional program have included an outdoor barbecue, a softball tournament, free entertainment, and a carnival.

The best known of all the folk festivals sponsored in North America by people of Germanic heritage are those in the

Pennsylvania Dutch Country, around Hershey and Kutztown, Pa. A one-day Pennsylvania Dutch Day at Hershey in 1949 attracted so many people, the festival was soon expanded to three days about the last weekend in August. Typical entertainment includes dialect and English programs, folk dancers and singers, lectures about the arts, customs, and folklore of the area, plowing contests, a pony show, an outdoor country auction sale, and a Pennsylvania German dialect church service. Regional food specialties include pretzels, bologna sausage, seven sweets and seven sours, and shoo-fly pie.

"Koom un Bring dei Freind Mit!" That is the welcoming slogan at the Pennsylvania Dutch Folk Festival established in Kutztown in 1950, and staged for about ten days during the first two weeks in July. There visitors ride Conestoga wagons, see seasoned craftsmen turn out baskets, brooms and barrels, make cider, do water witching, thresh with flails, and prepare schpotza from maple sugar. Bread is baked in an outdoor oven, and tent restaurants operated by Amish women's church groups serve rivvel soup, fastnachts, and vanilla pie. There are also a two-hour pageant of gay Dutch folklife, an Amish movie, jigging and hoe-down performances by championship sets, and free-for-all square dancing.

The Germans who settled among the hills of Missouri along the Missouri River in 1836 named their new home for Hermann, a German prince who helped free Germany from Roman rule almost 2,000 years ago. For many years they welcomed spring with a school picnic which eventually became such a popular event it was expanded into a two-day Maifest in 1952, at Hermann, Mo. Its purpose is to preserve the interesting German arts and culture brought over by the early settlers, and to encourage preservation and restoration of the town's old buildings. On a Saturday and Sunday early in May there are tours of old homes, craft shops, a museum and gardens, church suppers, folk dancing, a German songfest, church services, and a "Long, Long Ago" parade.

The week-long Bavarian Festival, an annual event in

116

Frankenmuth, Mich., during the second full week in June since 1959, is filled with activities. In 1966 the program included a chicken barbecue, parade, a drama titled "The Spirit of Frankenmuth," bicycle races, an ox roast, hootenanny, water shows, and a youth parade.

At Gimli, Manitoba, the first Monday in August has been Islendingadagurinn, Icelandic Day, since 1889. About 12,000 Icelanders immigrated to Canada between 1870 and 1890, with Manitoba as the focal point of the far-flung settlements which were established north and south of the border. Although there are few concentrations of Icelandic Canadians now, Winnipeg and Gimli, a resort and fishing community on the shore of Lake Winnipeg, unite to celebrate Icelandic Day with wrestling, sports, and the singing of English, Icelandic, and Scandinavian songs.

Once upon a time, Washington Island, off the tip of the Door County peninsula, in Wisconsin, was the largest Icelandic settlement in the United States. Some Icelanders still live there, together with Swedes, Danes, and Norwegians. Broad Lake Michigan, and its rocky cove-indented shoreline, make the region look a lot like the Old Country. There, too, a festival serves to keep traditions alive. The Scandinavian Festival on Washington Island takes two days, usually about the first weekend in August. The Lutheran Church often sponsors a smorgasbord on Saturday, and there is a dance program on Sunday. Usually the dance climaxes a summer-long series of Thursday evening recitals.

The traditional Irish Feis on the Bronx Campus of Hunter College, New York City, about the third Sunday in June, features Irish jigs, singing, band music, and oratory. Inaugurated in 1933 and staged at Fordham University for many years, it invariably attracts thousands of Irish-Americans. Hundreds of young people write poems, essays on Irish literature, and tales in Gaelic, and take part in athletic contests.

In the heart of New York City's original Italian neighborhood, between Chinatown and Greenwich Village on the

117

Lower East Side, there are two major celebrations along similar lines which celebrate the feast days of saints popular with those who migrated from Naples and environs, and recall the camaraderie, gaiety and vivacity for which the Neapolitans are known. For ten days in June, climaxing on June 13th, feast day of St. Anthony, the first of the two annual festas is centered on Sullivan St. The second, honoring San Gennaro, has been staged on Mulberry St. around the third week in September since about 1925. The thousands of Italian-Americans who participate in these festivals regard them as grand reunions. They drape the thoroughfares with garlands of electric lights and line the sidewalks with booths for souvenirs and southern Italian taste treats, such as calzone, a fried mixture of ricotta and mozzarella cheese and ham or sausage; zeppole, a dumpling fried in oil and dusted with sugar, and torrone, a hard candy studded with nuts. Featured activities of the two fairs include processions headed by statues of the saints being honored, and lots of Neapolitan, Sicilian, and popular American music.

Usually around the first Sunday in July residents of one of the few remaining "little Italys" in the Williamsburg Section of Brooklyn, N. Y., pay tribute to the Virgin Mary and St. Paulinus, a fifth-century bishop who is the patron saint of Nola, in the Province of Naples, Italy. Many of the Italian-Americans in Brooklyn trace their ancestry to Nola, which is at least 2,000 years old, so they fashioned their festa after the Dance of the Gigli, or lilies, in the old country, complete with bands, loud-speakers, a boat, men in Moorish costumes impersonating invading Saracens, and "lilies," which are extremely high steeples made of papier mâché, wood, and cloth adorned with holy statues and even a platform for musicians. The highlight of the celebration is the procession in which many men carry their lily burden through the streets to Our Lady of Carmel Church.

Since before World War II, Nisei, persons of Japanese descent, born in the United States and loyal to it, have staged an annual festival in Los Angeles' Little Tokyo. Customarily presented during the third week in August, the festival features judo, karate and sword tournaments, flower arrangements, a Cha-No-Yu tea ceremony, an Ondo parade of kimona-clad dancing girls and serpentine dancers with a "Mikoshi," or portable shrine, on their shoulders, and an art and photo show at the Koyasan Buddhist Temple.

Ybor City, Tampa, Florida's Latin Quarter, has its own purely Latin-flavored Fiesta in February or March, after other community frivolities have folded for Lent. Since 1927 the festival's Spanish folk songs, dances, gaiety, and cuisine have celebrated the traditional spirit of friendship enjoyed by Florida and Latin America. Latin debutantes serve as princesses; there are coronation ceremonies.

Although a Latin-type festival might seem out of character in Nordic Minnesota, since 1946 the people of Montevideo, Minn., have staged a fiesta around the third week in July as a tribute to the people of Montevideo, Uruguay. Typical programs include Latin dances, songs, folk costumes, a Pan American pageant, parades, and receptions for representatives from Uruguay. During the year school children in the two Montevideos exchange letters and discuss the fiesta in an attempt to promote goodwill and understanding.

The Norwegian "Syttende Day," May 17th, is probably the only Independence Day celebration in the world where there is not the slightest flexing of a military muscle. In Bergen, Oslo, and Trondheim, Norway, the big event is a parade of pupils and students singing school and folk songs. In Stoughton, Wis., a Norwegian-American community, the celebration is just as weapons-free. The weekend nearest May 17th is devoted to a party in Stoughton, founded in 1847 on the bank of the Yahara River by Luke Stoughton, an Englishman. Syttende Mai festivities begin with a parade, followed by a hootenanny, folk dancing, displays of Norwegian arts and crafts, and the serving of smorgasbord.

Petersburg, Alaska, has long been known as Little Norway

because of its predominantly Scandinavian population. The region also reminds one of the fjord-fringed coasts of Norway. As a rule, on May 17th, the Little Norway Festival established in 1958 salutes Independence Day in Norway as well as the first Pacific Coast halibut landing. Salmon bakes, saltwater fishing excursions, and smorgasbords are main events.

Polish-Americans who have settled in Montgomery, Minn., have had fun on Kolacky Day about the first Sunday in August since 1929. There is a big parade, the crowning of a queen, and other entertainment, all to honor the kolacky, a Bohemian biscuit. To show how much most Poles like the kolacky one of the big events of the party is a kolacky-eating contest.

Nova Scotia, appropriately, has several Scottish festivals between June and September. The most representative of all, though, is the Gaelic Mod at South Gut of St. Ann's, Cape Breton, around the second week in August. The Gaelic Mod began in 1938, and since has done the best all-around job of perpetuating Scottish customs, language, and traditions of any event in Canada. It is the festival to which clan chiefs have journeyed from Scotland, and where there are fine examples of dancing and playing the bagpipes. The Gaelic College of Celtic Folk Arts and Highland Home Crafts was created there by many Scots who were interested in it.

The flavor of Old Spain permeates some sections of the Sun Belt in the continental United States from Florida to California. Regularly since 1924 attempts have been made to recapture the fiesta flavor of the Days of the Dons in California with an Old Spanish Days Fiesta in Santa Barbara. The celebration lasts about five days during the full moon in August. Many residents sport Spanish and Mexican costumes to attend the pageant at the Mission, listen to music at an arena, or watch a procession of riders on horses wearing saddles heavily encrusted with silver.

Many Swedes were among the multitudes from northern Europe who were attracted to Minnesota's rich mineral deposits and forests in the mid-nineteenth century. They brought their old world customs with them, and some of the customs still survive, particularly in the field of festivals. Typical of the festivities is Svenskarnas Day at Minnehaha Park in Minneapolis around the third week in June, the period when Midsummer Day is celebrated in Sweden. As in Sweden, the major activity in Minneapolis is folk dancing.

The Swiss Cheese Center of Ohio is around Sugar Creek, and the people of the community have been celebrating that fact with a festival early each October since 1953. Swiss entertainment includes yodelers, accordionists, polka bands, wrestling, stone-tossing, street dancing, an antique auto procession, and a parade. Lots of Swiss cheese and other appropriate foods are available, and many Swiss-Americans wear canton costumes.

The first Swiss Cheese Festival in Middlefield, Ohio, was staged in June, 1958. Since then highlights of the annual celebration normally include a pony pull, barbecued chicken dinners, yodeling, square dancing, a Swiss Miss contest, street dances, a parade, bus tours to the nearby Amish country and a cheese factory, arts and crafts displays and sales, and a strawberry social.

Swiss Days became an annual event in Midway, Utah, in September, 1963. Swiss specialties, including handicrafts and sausages, are offered and there are also a music festival, a parade, a chuck wagon breakfast, art, flower and hobby shows, a beauty pageant, and a dance.

Welsh traditions have been celebrated at the annual Welsh Day in Bangor, Pa., on the first weekend in September since 1931. Bangor was founded by a Welshman and named for Bangor, Wales. Since Welshmen are fond of choral singing there is much harmonizing. It is customary for one of two services to be delivered in English, the other in Welsh.

The National Folk Festival has hopped, skipped, and jumped around the United States, and about the calendar, quite a bit since the first nationwide gathering took place in St.

Louis, Mo., in 1934. It has been staged for one or more years in Chattanooga, Dallas, Chicago, Wash., D.C., Philadelphia, Cleveland, Oklahoma City, Nashville, Covington, St. Petersburg, and Denver, at various times of the year. Indian dances, Tennessee singing games, dulcimer tunes, Negro spirituals and work songs, ballads, songs and dances brought to America by the English, French, Germans, and other Europeans, make up the program. Performers are picked for their ability, regardless of race, color, or creed. Prime aims of the festival are fun and the release of the spirit. It achieves them while maintaining a high standard of authenticity. The address of the National Folk Festival Association, Inc., is 710 Dupont Circle Building, Washington, D.C. 20036.

Western North Carolina's annual Mountain Dance and Folk Festival has been a standard event at the City Auditorium, Asheville, "along about sundown," the first week in August, since 1927. Spectators and participants are treated to several nights of square and buck dancing, ballad singing, mouth-harp and fiddle playing, and banjo picking by mountain people who travel from their homes in the Blue Ridge and Smoky Mountains. Contestants compete for cash and cups.

The preservation and perpetuation of the folklore of the Ozarks has been the task of a group of people in Eureka Springs, Ark., since 1948. Always staged in late October to coincide with the peak of fall foliage coloration, the Ozark Folk Festival offers string bands, square dancers, old gospel songs, fiddlers, banjo players, play party games, a Gay Nineties piano player, and jig dancers.

Early in April each year since 1949 young people from several counties of the southern mountains have gathered at the City Auditorium in Asheville, N.C., to participate in the annual Mountain Youth Jamboree. They sweep through the intricate patterns of the mountain square dances, and strum and sing the ballads and other melodies of their native hills and valleys.

Activities and dreams of the pioneers of West Virginia are recalled at the West Virginia State Folk Festival, Glenville, W. Va., during the fourth week in June. Inaugurated in 1950, it now offers an evening of drama and folk music, square dancing, exhibits, a spelling bee, a fiddlers' contest, a country auction, and old-time hymns.

One of the major events of the year at Stephen Foster Memorial on the bank of the Suwannee River at White Springs, Fla., is the Florida Folk Festival inaugurated in 1953 and usually staged on the first weekend in May. It gives visitors a chance to combine entertainment with a little instruction in the folk activity offered by communities, rural areas, and schools. This normally includes the older traditions brought in early days by the Czechs, English, French, Indian, Irish, Minorcan, Negro, Scots, and Spanish. Children's rhymes, customs, cowboy, farmer, lumber camp, and railroad folklore are emphasized, and so are indigenous ghost and witch stories, legends, and superstitions. Wood carving, whittlings, palmetto products, quilting, weaving, and pottery are displayed, and so are traditional foods of ethnic groups.

The inaugural Folk Festival, sponsored by the Newport Folk Foundation, Newport, R. I., in July, 1959, attracted an estimated 12,000 persons to the community's Freebody Park. The next year the total increased to 14,000, and it has been expanding ever since. Now the three-day program might include folk dancing, folktales and story telling interspersed with instrumental music, gospel, religious, American Indian and other folk music, topical songs, workshops on pertinent subjects, and demonstrations of folk crafts by American and Canadian craftsmen. A Children's Day program introduced in 1966 was so well received it probably will become a regular event.

The campus of Vincennes University, Vincennes, Ind., was the setting for the first Wabash Valley Folk Festival in mid-October, 1966. One of the highlights was a Folk Mass with music by students from St. Meinrad College, St. Meinrad. Participants in the general program included Charlotte Daniels, Anne Grimes, and John Jacob Niles.

Forest Festivals

THE FUN and frivolity of forest festivals are rarely associated with conservation and reforestation, yet without them there might be few forests in which to frolic. J. Sterling Morton, a Nebraskan who eventually became his state's Secretary of Agriculture, sensed this when he conceived the idea for Arbor Day while still a homesteader on a barren, treeless section of Nebraska in 1854. Obviously, timber was a scarce and valuable commodity in Nebraska then, so to Morton it just seemed right that one day each spring should be dedicated to public tree planting. He was unable to do anything about that, however, until he became a member of Nebraska's Board of Agriculture. Then he helped inaugurate Arbor Day on April 10, 1872, and in 1885 the annual observance was changed to April 22nd to honor his birthday. Arbor Day was introduced into Canada from the United States in 1890 to encourage an interest in forestry through the transplanting of trees and shrubs for the beautification of parks. In Nebraska the project was so successful from the very beginning that approximately one million trees were planted on the naked, windswept plains the first year, and an estimated 300 million during the next fifteen years. Today the 206,000-acre Nebraska National Forest is one of the largest man-made woods anywhere. It is also a place of pilgrimage and a source of seedlings for conservationists from countries where depletion of forests has created problems which seriously affect millions of people.

124

Nebraska is the only state in which Arbor Day is a legal holiday, although it is observed on various dates in a majority of the others. In Canada the dates for Arbor Day vary, but April or May are the customary months for it. In the States most observances are held in schools, although sometimes civic or patriotic groups honor the memory of deceased leaders with symbolic tree-planting ceremonies on the day. But it should have much greater significance than it has. It should be a time for festivities inspired by an awareness of our natural resources, and the need for conserving them. It could be a joyous holiday when we would glorify the faith and accomplishments of Morton as well as those of other Americans and Canadians who devoted their lives to developing rather than destroying our natural gifts. Such a list of Americans should certainly contain the name of Luther Burbank, the renowned plant breeder of Santa Rosa, Calif.; George Washington Carver, the agricultural chemist whose research at Tuskegee Institute, Tuskegee, Ala., won him international repute, and John Chapman, known affectionately as Johnny Appleseed because for forty years during the first half of the nineteenth century he roamed the wilderness in Pennsylvania, Ohio, Indiana, and Illinois planting innumerable apple orchards. Representative of the Canadians to be saluted for their contributions in these fields might be William Saunders, his son who became Sir Charles Edward Saunders, William Terrill Macoun, and Allan McIntosh. The senior Saunders achieved distinction in botany, entomology, horticulture, analytical chemistry, plant breeding, materia medica, and manufacturing chemistry. Sir Charles gave Marquis wheat to Canada, and helped make the Canadian prairies one of the world's great wheat growing areas. Dr. Macoun's specialties were fruit breeding and horticulture. McIntosh was the man who originated the McIntosh red apple.

To encourage the planting of trees the American Forestry Association, Washington, D.C., has compiled this list of Arbor Day dates in the United States: Alabama, second Friday in

Feb. Alaska, no formal observance. Arizona, Friday after Feb. 1st, in all counties except five which prefer the Friday after April 1st. Arkansas, first Saturday in Dec. California, March 7th. Colorado, third Friday in April. Connecticut, last Friday in April. Delaware, last Friday in April. Florida, third Friday in January. Georgia, third Friday in February. Hawaii, November. Idaho, third Friday in April. Illinois, last Friday in April. Indiana, last Friday in April. Iowa, last Friday in April. Kansas, last Friday in March. Kentucky, by proclamation of the governor. Louisiana, usually in January. Maine, last Friday in April. Maryland, usually first Friday in April. Massachusetts, last Friday in April. Michigan, late April. Minnesota, first Friday in May. Mississippi, Friday after first Monday in December. Missouri, Friday after first Tuesday in April. Montana, last Friday in April. Nebraska, April 22nd. Nevada, last Friday in April. New Hampshire, late April or early May. New Jersey, last Friday in April. New Mexico, second Friday in March. New York, last Friday in April. North Carolina, first Friday after March 15th. North Dakota, first Friday in May. Ohio, last Friday in April. Oklahoma, Friday after second Monday in March. Oregon, second Friday in February west of Cascades; second Friday in April east of Cascades. Pennsylvania, last Friday in April. Rhode Island, last Friday in April. South Carolina, first Friday in December. Tennessee, first Friday in March. Texas, third Friday in January. Utah, last Friday in April. Vermont, first Friday in May. Virginia, second Friday in March. Washington, late April or early May. West Virginia, second Friday in April. Wisconsin, last Friday in April. Wyoming, early spring. District of Columbia, third Friday in April. Guam, last Friday in October. Puerto Rico, Friday after Thanksgiving. Virgin Islands, last Friday in September. The National Arbor Day Committee, 63 Fitzrandolph Road, West Orange, N.J., a non-profit organization, has been encouraging the observance of Arbor Day since 1941.

A truck rodeo was added to the third annual Tall Timber

Days Festival at Stratton, Me., in mid-July, 1966. The event involves loading trucks with logs and racing to reach a goal in the shortest time possible. Other competitive activities included canoe races and tilting, log rolling and cutting, a parade, and street dances.

Nature's fecundity is particularly apparent in the forests in spring when seasonal festivals are woven around stands of rhododendron and laurel, or groves of dogwood with their fancy bracts of white or pink blossoms. It is in the autumn, though, that the forests in many states and across Canada are most flamboyant. Flaming fall foliage lures millions of Americans and Canadians deep into the woods to marvel at the brilliant golds, reds, and purples that perennially replace the tired summer suits of green. Invariably the invaders ponder the mystery of the phenomenon, even as scientists are also trying to discover the details of the interplay of factors underlying the foliage change.

Foliage tours are particularly popular in the northeastern United States and southeastern Canada, where one of the most majestic of all the gaily caparisoned trees is the red maple, the leaf of which now adorns the Canadian flag. In New England, fire and forest watchers chart the progress of coloration and relay the information to their state's tourist development bureau. In Massachusetts, southern New Hampshire, Vermont, Rhode Island, Connecticut, New York, New Jersey, Pennsylvania, and western Maryland, the peak of coloration is generally around October 10th to 15th. In the Midwest the first half of October is usually best. Farther south, in North Carolina, Tennessee, Virginia, West Virginia, Kentucky and the Ozark Mountains of Arkansas, Kansas, Missouri, and Oklahoma, coloration generally occurs during the last half of October. Across the Piedmont and Coastal Plains area of North Carolina it even lasts into November.

In Colorado aspencades and fall color weeks begin about the fourth week in September. Along the Pacific Coast, as elsewhere, coloration follows the sun southward. The best displays in the Pacific Northeast are normally from mid-September to mid-October. The height of coloration in northern California is in October, making itself noticed along the Redwood Highway, US 101, almost as soon as the month begins. In Central California, the spectacle can start as early as September 20th and last as long as mid-November, depending on the elevation. Near Longview, Tex., colors are best during November.

Around the last half of September when the Berkshire Hills in the vicinity of North Adams, Mass., are decked in vivid hues, the Fall Foliage Festival originated in 1947 entertains thousands of visitors. The celebration is launched with a blessing on Sunday and closes with a parade a week later. In 1966 the parade drew its inspiration from the Sunday comics. The week-long program was planned to include an air show, bowling tournament, art show, queen contest, country-western show and dance, a children's parade, and a dance for teenagers.

In recent years several communities in Vermont's "Northeast Kingdom" have teamed up to present a week-long Fall Foliage Festival late in September and early in October. As a rule the communities are Barnet Center, Cabot, Groton, Marshfield, Peacham, and Walden. The day allotted to Barnet Center might begin with a breakfast of fruit, pancakes with Vermont maple syrup, sausage and sweet rolls, featured tours, and an arts and crafts display all day, and conclude with a ham dinner. At Cabot, the program could start off with beef stew at noon; then a food, book, and handicraft sale; a foliage tour; visits to an old farm and cheese factory; and at sundown a turkey supper. Sometimes Groton features a lumberjack breakfast, trips to a furniture factory and an egg-marketing plant, a visit to Groton State Forest, and a chicken pie supper. Marshfield often offers a tour of the town, lunch, a tour of the countryside, and a Yankee supper. Peacham welcomes its guests with hot coffee in mid-town, then offers scenic tours, maple sugar on snow, visits to homes and historic buildings, and a New England boiled dinner. Walden specialties include demonstrations of Christmas wreath-making, sandwiches and homemade pie for lunch, a hymn-sing, farm tours, and a hot-dish supper.

A two-day Fall Foliage Festival inaugurated at Warner, N.H. in 1947 primarily to raise money for a living memorial to war veterans is now a regular event on the first weekend in October. Sometimes the hosts "turn back the clock" and stage a parade of antique fire equipment, vintage motor cars, and old-fashioned costume dances. Often, too, there are community auctions and a harvest ball.

Pennsylvanians play up the beauty of fall foliage in October with an Open House Tour in West Chester, an Autumn Leaf Festival in Clarion, a Fall Foliage Festival in Du Bois, and a Flaming Foliage Festival in Renovo.

Counties in northern Wisconsin cooperate with a full schedule of fall color tours by car or boat, cookouts and wild game dinners, and visits to a goose refuge and cranberry marshes, from mid-September until mid-October.

During October, Kalkaska, Mich., sponsors a Fall Round-up of Out-door Activities which includes guided motorcades each morning while the colors are at their best, and float or canoe trips on the Manistee River.

Annually around the first two weekends in October an Autumn Pilgrimage from Richmond, Va., to half-a-dozen churches and numerous houses and plantations serves to familiarize tourists with Tidewater Virginia.

Most typical of all the forest festivals are those which feature such woodsmen's activities as log chopping, birling, sawing contests, tree topping and felling, and climbing greased poles. All these events, plus woodcraft exhibits, pony rides, exhibition shooting, a horse show, barbecue, and equipment and machinery demonstrations are on the two-day Lumber-jack Roundup the second or third weekend in August at Branbury State Park, Lake Dunmore, Vt. A typical attraction at the Roundup might be a performance by an expert such as

World Champion Tree Climber Kelly Stanley, a lumberjack from the West Coast, who once shinnied up a spar tree in thirty-nine seconds. The Roundup, inaugurated in 1952, is sponsored by the Vermont Dept. of Forests and Parks in cooperation with Vermont wood-using industries. Its double duty is to entertain and educate laymen so they will understand the growing need for competent natural resources management, acquaint them with the pattern of modern timber harvest in the Green Mountains for which Vermont is named, and to publicize the important part the lumber and paper industries play in the state's economy. Also, on the educational level the Roundup is reported to underwrite the major portion of the costs of a ten-day Conservation Laboratory for Vermont teachers. In eleven years 277 teachers are said to have completed the course in natural resource management.

Woodsmen's Field Days has been an annual event at Tupper Lake, N.Y., each August since 1947. The show in the Adirondacks is nominally on a Friday and Saturday because it was founded by Rev. Frank Reed, who insists that Sunday should be a day of rest. On the program are horse-pulling contests, birling, water-skiing exhibitions, a parade and woodsmen's competitions which include bucksaws, chainsaws, tree felling, log-rolling, a tug o' war, and crosscut sawing.

To capitalize on the blazing backdrops of flaming foliage which cover the mountains of West Virginia like a crazy quilt, the people of Elkins have been staging a Forest Festival around the first weekend in October since 1930. Dedicated to the state's eleven million acres of forests, it offers parades, exhibits, wood-chopping and sawing contests, a riding tournament, entertainment, a queen's coronation, dances, and tours through Monongahela National Forest.

Men who wield axes and push saws for a livelihood in logging operations seem to enjoy testing their skills and competing with fellow workers before audiences at such forest festivals as the Timber Carnival in the natural amphitheater at Waverly Lake, Albany, Ore., for three or four days during the first week in July. A regular event since 1941, it now dangles about $7,000 in cash prizes before the contestants. Speed climbing and timber topping are big events, and there are also ax throwing, bucking, chopping, logrolling and jousting contests, baseball, horse shows, and dances.

Washington, nicknamed the Evergreen State because its famous fir trees are ever green, has long nurtured logging as one of its major industries. Perhaps the oldest of all lumberjack festivals is the Loggerodeo, which was staged at Sedro-Woolley for the first time in 1900, and is now presented annually about the first week in July. Bucking, splicing, and timber-falling and a rodeo usually are main events.

A Loggers' Jubilee has been a mid-August attraction at Norton, Wash., since 1939. Bucking, bulldozing, falling, high-climbing, power saw, splicing, tie-loading, and trailer-backing—eight important facets of the logging operation—are subjects for contests. At Norton climbers shinny up tall Douglas firs. The competition springs from the job of woodsmen who must climb trees, cut off the treetops, remove all limbs, and attach cables and blocks in preparation for their use as spar trees. The hand-bucking contest determines who is fastest at sawing a log approximately thirty-two inches in diameter. Since power saws are rapidly replacing handsaws in the woods there is a power-saw contest. In the hand-falling contest in which a tree is cut with an ax, fallers compete to see who can cut trees two feet in diameter the fastest. They must also make the tree fall in a specific direction so that it will drive a stake into the ground when it falls.

Canadian loggers decide their Dominion championships in July on All Sooke Day, at Sooke, B.C., a lumbering and farming town on the Sooke River, about fifteen miles west of Victoria. Canadian tree climbers are called high riggers. Otherwise the nomenclature and activities are similar to those at logging festivals in the United States.

131

Holiday Festivals

THERE ARE no national holidays in the United States because each state has the right to select the holidays it will observe. The President and Congress designate the holidays to be observed in the District of Columbia and by federal employees in all states. The legal or public holidays which all fifty states and the District observe are New Year's Day, Jan. 1st; Independence Day, the Fourth of July; Labor Day, the first Monday in September; Veterans Day, Nov. 11th; Thanksgiving Day, the fourth Thursday in November, and Christmas Day, Dec. 25th. Holidays in Canada are New Year's Day, Jan. 1st; Good Friday and Easter Monday, March or April; Victoria Day, the Monday before May 24th; Dominion Day, July 1st; Labor Day, the first Monday in September; Thanksgiving Day, the second Monday in October; Remembrance Day, Nov. 11th, and Christmas Day, Dec. 25th.

JANUARY

The observance of January 1st as the first day of a New Year began in 46 B.C. when Julius Caesar instituted the Julian Calendar named for him. Regularly since 1904 great crowds of Americans and their guests have thronged New York City's world-renowned Times Square on New Year's Eve to watch an illuminated ball slide down a seventy-foot pole to mark the final moments of the fading year and the arrival of the new one "on the dot." The edifice where this takes place was originally the Times Tower Building, but is now the Allied Chemical Tower. The dousing of the light is the signal that the New Year has begun.

132

Philadelphia, Pa., is very much alive on New Year's Day, if inclement weather does not cause the postponement of its renowned Mummers' Parade until the following Saturday. Silks, sateens and ostrich feathers in great profusion are the basic components of myriad extravagant costumes in one of the longest parades anywhere. It begins about nine A.M. and goes on and on.

Americans literally kick-off the New Year. From coast-to-coast on the afternoon of January 1st, as a rule, four major intercollegiate football contests—Sugar Bowl, New Orleans, La.; Cotton Bowl, Dallas, Tex.; Sun Bowl, El Paso, Tex., and Rose Bowl, Pasadena, Calif.—draw, all told, at least 300,000 spectators to their stadiums, and many times that number to television sets. In 1966 the Orange Bowl game was shifted to New Year's night. The New Year's Day bowl game tradition began at the Rose Bowl on January 1, 1916. The Orange, Sugar, and Sun Bowls date to 1936, and the Cotton Bowl to 1937.

The giving of gifts, especially to children, is still practiced by Puerto Ricans on Three Kings Day, or Epiphany, January 6th. However, the growing popularity of Christmas has curtailed the old-time fervor for Kings Day as a time for bestowing presents.

The first solemn Christian religious festival of the New Year is Epiphany, also called Kings Day and Cross Day, January 6th. It is observed with much ceremony, especially by the Greek Orthodox Church. Since it commemorates the baptism of Christ by John the Baptist in the River Jordan, the descent of the Holy Spirit in the form of a dove, and the recovery of the cross under Constantine, diving for crosses tossed into streams by high priests, and the releasing of caged doves, have become a Greek tradition. In Tarpon Springs, Fla., where Greek sponge divers settled years ago to follow their trade, the rites are performed on the shore of a bayou. The observance begins with mass at the church of St. Nicholas. The archbishop and his subordinates lead a procession through streets brightened with flags, bunting, and religious banners. At the water's edge a picked group of youthful divers waits to perform the final act of the ceremony, the recovery of the cross. Their lithe, bronzed bodies are in sharp contrast to the resplendent robes and golden cross of the bishop. He gently releases a white dove, casts a small gold cross into the water, and blesses the divers as they plunge into the stream to retrieve it. The one who finds the cross receives a special blessing. That night there is music, singing, dancing, feasting and merrymaking in the finest holiday tradition. A typical menu might include salty green cheese, wine, honey cakes, and coffee.

Once every four years, Washington, D. C., is the site of the most important ceremony of the nation: the inauguration of the President of the United States. He and the Vice-President are sworn into office at noon of the 20th of January following the national presidential election the preceding November. The Chief Justice of the United States officiates, inducting the Vice-President-elect into office first so that if the President is disabled before he has been sworn in, a duly installed Vice-President will be able to pick up the reins of government. After the new Chief Executive takes office he delivers his inaugural address. Then a long parade of floats, bands, and marching units usually takes several hours to pass the reviewing stand. Inauguration Day is climaxed with official dances.

FEBRUARY

The bonfires that burn on plantations in Puerto Rico the night of February 2nd, celebrate two occasions: the feast day of La Virgen de la Candelaria, and the beginning of the five-month sugar harvest, or zafra, as the Puerto Ricans call it.

The birthdays of two revered Americans born in February are marked with special ceremonies that month. Abraham Lincoln's birthday is February 12th, and George Washington's on February 22nd. Invariably, Lincoln's memory is honored at Cooper Union, in New York City, where he delivered an historic address in Febraury, 1860, before he received the Republican nomination for the presidency, and there are annual pilgrimages to his grave in Springfield, Ill. George Washington is still the favorite son of Fredericksburg, Va., where a Washington's Birthday Party usually features the planting of a cherry tree, a pie-baking contest, and throwing silver dollars across the Rappahannock River. The dollar-pitching is an imitation of a stunt Washington is believed to have performed. Laredo, Tex., and Nuevo Laredo, Mexico, team up to stage a Washington's Birthday Party, complete with an international parade and dances.

MARCH

Discovery Day in Guam on March 6th, recalls the arrival of Magellan there on that date in 1521. The anniversary was celebrated before World War II, but after the conflict it was not revived until 1964. Now on March 6th, pleasure craft gather at Agana and proceed down the West Coast to Umatac where everyone participates in an all-day fiesta.

Since Easter can arrive as early as March 23rd, or as late as April 25th, it is feasible to describe it in March. The decision to observe Easter on the first Sunday following the fourteenth day of the Paschal Full Moon was decided in A.D. 325 by the first council of the Christian Church at Nicaea, Bithynia, once a part of Asia Minor, now in Turkey. Although the Paschal Moon is the first full moon after March 21st, it does not always coincide with the astronomical full moon. So, the ancient mathematicians devised a Golden Number Rule with 19 as the key to determine the date of Easter for any year, centuries ahead. The Sunday after the date indicated by the Golden Number Rule is Easter. If that date occurs on a Sunday, Easter is observed a full week later. Therefore, Easter occurs from one to seven days after the date indicated by the Golden Number Rule. The following exercise in long division illustrates how the date of Easter in 1966 was determined:

$$
\begin{array}{r}
103 \\
19\sqrt{1966} \\
19 \\
\hline
66 \\
57 \\
\hline
9
\end{array}
$$

Always add   1

In 1966 the Golden Number was   10

The Golden Number for 1966 was ten. The Paschal Full Moon occurred on April 5th. The Sunday following the Paschal Full Moon that year was April 10th. If April 5th had occurred on a Sunday in 1966, Easter would have been observed a full week later, on April 12th. Here is the list of Golden Numbers one through nineteen, inclusively, assigned to dates in March and April, when the Paschal Full Moon occurs during its 19-year cycle: *1*, April 14. *2*, April 3. *3*, March 23. *4*, April 11. *5*, March 31. *6*, April 18. *7*, April 8. *8*, March 28. *9*, April 16. *10*, April 5. *11*, March 25. *12*, April 13. *13*, April 2. *14*, March 22. *15*, April 10. *16*, March 30. *17*, April 17. *18*, April 7. *19*, March 27.

The Easter Fires celebration on the night before Easter at Fredericksburg, Tex., has developed into one of the Lone Star State's oldest, more unusual festivities. On Easter Eve, around 1846, a group of Commanche Indians assigned by their Chief to keep a group of white settlers under surveillance, built several bright watch fires to warm themselves. When the frightened children of a newly arrived family asked their mother why the fires were burning, she told them that rabbits were boiling Easter eggs. After the settlers signed a peace treaty with the Commanches the story became folklore. Now each Easter Eve school children present a pageant based on the tale, and Boy Scouts tend fires.

Several hours before midnight on Easter Eve thousands of people begin to assemble on the hillsides at Holy City in the Wichita Mountains some 22 miles northwest of Lawton, Okla. They go equipped with warm clothing, blankets, sandwiches, and hot coffee, prepared to spend the night watching the admission-free "Oklahoma Oberammergau," an Easter pageant based on the traditional Passion Play, and presented on a mammoth natural stage annually since 1926. The area bears an extraordinary resemblance to the Holy Land in the Middle East, so the full-size reproductions of a number of Biblical landmarks such as the inn and the manger, the walls and city gates of Jerusalem, the Judgment Hall, the Upper Room, and Mt. Calvary, are convincing. The six-hour pageant usually begins at midnight and is timed to reach its climax at sunrise.

When devout Moravians who founded the village of Salem, N. C., in the 1770's decided to start the community off right with a sunrise service on Easter morning, April 11, 1773, they did not realize that they were inaugurating what would become one of the foremost types of church services among Christians in America. While many of the latter day Easter morning services throughout the United States have taken on gaudy trappings, the Moravians continue to present a model of simplicity. Thousands of people gather before dawn in front of the Old Home Moravian Church on Salem Square in Winston-Salem to await the traditional salutation which opens the service, "The Lord is Risen!" They sing joyous hymns of Christian faith and hope, and as day breaks they walk quietly in long lines along the short blocks to God's Acre, the Moravian cemetery. There they reaffirm their belief in a resurrected and eternally reigning Lord. Elsewhere in North Carolina, Easter sunrise services often are held at Asheville, Bald Mountain, Boone, Hatteras Island, Murphy, and Wayah.

137

The first Easter Sunrise Service in Southern California took place on Mt. Rubidoux, near Riverside, April 11, 1909, exactly 136 years after the Moravians held the first one in America in 1773. The most elaborate service of all in California, however, has been staged regularly at Hollywood Bowl, Hollywood, since 1921. The audience begins to stream into the bowl at midnight on Easter Eve. The amphitheater is moderately lighted all night, and the benches are filled with drowsy figures. Daylight reveals hundreds of calla lilies in front of the band shell, then shortly after dawn a "living cross" of some 250 teen-agers, a choir of adults, an organist, and a symphony orchestra present a musical program. As the sun comes over the mountain, blasts from trumpets touch off the service. Since Southern California is a fertile field for this type of religious program there are probably more of them in this region than anywhere. In the vicinity of San Diego, it is customary for services to be held at such places as the foot of Sierra Cross in Presidio Park, on top of Mt. Helix, at the Mt. Soledad Memorial Cross; at Oceanside Beach Stadium, at Camp Pendleton's outdoor theatre; at Inspiration Point in Julian; at Easter Mountain in Borrego Springs; and even aboard Navy vessels at anchor in San Diego Bay.

The Garden of the Gods, Colorado Springs, Colo., has been the site of the best-known Easter Sunrise Service in Colorado since 1921.

A half-hour program, usually broadcast over a nationwide network, is filled with hymns, prayers, scripture reading, a brief sermon, and detailed descriptions of various parts of Grand Canyon to emphasize its majestic splendor and cathedral-like solitude when the annual Easter Sunrise Service inaugurated there in 1919 is heard 6:30–7 o'clock Easter morning. The Grand Canyon is in Arizona.

There are several services in the vicinity of Phoenix and Wickenburg, Ariz. Some of them are staged with the minister and his congregation seated on horseback.

During the 1870's, soon after the summer vacation season

ended early each September at Atlantic City, N. J., the city fathers would have the resort's boardwalk stored away in a barn for the winter to protect it from storms and high water. It was then erected again in late spring. In 1876, though, the planks were put up sooner than usual in the hope of attracting some of the tourists from Philadelphia's Centennial Exhibition. To encourage the tide of tourism to roll onto the famous beaches ahead of its customary time the now traditional Easter Parade on the Boardwalk was introduced. These days about a dozen women in the Paschal procession are given prizes for wearing what several judges consider the most attractive chapeaux in the crowd. Famous impromptu Easter fashion parades also take place at St. Augustine, Fla., along Michigan Blvd., Chicago, Ill., at Asbury Park, N.J., and especially on Fifth Ave., New York City. A handsome backdrop for seasonal finery at the Easter Parade on Fifth Ave. is the lavish arrangement of plantings in Rockefeller Center. Easter flower shows in the Channel Gardens started in 1934. Through 1940 spring flowers and flowering trees were shown. Since 1941 Easter lilies have been used.

Easter is visiting day among residents of American and Western Samoa. Sports competitions between the people of the two Samoas are staged either at Pago Pago, American Samoa, or Apia, Western Samoa.

One of the longest of all the annual parades in New York City salutes St. Patrick on his day, March 17th. Then thousands of Americans of Irish descent march up Fifth Ave. past St. Patrick's Cathedral and reviewing stands beside Central Park. Such celebrations were staged in New York as early as 1762, and possibly as long ago as 1684.

St. Patrick's Day is one of the more important annual events in Boston, Mass., which has a large Irish-American population. The first of the observances in Boston took place on March 17, 1737, when leaders among Irish Protestants organized The Charitable Irish Society. In recent years the festival has come to be identified with Irish Catholics. When the British evacuated Boston on March 17, 1776, General George Washington designated "Boston" as the password for the day, and "St. Patrick" as the countersign.

APRIL

Pan American Day, April 14th, presents a happy challenge to all members of the Pan American Union, or Organization of American States, to glorify the heroes of peace and others who have made heroic contributions to man's store of knowledge. It was on April 14th, 1890, that the First International Conference of American States met in Washington, D.C. Since then celebrations have been staged mostly in Latin American countries, or in states where there is a sizable Spanish population. In 1947, Lakewood, near Long Beach, Calif., began celebrating Pan American Festival Week as a means of stimulating deeper friendships among the Latin American countries. There are flag exchange ceremonies, luncheons, dinners, dances, a float parade in which members of the counselor corps from nearby Los Angeles participate, and a fiesta at which art and cultural exhibits, Latin American entertainment, Latin foods, and sports contests are featured.

What is now American Samoa came under the Stars and Stripes as a result of a convention with Great Britain and Germany on Dec. 2, 1899. Flag Day, April 17th, commemorates the raising of the first American flag on that date in 1900. For more than fifty years the Navy had jurisdiction over the islands. However, on July 1, 1951, their administration was assigned to the Dept. of the Interior. The Department appoints a Governor and a Secretary. A bicameral legislature is one aspect of the local constitutional government. In 1964, at the behest of imaginative, energetic Governor H. Rex Lee, the islands obtained from the U.S. Government one of the first comprehensive educational television systems anywhere. On Flag Day, a Samoan flag flying from the same pole as the American flag, waves over a crowd gathered to hear speeches, prayers, the playing of anthems, and watch a parade. Often the holiday fare includes boat races, coconut-husking contests, dancing, fire-making, and a tug-o'-war.

Patriot's Day, April 19th, rivals St. Patrick's Day for popularity in Boston. It commemorates the start of the War for Independence in 1775, when a strong force of British regulars was repulsed by farmers known as Minutemen after Paul Revere made his famous ride to alert the patriots. The route of the ride is traced by participants in a twenty-six-mile marathon sponsored by the Boston Athletic Association since 1896.

MAY

In 1776, Rhode Island stole a march on some of the other colonies by severing connections with England on May 4th, two months before the Declaration of Independence became unanimous. The state now commemorates that gesture of defiance with a Heritage Week early in May, at which time it usually calls attention to its cultural and commercial attributes. Among the long-established festivities in Rhode Island are the May Day Breakfasts which have been sponsored by the Grange and churches since 1867. As the title suggests, the breakfasts are served on May 1st.

To the everlasting credit of Miss Anna Jarvis, who originated Mother's Day on May 10th, 1908, she emphatically deplored the commercialism which eventually infested the day of tribute. Miss Jarvis suggested the initial observances in Philadelphia, Pa., and Grafton, W. Va., to honor her own mother, Mrs. Anna M. Reeves Jarvis, who died in Philadelphia, May 9, 1905. In 1914, Congress authorized the President to designate as Mother's Day the second Sunday in May. Miss Jarvis died in West Chester, Pa., Nov. 24, 1948.

Indians served by the Mission San Antonio de Pala, near San Diego, Calif., have been celebrating the Feast of Corpus Christi regularly since about 1817. The occasion is a holy feast of obligation in the Roman Catholic Church which

141

occurs sixty days after Easter. Its purpose, according to Catholic doctrine, is to give praise and honor to God really present in the Blessed Sacrament. As it does in most places, the observance at Pala is staged on the Sunday following the actual feast day, which is a Thursday. The Indians are called to worship at solemn High Mass by ringing of the bell in the old campanile in front of the Mission. After Mass, young Indian girls wearing white dresses lead a procession, scattering flowers as they go. They are followed by church dignitaries in religious robes, and Indians from the area. Three times along its route the procession stops at altars made of flowers, fronds, and ferns. After the procession there is a barbecue, Indian games, and other fiesta activities. Mission San Antonio de Pala, founded in 1816, is the only mission still serving its original purpose of ministering to the Indians. In Indiana, for more than 100 years seminarians and parishioners in Oldenburg have given more than the customary attention to the Feast of Corpus Christi by staging a procession through the tree-shaded lanes of the community, while monks of St. Meinrad's Abbey, St. Meinrad, have conducted their Procession of Corpus Christi since the monastery was founded in 1854.

Beginning on the third Saturday in May, 1950, Armed Forces Day supplanted the separate U. S. Army, Navy, and Air Force Days. The two-fold purpose of Armed Forces Day is to familiarize Americans with the state of defense, and to encourage public interest in all branches of the service, including the Coast Guard and Marines.

Victoria Day, which began in Canada as Empire Day, was originated by Mrs. Clementine Fessenden. One day in 1896, she attended a memorial for her late husband, Rev. E. J. Fessenden, conducted by the Wentworth Historical Society, Hamilton, Ont. On that occasion the Society made an honorary member of Mrs. Fessenden's young granddaughter as a tribute to the memory of her grandfather. This prompted the idea that other children might like to hear about the noble deeds of those who had demonstrated their devotion to the Empire at home and abroad. As a result, the first Empire Day was observed May 25, 1897. Appropriate exercises were held on the last school day preceding May 24th, which was Queen Victoria's birthday. Queen Victoria was born at Kensington Palace, May 24, 1819. She became queen June 20, 1837, was crowned in June, 1838, and died Jan. 22, 1901, at Osborne Palace. Her birthday having been celebrated for sixty years, the people of the British Empire continued the habit. In 1904, May 24th was set aside for special services by school children of Canada in honor of Great Britain and her heroes. By legislation passed in 1952, Victoria Day is celebrated on the first Monday preceding May 24th.

Although many Americans call their communities the birthplace of Memorial Day in the United States, in 1966 Waterloo, N.Y., was chosen for that honor by proclamation of President Johnson and the adoption of Concurrent Resolution 587 by the United States Senate and the House of Representatives which states that "the Congress of the United States, in recognition of the patriotic tradition set in motion 100 years ago in the village of Waterloo, New York, does hereby recognize Waterloo, New York, as the birthplace of Memorial Day." The people of Waterloo based their claim to the distinction on the actions of Henry C. Welles, a druggist, and General John B. Murray, the Clerk of Seneca County, in 1865. That year they encouraged their fellow townsfolk to remember the day by decorating their graves and shutting down shops and other businesses a full day as a sign of respect for their nation's war dead. So, on May 5th, in 1866 and 1867, flags in Waterloo were flown at half-mast and there were other signs of public mourning, including pilgrimages to the cemeteries where flowers were distributed and memorial services were conducted. However, even though May 5th was Waterloo's first choice for the annual observance, in 1868 when the Federal Government approved May 30th as the date for the annual observance, Waterloo's citizens accepted the decision gracefully.

Order No. 11, issued by Gen. John A. Logan, Commander of the Union veterans' Grand Army of the Republic, three years after the close of the Civil War, inaugurated Memorial Day in the United States. The order designated May 30, 1868, as the date for strewing with flowers or otherwise decorating the graves of those who died in defense of their country during the recent rebellion. Among an estimated 5,000 persons at the first observance in Arlington National Cemetery, Va., just across the Potomac River from Wash., D. C., were Generals Ulysses S. Grant and James A. Garfield, who subsequently became Presidents. Since that first Memorial Day every President of the United States has played a prominent role in the solemn ceremonies. Next to Arlington, a favorite place for Presidents to salute the honored dead is Gettysburg National Military Park, Pa. That was where Lincoln delivered his immortal Gettysburg Address on November 19, 1863. In spirit it foreshadowed Memorial Day. To emphasize the fact that Memorial Day, or Decoration Day as it is also known, is for flowers, the Fleet of Flowers celebration at Depoe Bay, Ore., each May 30th since 1948, has been a tribute to those who have lost their lives at sea. Flotilla No. seventy-eight of the U.S. Coast Guard Auxiliary begins its service on shore about ten A.M. There is usually religious and patriotic music, volleys are fired, then participants get aboard flower-laden fishing vessels and sail out to sea. There the parade of boats forms a circle around an anchored Coast Guard cutter. Often military planes fly past, dip their wings in salute, and even drop blossoms as the boats' passengers toss bouquets and wreaths overboard. Meanwhile, across the nation veterans' organizations regard Memorial Day as one of the major patriotic occasions of the year. Their color guards, drum and bugle corps, and drill teams parade, and their buglers blow taps to conclude ceremonies at cemeteries and war memorials.

The title of father of Flag Day in the United States was long ago given to William T. Kerr, who was credited with founding the American Flag Day Association in 1888 while he was still a school boy in Pittsburgh, Pa. His lifelong dream of an annual salute to the flag became a reality in 1949 when President Truman signed a bill designating July 14th as Flag Day, because it was on June 14, 1777 that the Continental Congress adopted the Stars and Stripes as the official flag of the new nation.

Mrs. John Bruce Dodd, Spokane, Wash., became the mother of Father's Day when she persuaded the Ministerial Association of that city to honor fathers with special services for the first time on June 19, 1910. The inspiration for the tribute is said to have occurred to Mrs. Dodd as she remembered how her own father successfully reared a family of small children after the death of his wife.

The passing of the Organic Act by the Congress of the United States on June 22, 1936, which granted civil government and universal suffrage to the U.S. Virgin Islands, also prompted the Islands' tenth legislature to declare June 22nd an annual holiday.

Appropriately, for many generations Puerto Ricans and their guests have been celebrating June 24th, the feast day of St. John the Baptist, for which the capital was named, by taking a dip in the Caribbean on St. John's Eve to commemorate the saint's baptisms. Often bonfires which illuminate the seashore burn the whole night through. In recent years the celebration has expanded to include street dances, parades, and other carnival events.

The greatest popular manifestation in Montreal, Canada is the "Fêtes de la Saint-Jean-Baptiste," the French-Canadian national holiday in honor of St. John the Baptist, patron of Quebec Province, on June 24th. In 1964 the celebration organized by the St. Jean Baptiste Society extended the customary one-day event to eight days, and used the theme "French-Canada, 20th Century Reality," to emphasize an identification of French-Canadian language, culture, and folklore in the area. It is not unusual for the festival to include a musical revue featuring leading artists from France and other nations where French is the mother tongue; a White Ball for which women wear white gowns and men don formal white ties and tails; a Gala National Show featuring band competitions, bugle corps, choral music, and folk dancing; a Mass on the square in front of historic Notre-Dame Church; a "Sound and Light" presentation; the Guillaume Couture oratorio, "Jean le Precurseur," based on the life of St. John the Baptiste, in its entirety at Montreal's new concert hall, Place des Arts; a "Communion of bonfires" across the province from Manicougan in the east to the Ontario border, and on both banks of the St. Lawrence River; the longest, gayest, most popular parade in the province; and a mass ball called "La Fête Dans l'Île" on St. Helen's Island in the St. Lawrence River, site of the 1967 World's Fair created to mark the anniversary of Canada's Confederation.

JULY

Among the bonds which link the United States and Canada in comradeship is the history of their independence. Both obtained freedom from the same guardian, England; both celebrate their sovereignty in July; and both consider Britain their best friend and staunchest ally. The thirteen American colonies declared for independence on July 4, 1776, then fought the good fight to achieve it. The Dominion of Canada evolved less dramatically. In 1864, representatives of New Brunswick, Nova Scotia, Ontario, and Quebec, met in Charlottestown, Prince Edward Island, to consider confederation. After some three years of discussion, persuasion, and compromise, confederation became a reality. Dominion Day was proclaimed on July 1, 1867.

Since the summer of 1959, Detroit, Mich., and Windsor, Ont., Canada, have been staging an International Freedom Festival which salutes both Dominion Day and the Fourth of July. Actually, it took much longer to bring off this cooperative celebration than it took the Canadians to confederate. The idea of a hands-across-the-border patriotic party which occurred to Paul Lutzeler in 1930 while he was a journalism student at what is now Wayne State University, Detroit, took almost thirty years to materialize. However, when Lutzeler's suggestion was accepted it was developed with enthusiasm. From the very beginning dignitaries of both nations have participated in major events. The J. L. Hudson Co., Detroit, sponsors a spectacular fireworks display from barges anchored in the Detroit River, midway between Canada and the United States, and there are many events in Detroit and Windsor to provide entertainment for tens of thousands of spectators on both shores. Among the activities are contests to select Miss Freedom Festival, a competitive art exhibit, a pleasure craft water parade, concerts, parades, baton-twirling contests, puppet shows, kite-flying contests, sky diving, foreign folk festivities, square dancing, hootenanny, water polo, a horse show, and an international Gold Cup Powerboat race.

While all Canadians observe Dominion Day, July 1st, the ten provinces and the Yukon Territory also celebrate their own provincial anniversaries. Among them are, from East to West: Newfoundland—Commonwealth Day, May 24; Discovery Day, anniversary of Cabot's landfall in 1497, June 21; Memorial Day, July 5th; Nova Scotia—John Cabot Day, Cape North, June 26th; Natal Day, Annapolis Royal, Aug. 1st; Dartmouth, Aug. 11th: New Brunswick—Natal Day, Moncton, Aug. 14th; Ontario. Victoria Day, Woodstock, May 24th. Yukon Territory—Victoria Day, Whitehorse, May 24th, Discovery Day, Aug. 17th.

Millions of Americans participate in a wide variety of patriotic celebrations and watch many championship sports events on July 4th, Independence Day. Traditional ceremonies are held at Independence Hall, Philadelphia, Pa., and on the Washington Monument Grounds, Wash., D. C., there is a program of music, popular entertainment, a speech by a prominent citizen, and a fireworks display.

July 4th is not only American Independence Day on the U. S. Virgin Islands. It is also a time for celebrating the anniversary of the abolition of slavery which occurred on July 3, 1848, almost seventy years before the United States purchased the islands from Denmark, on March 31, 1917.

In Guam, the celebration of Independence Day, July 4th, and Liberation Day are similar. At Agana there are patriotic parades, carnivals, and dances. Liberation Day, July 21st, observes the return of U. S. Forces to Guam in 1944, and the subsequent liberation of the island from two-and-a-half years of Japanese domination.

Since July 25, 1952, when Commonwealth status was created for Puerto Rico, the anniversary titled Constitution Day has been celebrated especially in San Juan. In Santa Isabel and Cabo Rojo there are sailing regattas.

In the U.S. Virgin Islands, July 25th is Supplication Day. Then islanders attend churches to pray for deliverance from hurricanes. Three months later, on Oct. 25th, it is a local tradition to give thanks for having been spared from severe storms.

The feast of Santiago Apostal, July 25th, is celebrated enthusiastically with parties and dances in Loiza Aldea, P.R., for three days before and three days after the actual holiday because St. James is the patron of the town.

AUGUST

Remembering the example set by Great Britain as long ago as 1871, at least, when Lord Avebury's Bank Holidays Act included the first Monday in August as an official bank holiday, many communities in Canada hold a civic holiday on that day.

August is the traditional time for community reunions called Old Home Week in New England, New Brunswick, and on Prince Edward Island. The practice began in 1899 when Governor Frank West Rollins introduced it to New Hampshire. Communities were urged to invite their wandering native sons to return home for a visit during the last week in August. Bonfires were lighted on hilltops after the fashion of the Scots summoning the clan, and fireworks were set off on the mountain peaks. Sometimes there are town socials, baked bean suppers, and square dances.

SEPTEMBER

In Canada, whenever there is a discussion about the origin of Labor Day, or Labour Day as the Canadians write it, Canadians like to point to the record which indicates that "the Toronto Trades Assembly, perhaps the original central labour body in Canada, organized the first North American 'workingman's demonstration' of any significance for April 15, 1872." According to a report by Clifford A. Scotton, editor of Canadian Labour, the official journal of the Canadian Labour Congress, Ottawa, minutes of the Assembly show that the coachmakers, coopers, iron moulders, bookbinders and brass founders were among the unions which took part in a parade to the Toronto Exhibition Grounds on that date. Labour Day marches, now staged on the first Monday in September, still wind up at the exhibition grounds where the gigantic Canadian National Exposition, incorporated in 1879, takes place late in August and early in September. How much the status of trade unions has changed since 1872 becomes obvious to anyone who learns that the parade and rally were staged then to call for abolition of the law which decreed that "trade unions were criminal conspiracies in restraint of trade." Scotton points out that "the freedom of twenty-four imprisoned leaders of the Toronto Typographical Union, on strike to secure the nine-hour working day, was the immediate purpose of the parade, on what was then Thanksgiving Day in Canada." Apparently, "It was still a crime to be a member of a union in Canada although the law of criminal conspiracy in restraint of trade had been repealed by the United Kingdom Parliament in 1871 by passage of the Trade Union and Criminal Law Amendment Acts."

Prophetically, since Labour Day eventually became an annual event on the first Monday in September, on September 3, 1872, the first Tuesday in the month, seven unions in Ottawa took part in a parade "more than a mile long." It "wound its way to the home of Prime Minister Sir John A. MacDonald where the marchers hoisted him into a carriage and drew him to Ottawa City Hall by torchlight. "The Old Chieftain," aware of the discontent of workers with the laws which made unions illegal, in a ringing declaration from the steps of the City Hall, promised the marchers that his party would 'sweep away all such barbarous laws from the statute books.' " The offending regulation was repealed by the Canadian Parliament in 1872. Nevertheless, the traditional salute to labour launched by the Toronto Trades Assembly in April, 1872 continued into the early 1880's. "In 1882," Scotton reports, "the Toronto Trades and Labour Council, successor to the Toronto Trades Assembly, decided to organize the annual demonstration and picnic for July 22. The Council sent an invitation to Peter J. McGuire, of New York, requesting his services as a speaker for the occasion. McGuire was the founder and general secretary of the United Brotherhood of Carpenters which had been organized the previous year." The American was to share the platform with Daniel J. O'Donohue, an Irish immigrant printer, who was elected to the Ontario Legislature in 1874. However, McGuire is reported to have sent a telegram to the President of the Trades and Labour Council, who was in charge of ceremonies at the Exhibition Grounds, regretting that "a sudden and dangerous accident" to his wife prevented him from being present. The "unequalled success" of the celebration has been summed up by Scotton in this way:

"At noon on July 22, 1882, the parade set off from the Albert Hall. Delegates from twenty-three unions and the TTLC swelled the ranks of marchers to between 3,000 and 4,000. The old *Toronto Globe,* in a story headed, 'Monster Demonstration,' estimated that 50,000 Torontonians watched the parade swing by with its military and civil bands, its floats, banners and ribbons headed by a parade marshal on horseback." Now, in Canada as well as in the United States, labour's day has given its name to the last holiday weekend of summer. Regattas, such as those staged at Fort Williams-Port Arthur and Sarnia, Ont., are numerous, and a representative Labour Day parade in Toronto winds up, as usual, at the Canadian National Exposition.

Appropriately, New York City, where a holiday dedicated to American labor was introduced in September 1882, has one of the major mass celebrations of the event. As a rule, about ten A.M. on the first Monday in September, floats, bands, and thousands of marchers affiliated with the AFL-CIO, gather at 26th St. and Fifth Ave. to begin the long march up the avenue to 65th St. Similar parades are conducted in other industrial cities, such as Detroit and Chicago, thus fulfilling the dream of Peter J. McGuire, a native of New York City and a union carpenter by trade, when on May 8, 1882, he suggested to the newly organized Central Labor Union that it dedicate one day a year to the greater glory of the laboring class and call it Labor Day. He chose the first Monday in September because that day is approximately midway between two major American holidays, July Fourth and Thanksgiving Day, the fourth Thursday in November.

The home base for Defender's Day on Sept. 13th is Fort McHenry National Monument and Historic Shrine, Baltimore, Md. It was the repulse of a British naval attack against the fort on Sept. 13 and 14, 1814, that prevented the capture of Baltimore, and inspired Francis Scott Key to pen the poem which eventually became the lyrics for "The Star Spangled Banner." A reenactment of the Story of the Flag was a highlight of the 150th Defender's Day Ceremony in 1964. However, the most exciting part of any commemorative program is the simulated bombardment of the fort with "bombs bursting in air" in the manner that thrilled the author of America's national anthem. Key and a federal agent for the exchange of prisoners had sailed from Baltimore to persuade the British to release Dr. William Beanes, who had been seized for alleged violation of "good conduct." During the attack the Americans were on a vessel at the rear of the British fleet, but able to witness the bombardment. As it progressed, Key made a rough draft of the poem, and completed it the next day. Credit for popularizing "The Star Spangled Banner" has been given to Col. Caleb Carlton, Commander of Fort Meade, Md., where, in 1892, he ordered it played at the close of all parades and concerts. In 1916, President Wilson ordered it played at every U.S. Army Post retreat, and the song was designated the national anthem by Act of Congress on March 3, 1931.

OCTOBER

On or about Oct. 4th, the feast day of St. Francis of Assisi, the patron of Cupeno Indians, there is a children's festival at the Mission San Antonio de Pala, some twenty-five miles east of Oceanside, Calif. In the morning there usually is a solemn High Mass and a procession. In the afternoon there are Indian games, contests and tribal dances in costume.

Canadians contend that the first formal Thanksgiving service in North America was held in Newfoundland in 1578 by Sir John Frobisher after the very first immigrants to settle in the New World landed there safely. However, it was not until

152

1879 that Canada began setting aside one day each year on which to offer thanks, particularly for a successful harvest. For a while, Canada and the United States observed Thanksgiving on the same Thursday in November. Eventually, though, Canadians decided that Thursday did not give commercial travelers enough time to get home for family reunions, so they moved Thanksgiving to Monday to create a three-day weekend. Even the Monday on which Canada's Thanksgiving is held has been shifted about the calendar. After World War I, Thanksgiving was a part of the Armistice celebration and was held in the same week as November 11th. In 1931, however, it was felt that November is too late in the year for an authentic harvest celebration, so the date was moved to the second Monday in October, which is now the accepted date.

The dates of the Columbus Day Parade and the "Festa Italiana" in San Francisco, Calif., are determined each year by the Columbus Day Celebration Committee. Although the parade is always scheduled on the Sunday preceding or following Columbus Day, Oct. 12th, the city's special events calendar is taken into consideration to avoid major conflicts. Typical activities might include a pageant depicting the coronation of Queen Isabella and the commissioning of Columbus's voyage which led to the discovery of the New World in 1492, the North Beach Street Fair, a Waterfront Cavalcade based on the life of Columbus, a parade, ceremonies at the statue of Columbus on Telegraph Hill, a banquet, and a ball.

It is fair to estimate that the observance of Children's White Sunday, primarily a religious event on the second Sunday in October, began in Samoa as long ago as 1840, since missionaries arrived there in 1830 and promptly converted the natives to Christianity. On the feast day it is traditional for children to dress in white, wear garlands of flowers, and sing as they march to church. The youngsters might also be called upon to recite a bit of scripture. They usually receive gifts, and are given the place of honor at family dinners.

A splendid opportunity to put the accent on the positive in

the field of festivals by dramatizing the achievements and brotherhood of man has been waiting to be developed ever since the representatives of forty-six countries drew up the United Nations Charter at San Francisco, Calif., April 25 to June 26, 1945. On Oct. 24, 1945, the charter was ratified. Thus the world organization, and United Nations Day, came into being. Normally, the celebration of UN Day throughout the world has been done on a community basis, with assists from the UN Dept. of Public Information, if required. However, most observances have been on the level of folk dancing and singing. An elaborate entertainment of this type, with special band music, songs, and dances of many nations, is presented from time to time during UN Week in October on the Lower Plaza of Rockefeller Center, New York City. There member nations' flags are displayed from Good Friday through November. By the end of 1966 the total was 122 flags. John D. Rockefeller, Jr., whose foresight created the monumental Rockefeller Center in the 1930's, gave eight million dollars for the land on which the UN Headquarters are located in New York.

The House of Pacific Relations founded during the 1935–36 exposition in Balboa Park, San Diego, Calif., displays some of the art and cultural activities of about twenty nations during the Fall Fiesta of Nations. The celebration is a salute to United Nations Day, which is Oct. 24th, because the charter came into effect Oct. 24, 1945.

The juvenile practice of cadging coins at Halloween with a plea for a trick or a treat was boosted to the status of a good deed in 1965. After the United Nations Children's Fund was awarded the Nobel Peace Prize it was disclosed that some of the American youngsters who gave to the fund had collected their donations via trick-or-treat on Oct. 31st.

Community Halloween Festivals on Oct. 31st have done much to curtail vandalism which was customary on that occasion. Some credit the people of Anoka, Minn., with organizing the first citywide supervised Halloween Party in 1920. Other communities adopted similar plans soon after. A celebration which has been setting a fine example for community cooperation at Halloween since 1923 is the one at Anaheim, Calif. There youngsters and grown-ups alike lose themselves in masquerades, and everybody's energy is guided into non-destructive channels, such as parades, games, and contests. A typical program might begin with a Costume Breakfast, stage entertainment, costume judging and awarding of trophies, a kids' parade, kids' day at a recreation amusement park, a show window decorating contest, and the annual Pumpkin Bowl football game. Often on the second night there is an hour of entertainment and a two-hour Festival of Sports Parade.

NOVEMBER

To salute the memory of departed warriors who died defending their country, Canadians observe Remembrance Day on Nov. 11th, the anniversary of the end of World War I in 1918. On Remembrance Day, 1966, an estimated 10,000 persons stood in silence under cold, overcast skies to watch the placing of wreaths at the base of the National War Memorial, Confederation Square, Ottawa, Ont.

To honor the quick and the dead among their nation's war veterans Americans supplanted Armistice Day with Veterans Day as a patriotic holiday on Nov. 11, 1954. The focal point for the foremost ceremony in the United States are the tombs of the Unknowns in Arlington National Cemetery, Va., just across the Potomac River from Wash., D. C. If the President is in the capital it is customary for him to place a red, white, and blue wreath at the shrine. Invariably representatives of all branches of the service stand behind the tombs as honored witnesses of the ceremony that takes place at eleven A.M., the hour the cease-fire went into effect along the Western Front in Europe to end World War I. On Veterans Day, 1963, President John F. Kennedy, a Navy veteran, led the nation's tribute before an audience estimated at 5,000. Hatless, he walked to the tomb accompanied by the speaker of the day, a Medal-of-Honor winner, Gen. David M. Shoup, Marine Corps Commandant. An Army sergeant helped the Chief Executive place a huge wreath on a stand as the spectators maintained a respectful silence. That was just eleven days before President Kennedy was assassinated in Dallas, Tex., and exactly two weeks before he was buried at Arlington, virtually in the shadow of the national memorial.

What is perhaps the most exotic observance of Veterans Day takes place on November 11th at Indian City, Anadarko, Okla., where Indian warriors perform a ceremony that antedates the coming of the white man to North America. It is performed by members of the Ton-Kon-Ko, the Kiowa Society of the Black Legs. Although the U. S. Army disbanded the fraternity after vanquishing the Kiowas some seventy-five years ago, it was reorganized following World War II to salute the braves who acquitted themselves so well in combat.

New Englanders have been celebrating Thanksgiving since Gov. William Bradford and the Pilgrims observed it there in 1621. George Washington was the first President to proclaim a nationwide Thanksgiving when he set aside the last Thursday in November, 1789, for that celebration; but six years passed before he proclaimed another. From then until President Lincoln, by proclamation, established America's annual Thanksgiving observance in 1863, the holiday occurred spasmodically. In the main, the American Thanksgiving is a time for worship, feasts, and family reunions. However, more and more across the country it seems that Thanksgiving Day, and the weekend which follows, are becoming known as the period of the big toy parades. The parades were introduced at Philadelphia, Pa., in 1920, when Gimbel Brothers inaugurated a procession glorifying toyland and characters from juvenile fiction. Whether or not this was one of the secrets the two major department stores, Gimbels and Macy's, are supposed to keep from one another is not known. However, the Gimbels project proved to be so successful Macy's launched an annual Thanksgiving Day parade in New York City in 1924, and the rest is toyland history.

In Canada, the T. Eaton Co. sponsors a mile-long parade in Toronto, Ont., in mid-November, and usually restages the toyland procession in Montreal a week later.

The sight of many motion picture and television actors passing in review on some forty festooned floats gliding along Hollywood Blvd., in Hollywood, Calif., is a dream-come-true for a multitude of movie and television fans the night before Thanksgiving. The big, brassy, hour-and-a-half parade has been a popular attraction since about 1926. The world-famous Hollywood Blvd. becomes Santa Claus Lane for the Christmas shopping season, and is gaily decorated with colored lights and ornamental Christmas trees. Santa Claus leads the procession in an expensive tinsel-covered sleigh, and other celebrities follow him.

DECEMBER

The procession in honor of Our Lady of the Immaculate Conception at Agana, Guam, on Dec. 8th, is one of the more impressive religious observances staged regularly on the island. Throughout the year at celebrations honoring patron saints of various villages there are water buffalo races and other sports events as well as religious services. As a rule the party takes place on Saturday and devotions on Sunday.

Countless customs are bound to embellish a festival that is as old as Christmas is. Many of them represent quiet, peaceful attributes of the occasion, such as the ancient ceremonial dances performed by some Indians in New Mexico after they attend Christian religious devotions, and the posadas along the Mexican–United States Border enacted by people of Spanish or Mexican descent between Dec. 16th and 24th. Las Posadas, the lodgings, dramatize the difficulties encountered by Mary and Joseph as they sought shelter in Bethlehem. The symbolic pilgrimages take place on the nine nights before Christmas because the journey of Mary and Joseph is supposed to have taken nine days.

The only major outdoor Christmas Eve program of caroling and tableaux in a National Park is the one inaugurated in 1931 at Hot Springs National Park, Hot Springs, Ark., by Elizabeth Bowe Sims.

The oldest continuing activity at the Rockefeller Center Plaza in New York City is the Christmas tree and seasonal display of flowers in the Channel Gardens, which were so named because they separate the British and French Buildings. The first informal tree was set up by workmen in the excavation for the British Empire Building in 1931. The first formal tree was erected in 1933 on Rockefeller Plaza, and has been continued yearly without interruption. In 1966, the tree from the Petawawa Forest Experiment Station, 120 miles north of Canada's capital city of Ottawa, was the first Center tree to come from Canada, and the first to come from outside the United States. The gesture was a tribute to Canada's forthcoming centennial in 1967. At the thirty-fourth annual tree lighting on Dec. 9th, 1966, Hugh Downs, the host of NBC-TV's "Today Show," was master of ceremonies. To entertain the huge crowd assembled around the skating rink there were three talented figure skaters from Canada, and the Little Singers of Mount Royal, a thirty-seven-voice boys' choir from St. Joseph's Oratory, Montreal, that sang traditional French carols.

The contemporary Christmas Festival at St. Croix, V. I., had its counterpart in early Virgin Islands history. Before slavery was abolished there in 1848, while the islands were owned by Denmark, public celebrations were forbidden the slaves, especially in St. Croix, the seat of the local government. The one exception was Christmas, so the slaves grasped that opportunity each year to have fun, practice ancient African customs, dress up, masquerade, promenade, prance, sing, and dance. However, as the natives moved away from slavery the old-time communal Christmas party languished, because the younger generations deemed it primitive, unsophisticated, and a painful reminder of slavery times. About 100 years later, though, Ann Brodhurst is said to have campaigned to revive the Christmas Festival. Her efforts were successful, so the first celebration in the current series was staged in 1952. Between Dec. 16th, 1966 and Jan. 7th, 1967, the Christmas Party at Christiansted and Frederiksted included a queen contest, festival formal, coronation, steel bands, concerts, parades, and dances.

The Christmas Pageant of Peace which begins about Dec. 20th in Washington, D. C., has been an annual event since 1954. As a rule the President of the United States launches it by lighting the National Christmas Tree and delivering a short address. The tree is at the head of a path which is flanked by trees representing the states and territories of the United States. Reindeer, burning yule logs, a manger scene, music and drama on an outdoor stage, and choral and instrumental groups from different parts of the nation are featured during the celebration.

In Victoria, B. C., which is often described as being more English than England, an Olde English Elizabethan Yuletide is a Christmas time attraction. Carolers in period costumes stroll the corridors of some hotels; there are yule log ceremonies and the procession of the boar's head. Similar festivities are staged at Harrison Hot Springs, B. C.

In 1922, several men in Colorado Springs, Colo., formed the AdAman Club, intending to Add A Man to membership each year, and ascended 14,000-foot Pike's Peak to welcome the New Year with fireworks. Still an annual event, the trek begins on New Year's Eve. The pyrotechnical displays at midnight are visible in Colorado Springs, weather permitting.

Indian Festivals

THE SEMINOLES who gather at Moore Haven, Fla., around the first weekend in March to celebrate Chalo Nitka, which is Seminole for "day of the big bass," could be the new rich among Indians, if a decision handed down in their favor in May, 1964 by the Indian Claims Commission for land taken from their ancestors is sustained. Federal attorneys have contested the decision which upheld the Seminole Tribe's claim to ownership of nearly 90 percent of Florida's 37.5 million acres which was taken from them as a result of the Seminole Wars of 1816–18, 1835–42, and 1855–58. During and after the wars some 4,000 Seminoles were rounded up and shipped to Oklahoma, but a band of determined, wily natives of the Big Cypress Swamp and the Everglades never gave in. They signed no peace treaty. They merely retreated into the saw-grass marshes, and did not even recognize the U. S. Government until 1938. In a sincere attempt to rectify mistakes made by the Government in its dealings with Indians, especially during the nineteenth century, Congress established the Indian Claims Commission in 1945. Since then the Commission is reported to have awarded more than $100-million to various tribes, but nothing to an estimated 1,500 Seminoles still in Florida, and another 3,500 in Oklahoma. In 1949 they filed their claim with the Commission, which announced its approval five years later. The sum being considered was established by a Government appraisal of the approximately thirty-two million acres of Florida real estate taken from the Seminoles about 150 years ago. At that time the property recently seized from the long-entrenched Indians was sold for as little as $1.25 an acre. Should the ancient antagonists settle for this figure, as has been recommended, the estimated 32 million acres under dispute would fetch about $40 million for the Seminoles. If that amount is prorated among the estimated 5,000 claimants, each would receive around $8,000. Now some of them live in thatched-roofed, open-sided Chickees on the Dania Reservation, a Federal area about twenty miles north of Miami, while others prefer the Federal reservations at Brighton, northwest of Lake Okeechobee, Big Cypress, to the south, or a State reservation adjoining Big Cypress. Many Seminoles work on farms near the reservations, but quite a few capitalize on their uniqueness by maintaining Indian villages along the Tamiami Trail where they sell handcrafted souvenirs. Moore Haven is on the western shore of Lake Okeechobee. The Seminoles who participate in the Chalo Nitka Festival there around the first Saturday in March compete in athletic contests, tribal dances, and the crowning of an Indian Princess. For all comers, though, the big attraction is the trophy awarded for catching the biggest bass, a freshwater game fish that is plentiful in the Okeechobee region. Contestants have from mid-January till the eve of the festival to register their catches. The man and woman who catch the largest bass during the seven-week period are crowned King and Queen of the Bass. As a rule there are also a parade, rodeo, and a barbecue.

Choctaw Chief Alan Wright has been credited with having named Oklahoma when the area was chosen as a settling place for Indians in the 1800's. A literal translation of the word is "home of the red man." The state's Indian population of approximately 65,000 is second only to Arizona's estimated 84,000. Quite a few Oklahoma Indians became wealthy when oil was discovered on their land. However, rich or poor, many Indians in Oklahoma and elsewhere perpetuate the ancient tribal customs. Some do so for sentimental reasons, others because the practice provides a way to entertain tourists. Each summer since 1932, lately during the third week in July, an estimated 3,000 Indians from the Apache, Arapaho, Caddo,

Cheyenne, Comanche, Delaware, Kiowa, Otoe, Osage, Pawnee, Seminole, and Wichita tribes have gathered at Anadarko, Okla., to stage their very impressive American Indian Exposition. This authentic all-Indian show is witnessed by an average of 10,000 white men on each of its six days. The Exposition usually opens officially about one P.M. on Monday with a big parade that meanders from the grounds through the downtown district and back in time for a program of Indian dances, games, skills, and horse racing. Two distinct sets of night performances are as different from each other as they are from the afternoon shows. As a rule, on Monday, Wednesday, and Saturday, a pageant in Redman Foundation Amphitheater depicts the story of the Southwest and Great Plains Indian Tribes. War dance elimination contests, tribal and ceremonial dances are staged Tuesday and Thursday nights, and the National Championship War Dance finals take place on Friday night. For most occasions the Indians don their feathers, furs, and bead-encrusted buckskins. Princesses dressed in tribal costumes are presented at each performance. An annual ceremony since 1952 when the National Hall of Fame for Famous American Indians was opened has been the dedication of busts of cherished redmen. There you will see likenesses of such stalwarts as Sequoyah, who invented the Cherokee alphabet; Charles Curtis, a Kaw Indian who was Vice-President of the United States when Herbert Hoover was President; and Alice Brown Davis, a Seminole believed to have been the only woman American Indian Chief.

During June, July, and August many of the several dozen Indian tribes domiciled in Oklahoma stage pow-wows. The contemporary campouts, often complete with tents made of synthetic materials and illuminated by power from portable generators, feature time-honored tribal councils, ceremonial rites and dances, and the sale of souvenirs to curious whites. Oklahoma communities in which they usually take place for a few days each summer include Carnegie, Clinton, Okmulgee, Pawnee, Ponca City, Quapaw, Stroud, and Tulsa.

Indian pow-wows have such an appeal for tourists the Inter-Tribal Indian Ceremonial inaugurated at Gallup, N. M., in 1921, is one of that state's major annual attractions during the second week in August. Then hundreds of Indians from a couple of dozen tribes congregate at the ninety-acre Lyon Memorial Park in the mesas on the northeastern part of town, parade daily in full regalia, dance, chant, and perform ancient rites for interested audiences. Among the traditional performances are the Devil, Basket, Buffalo, Corn, Eagle, and Feather dances. There are tribal athletic contests, and a large Navaho sand painting which plays an important part in the tribe's rituals. Zuñi girls stage a beauty show. Indian men compete in a rodeo, and soloists and choral groups sing ancient songs. Often the grand finale is the Navaho Fire Dance, a purification rite ordinarily staged as the climax of an age-old healing ceremony; or the thrilling Volador dance, of Mexican origin, in which performers tied with ropes fastened to the top of a tall pole, plunge earthward and describe wide circles in the air as the slowly unwinding rope lowers them gently to the ground.

According to the decennial tabulation published by the U. S. Bureau of the Census in 1960, New Mexico's Indian population of almost 57,000 is less than the estimated 65,000 in Oklahoma, or the approximately 84,000 in Arizona. Nevertheless, of the three states, New Mexico makes the most of its Indian heritage, as far as appealing to tourists the year round is concerned. New Mexico's Tourist Bureau in Santa Fe and the Albuquerque Chamber of Commerce distribute lists of dates and places of some three dozen fiestas scheduled in the state throughout the year. A majority of the events reflect religious practices which began eons ago, while others reveal definite commingling of pagan and Christian rites where the tribes have accepted Christianity. An obvious example of blending rituals is the Spring Corn Dance, an age-old supplication for fertility. It is the ceremonial dance at Easter time by Indians of the Cochiti, San Felipe, and Santo Domingo Pueblos. Men and women in ceremonial garb dance to the rhythm of tom-toms and chant their prayers for good crops and wild game. With a statewide average of at least three festivals a month, the Indians of New Mexico dance a lot. They dance the New Year in with either the Buffalo or Deer Dance, then they dance some more on January 6th, to celebrate the Christian Feast of Epiphany and the installation of new governors at Indian pueblos. The governor's symbol of office is a cane which was presented by President Lincoln.

Despite the fact that New Mexico has a superabundance of fiestas featuring Indian dances, much of the credit for preserving the dances belongs to caucasian folklorists, dance specialists, and hobbyists. A notable example of a hobbyist whose avocation literally became his vocation is J. F. "Buck" Bushears, a railroad contractor and scoutmaster, of La Junta, Colo. While a student at Colorado College he became interested in Indian lore, then combined his hobby with scouting in 1933. Bushears encouraged his charges to do research on costumes and rituals, then divided them into three groups. The Kiowas and Sioux concentrated on dances, the Navajos on music and drums. All the boys must make their own costumes, or obtain the beads, buckskins, quills, and rawhide from Indians. The scouts called themselves Koshares, a Pueblo Indian word for clowns or playmakers. They have become so adept that now they present many shows each year in the 200-capacity stockade behind their Kiva, or in communities across the land when they receive invitations to perform at conventions or festivals. The big Koshare festival of the year, however, is the Winter Night Ceremonial, usually on the Saturday and Sunday between Christmas and New Year's. Sometimes Koshares who have grown to manhood bring their wives and offspring to the festival, and the whole family joins in the fun.

An Indian dance once performed in jest by civic leaders of Prescott, Ariz., eventually became for them a subject of serious study. The pseudo redskins call themselves the Smoki —pronounced Smoke-eye—people. Their annual Snake Dance on the first Saturday in August which falls in the dark of the moon is one of the better-known annual events in Arizona. It began in 1921 with a burlesque of the Hopis' supplication for rain, a dance in which live rattlesnakes are used. The white men settled for harmless bull snakes, yet the performance made an impression. Now a typical six-part program might include an example of sand painting, a Sun Basket Pole Dance, the Kachina Dance, Ceremonial Flute Dance, Scalp Dance, and the inevitable Smoki Snake Dance. Money earned by the festival, which was first staged to finance the city's long-established rodeo and Frontier Days, now helps maintain a clubhouse and a museum for Indian relics, costumes, and other ceremonial paraphernalia valued at several thousand dollars.

Several thousand Indians from many tribes attend ceremonial dances and an all-Indian rodeo at Flagstaff, Ariz., during the first week in July. Only Indians take part in the daily parades, rodeo, wild cow milking, bareback cowpony races, papoose contest, girls' beauty pageant, and nighttime ceremonials which have become a part of the annual event begun in 1929. At the Museum of Northern Arizona, near Flagstaff, arts and crafts of the Hopi villagers are displayed and sold.

The Hopi Indians' prayers for rain, as demonstrated in the famous Snake Dance in July and August, are particularly pertinent since corn is their principal crop. The exact dates and locations of the religious ceremony are made known just about ten days before it takes place. The organization that receives first word of the date is the Winslow Chamber of Commerce, P.O. Box 621, Winslow, Ariz. Hopis remind visitors that although they welcome guests, they also reserve the right to deny admission to anyone. Also, because of the religious nature of the ceremony the Hopis object to picture taking, sketching, or writing notes. Their guests are advised to leave all cameras behind; that they are witnessing a sacred religious ceremony, and must stay in the seats assigned them so they will not interfere with or desecrate the ritual in any way.

Every summer around the second or third week in July on the Blackfoot Indian Reservation at Browning, Mont., the annual North American Indian Days attracts several thousand spectators who watch Indian dances, ceremonials, games, parades in which participants wear tribal costumes, and a pageant of the Blackfeet which begins with the creation of man and ends with the signing of the treaty the tribe made with the U.S. Government. Recently, a restaging of the Medicine Lodge and Sun Dance, which emphasizes the power of the medicine men and women and the purification of Indian braves, was presented after an absence of several years.

All American Indian Days, usually staged during the first week in August at Sheridan, Wyo., is supposed to have originated around 1955 to provide background material for the presentation ceremonies of the George Washington Honor Medal by the Freedom Foundation to the community of Sheridan for outstanding achievement in human relations. Interdenominational religious services, a parade, Indian games such as archery, lance throwing and races, an arts and crafts exposition, a buffalo barbecue, dance contest, and the selection of a Miss Indian-American Princess are highlights of the festival. Contestants in the Miss Indian-American Princess contest are judged for beauty, poise, Indian characteristics, education, and dedication to the welfare of their people.

Indian Days at Banff, Alta., usually staged for four days in mid-July immediately after the famous Stampede at Calgary, is one of the better known annual Indian celebrations in Canada. Indians trek from their haunts on the Canadian plains to lodge on the Banff sports grounds in the lee of the Cascade and Rundle Mountains of the Rockies. The annual pow-wow devoted to worship, sports, and dances is believed to have originated during the rainy summer of 1889 when the

166

swollen Bow River overflowed and washed out a railway line, thus stranding trainloads of vacationers at Banff. To entertain their frustrated guests the people of Banff persuaded a few Indians, who had been wise enough to spend the summer in a cool mountain retreat on purpose, to present a program of Indian lore. The impromptu festival was so well received it became an annual event. Indians from the Blackfoot, Blood, Cree, Poigan, and Stony reserves stage their own archery contests, parades, and rodeo in the daytime, and at night they don loincloth and feather bustles, twirl hoops from wrists and ankles to the rhythm of tom-toms, and perform the Owl and the Chicken Dance.

In the shadow of the Livingstone Range of the Canadian Rockies of southwestern Alberta, is the largest Indian Reservation in Canada. Approximately half the size of Holland, it is home to an estimated 2,500 members of the Blood Tribe whose livelihood is derived principally from farming and ranching. Although some Bloods were baptised by Christian missionaries a hundred years ago, each summer those who cling to the faith of their ancestors perform an age-old ritual called the Sun Dance. The ceremony usually takes place in August, but the exact dates of the two-week celebration vary from year to year. Regulations require that visitors secure a pass from the Superintendent, Blood Indian Agency, Cardston, Alberta, Canada, before going on to the reservation. This formality is enforced to protect the Indians against those who might make trouble by their failure to realize that the Sun Dance is essentially a religious gathering, and not a medicine show.

Since 1949, as the slanting rays of the late afternoon sun on the second and third Fridays and Saturdays in August penetrate a stand of maples surrounding a natural amphitheater on the Six Nations Reserve near Brantford, Ont., the Indians who live there have dramatized stories related to the history of the five tribes which were members of the confederacy of Iroquois—the Cayugas, Mohawks, Oneidas, Onondagas, and

Senecas—plus the Tuscaroras. One year a typical pageant, "The Iroquois League of Peace," depicted the founding of the Iroquois Confederacy, a precurser of the twentieth century League of Nations. The prime purpose of the dramatizations is to remind members of the Six Nations of their heritage, but interested spectators of other races are welcome, too. Usually visitors get a glimpse of a Six-Nations village as squaws perform the age-old chores of pounding corn, weaving baskets, and lacing moccasins.

Music Festivals

As NORTH Americans have moved away from the pioneer period familiar to their forebears they have developed more and more organized cultural activities, such as concerts and other musical events. Appropriately, this development is rooted in New England where the Worcester Music Festival, Worcester, Mass., the oldest in North America, has been an annual event since 1858. A typical festival in the Worcester Memorial Auditorium during the last week in October includes five concerts. In 1966, the Detroit Symphony conducted by Sixten Ehrling made its ninth appearance at the festival. The Worcester Chorus sang, and there was a concert for young people on Saturday morning.

The growth of music at the annual Chautauqua, Chautauqua, N.Y., during June, July, and August is noteworthy. Founded in 1874 by Bishop John H. Vincent and Lewis Miller as an educational idea, the Institute pioneered in adult education, and its programs have since included lectures by nationally and internationally known authorities. In 1949, Artie Shaw, band leader, played the world premiere of Norman Dello Joio's clarinet solo concertante for clarinet and orchestra, with the Chautauqua Symphony Orchestra conducted by Franco Autori. In 1966, the musical schedule included chamber music, opera, and symphony concerts. Audiences applauded "Abduction from the Seraglio," "Albert Herring," "Barber of Seville," "Rigoletto," and "My Fair Lady."

The Ann Arbor May Festival maintained by the University Musical Society of the University of Michigan, Ann Arbor, has been firmly established since 1894 when it was founded by Albert A. Stanley. At the 73rd annual festival, May 5th to 8th, 1966, 6 concerts in Hill Auditorium marked the 30th anniversary season of Eugene Ormandy as Musical Director of the Philadelphia Orchestra and conductor at the Ann Arbor May Festival. Thor Johnson was guest conductor, and Lester McCoy chorus master for the University Choral Union. The University Musical Society was organized during the winter of 1879–80 and was incorporated in 1881 to maintain a choral society and an orchestra, to provide public concerts, and to organize and maintain a school of music. The University Choral Union was the outgrowth of a "Messiah Club" made up of singers from several local churches. In addition to its "Messiah" concerts, since 1894, it has performed at the annual May Festivals, offering a wide range of choral literature over the years. The chorus membership numbers about 300 singers, including townspeople and students. Because the trimester plan has advanced the date of commencement to late in April or early in May, the Ann Arbor May Festival will be staged during the fourth week in April. The sponsors feel obliged to hold this important event while the students are still on campus so they may be in the audience or may participate in the Choral Union chorus performing with the Philadelphia Orchestra.

Chamber and orchestra music concerts supervised by the Yale Summer School of Music and Art are presented on Friday evenings during July and August in the 1,200-seat Music Shed on the Ellen Battell Stoeckel Estate, Norfolk, Conn. Although festival music has been heard there from time to time since the auditorium was built in 1906, the current series began in 1960. At the concerts in 1966 Gustav Meier conducted the Yale Summer Session Orchestra.

The summertime South Mountain Concerts, near Pittsfield, Mass., date to 1918, when Mrs. Elizabeth Sprague Coolidge established her Berkshire Festivals of Chamber Music there. The chamber music hall she had built is noted for its excellent acoustics. Still in force is Mrs. Coolidge's policy for encouraging contemporary composers and presenting modern music. As a result, between 1918 and 1966, world premieres or first American performances of more than 200 important chamber music works were presented there. On the list are compositions by de Falla, Hindemith, Martinu, Ravel, Schonberg, and Villa-Lobos. Among the artists and musical groups which have appeared at South Mountain are Leonard Bernstein, Myra Hess, Rudolf Serkin, the Budapest Quarter, Juilliard String Quartet, and New York Pro Musica. In 1955 Young Audience Concerts were inaugurated. Some forty such concerts are given in public schools each spring and fall. Mrs. Coolidge is also remembered from time to time whenever the Coolidge Foundation Festival is held in the Library of Congress, Washington, D. C., where it was presented for the first time on Oct. 28–30, 1925. The festival is not an annual event. The most recent one was in 1964, and the next has not been scheduled. However, the concerts always encompass Mrs. Coolidge's birthday, Oct. 30th.

The Maverick Sunday Concerts at Woodstock, N.Y., from about the Fourth of July to Labor Day, have been a summertime attraction since 1916. In 1966 the emphasis was on selections for string instruments. Among the ensembles which played there then were the Berkshire, Curtis, Kohon, New Chamber, and Salzburg String Quartets.

On June 23, 1918, Adolph Lewisohn founded the famous Stadium Concerts at the new Lewisohn Stadium which he had given to City College of New York, and thereby set a pattern for many summer concerts elsewhere. Through the years the concerts established several admirable precedents for out-of-season cultural enterprises in all parts of North America, such as designating a symphony orchestra of the calibre of the New York Philharmonic the performing organization as long ago as 1923. Also, the Stadium served as the launching place for the careers of many prominent artists, among them Marian Anderson, Eugene Ormandy, William Kapell, and George Gershwin, who played his Concerto and Rhapsody in Blue there several times. At the close of the forty-ninth season in 1966 the series was discontinued because the stadium was to be razed to make way for new academic structures. While that marked the close of a distinct phase in the cultural life of New York City, which had been championed diligently for many years by Minnie Guggenheim, it did not mean the end of summer concerts in Manhattan by the Philharmonic-Symphony Orchestra. In fact, the Philharmonic Symphony Society of New York, which was founded in 1842, has increased its participation in community activity since 1962 when it moved into the new Philharmonic Hall at Lincoln Center for the Performing Arts. In the spring of 1963, Promenade Concerts were inaugurated primarily to give New York more "off season" music. Program works are mainly of a light classical nature, and in 1966 they were conducted by Morton Gould, Andre Kostelanetz, and Sir Malcolm Sargent. The first summer festival of purely classical music with a particular theme was the French-American Festival, presented at Philharmonic Hall in cooperation with the Government of France, during the last half of July, 1965. The conductors were Leonard Bernstein, Aaron Copland, Duke Ellington, Lukas Foss, Darius Milhaud, and Charles Munch. Then, in August, 1965, for the first time the N. Y. Philharmonic performed twelve admission-free public parks concerts which were so well attended and applauded so enthusiastically plans were made to continue them on an annual basis. A Festival of Stravinsky, conducted by Ernest Ansermet, Leonard Bernstein, Robert Craft, Lukas Foss, the Artistic Director of the Festival, Kiril

171

Kondrashin, and Igor Stravinsky, paid tribute to the composer's heritage and his legacy, in July, 1966.

Even as the demise of the Stadium Concerts was confirmed late in the summer of 1966 it was announced that they were to be succeeded the following summer by an extraordinary program of cultural events to be called the Lincoln Center Festival '67. Within the new framework, the N.Y. Philharmonic will continue its role as the representative orchestra, and all the events during the two-month festival will be presented in Philharmonic Hall and other buildings that comprise the city's handsome, pace-setting Lincoln Center for the Performing Arts. The perfection and acceptance of air-conditioning, which was at the experimental level for many years after the Stadium Concerts were started, makes it feasible now to offer entertainment indoors on the warmest summer evenings in New York. A promised highlight of Lincoln Center Festival '67 was the Hamburg Opera, the first full foreign opera company ever to appear in the United States. In the repertoire were Hindemith's "Mahis der Maler," Berg's "Lulu," Janacek's "Jenufa," Giselher Klebe's "Jacobowsky and the Colonel," Schuller's "The Vision," Stravinsky's "Rake's Progress," and a concert version of Weber's "Der Freischutz"; the Metropolitan Opera performing "La Traviata," "Lohengrin," "La Giaconda," "Die Zauberslote" ("The Magic Flute") in German, and "The Masked Ball." Yehudi Menuhin was to conduct the Bath Festival Orchestra, which was founded in Bath, England, in 1958. The world-famous 115-member l'Orchestre de la Suisse Romande, founded in 1918 by Ernest Ansermet, was to be conducted by him in its first appearance in New York. There would also be ballet, drama, films, and poetry. The mere prospect of having a cultural event as prodigious as the Lincoln Center Festival succeed her beloved Stadium Concerts must have indeed gratified the soul of Minnie Guggenheim.

The standard pattern of concerts for Symphonies Under the Stars, presented regularly in Hollywood Bowl, Hollywood,

172

Calif., during July and August since 1922, includes ballet, light opera, soloists, and programs devoted to the works of popular composers such as Gershwin, Porter, Rogers and Hammerstein, and Lerner and Lowe.

Contributions and bequests have sustained free concerts each July and August in the Prosellis Bowl, Redlands, Calif., since 1924. More than forty years later the Redlands Community Music Association, Inc., provided some twenty evenings of musical entertainment which included ballet, concerts, light opera, opera, and symphonic music. It also presents winners of the annual Redlands Bowl Auditions.

A major musical attraction from the last week in June to about the third week in August since 1928 has been the National Music Camp, Interlochen, Mich., affiliated with the University of Michigan. Performers are selected from among the junior, high school, and university divisions, and there are also faculty concerts. In 1964 the first Interlochen Arts Festival featured Eugene Ormandy and the Philadelphia Orchestra. A highlight of the 1966 season was the world premiere of "Songs of Walt Whitman," composed by Norman Dello Joio.

Music Mountain, Falls Village, Conn., was founded in 1930 by the late Jacques Gordon, then concertmaster of the Chicago Symphony under Frederick Stock, as the headquarters for his Gordon String Quartet. After Mr. Gordon's death in 1949, Music Mountain became the summer home of the Berkshire Quartet. In winter the Quartet is in residence at Indiana University, Bloomington, Ind. The type of music presented on Saturdays for ten weeks each summer usually beginning on the first Saturday in July, has always been music for string quartet. The 300-seat concert hall and the cottages at Music Mountain stand on the organization's own property, a low hill with views of the rolling Connecticut countryside all around.

Mrs. Sigmund Stern, philanthropist, gave a eucalyptus grove at 19th and Sloat Blvd., San Francisco, to the city in 1931. On July 4, 1932, the first of the Stern Grove concerts for children was presented, and in 1938, Mrs. Stern formed the Stern Grove Music Association to present free concerts for adults each Sunday afternoon for ten weeks beginning in mid-June. Programs presented in the shade of the towering trees during the 1960's have included such popular attractions as Arthur Fiedler and the Pops Orchestra, the San Francisco Opera Ring in "Guys and Dolls," the Oakland Light Opera in "The Merry Widow," the Lola Montez Spanish dancers, the San Francisco Symphony, the California Youth Symphony, San Francisco Lamplighters in "Yeoman of the Guard," the San Francisco Opera "debut" stars in "La Boheme," and the Pacific Ballet.

When the current series of summertime festivals began in 1936 at Ravinia, an idyllic spot on the north shore of Lake Michigan some twenty-five miles from Chicago's Loop, the area was considerably more rural than it is now. The Chicago and Northwestern, once a popular rail link between the city and the suburb, has been virtually supplanted by automobiles which whisk over broad highways to and from the festival park. Yet between mid-June and early August, concert-goers still picnic on the tree-shaded acres, and the festival continues to do business on the site first used for festive gatherings in the 1890's to attract prospective home builders. Periodically at Ravinia, as at all continuing festivals, the format is updated. Major innovations introduced in 1964 included the signing of the Japanese conductor Seiji Ozawa as musical director and resident conductor, the lengthening of the festival's season of symphonic and popular programs from six to seven weeks, and the addition of Sunday afternoon "Four O'Clocks" concerts, a new season of theatre to the traditional schedule of music, and a week of ballet. From late June until mid-September, 1966, concerts featured the Chicago Symphony Orchestra, Janis, George London, Roberta Peters, Szeryng, and Van Cliburn. A new format announced for the 1967 Ravinia Festival promised a greater number of events and a

174

greater variety of the performing arts than in former festivals. Among the additions were a new series called "Mondays at the Murray," performances of music, dance, and theatre at Ravinia's Murray Theatre, and "specials" in the large pavilion on Tuesday nights.

The Berkshire Music Festival at Tanglewood, near Lenox, Mass., is a perpetual musical monument to the eminent Russian-born conductor Serge Koussevitsky. Held since 1937 at the former estate of Nathaniel Hawthorne, the festivals were begun in 1934 at a farm in Stockbridge, and for two summers Henry Hadley conducted an orchestra composed largely of members of the N. Y. Philharmonic Symphony. In 1936 the festival was taken over by Koussevitsky and the Boston Symphony Orchestra, which was founded in 1881 by Henry Lee Higginson, a Boston banker who helped finance it until 1918. Then it became a nonprofit institution supervised by a board of trustees. In 1938, the Music Shed at Tanglewood, designed by Eero Saarinen, was opened. From the air the Shed resembles a cream and black grand piano tucked among the green, tree-clad Berkshire Hills. It seats at least 6,000 spectators, and, weather permitting, another 6,000 can lounge on the lawn outside. In 1940, Koussevitsky launched a summer school, the Berkshire Music Center, in combination with the festival. During July and August, 1966, the festival presented twenty-four concerts in the Music Shed on Friday and Saturday evenings and Sunday afternoons, with Erich Leinsdorf as music director. Guest conductors included Sir Adrian Boult, Sixten Ehrling, Szymon Goldberg, Seiji Ozawa, Thomas Schippers, and Stanislaw Skrowaczewski. Also in 1966, for the third consecutive year, a festival within a festival was staged when the Festival of Contemporary Music inaugurated in 1964 by members of the Berkshire Music Center, and open to the Friends of the Berkshire Music Center, was held Aug. 14th to 18th. Sponsored by the Music Foundation in cooperation with the Fromm Music Foundation of Chicago, the 1966 concerts featured the world premieres of four compositions commissioned by the Music Center.

Although most Summer Music Festivals staged in June, July, and August since 1939 at Brigham University, Provo, Utah, have featured string quartets, recently more and more vocal selections have been added.

The 1966 series of admission-free concerts in June and July at Houston, Tex., was the 27th season by the Houston Summer Symphony. The twenty-one concerts were conducted by Clyde Roller.

The admission-free American Music Festival, in the National Gallery's East Garden Court, Washington, D. C., each spring since 1944, still attracts capacity audiences. At the 23rd annual festival on seven Sunday evenings in May and June, 1966, there were orchestral, piano, vocal, and chamber music concerts. The series was under the direction of Richard Bales who conducted the National Gallery Orchestra in two of the concerts. The programs included works by forty composers. On the lists were first performances of compositions by Richard Bales, Emma Lou Diemer, Robert Evett, Joseph Ott, Robert Parris, and Russell Woollen.

In 1945 the Brevard Music Center, Brevard, N.C., began sponsoring an annual music festival on the second and third weekends in August. Now under the management of Converse College, in 1966 the festival which took place during July and August offered "Don Pasquale," "La Boheme," "La Traviata," and "My Fair Lady."

The international flavor of the music which has been presented each summer at the Caramoor Festival, Katonah, N.Y. since 1946, reflects the universal interests of the late Walter Tower Rosen and his widow, Lucie Rosen, who inaugurated the festival on their lovely estate, Caramoor. After Mr. Rosen's death in 1951, the Walter Rosen Foundation assumed management of the event. The 1966 season in June and July featured the American premiere of Benjamin Britten's "Curlew River," Mozart's "Bastien and Bastienne," Levy's

"Escorial," and Donizetti's "Requiem for Bellini." The park of Caramoor, where the 1,500-capacity theatre is situated, is a romantic expanse of lawns and woods. It can be visited on special weekends in addition to the festival period by applying for permission.

When the late Walter P. Paepcke sought a site for an institute that would help modern man reassert the pre-eminence of the human spirit, he found his ideal at Aspen, Colo. It is a valley town away from the seaboard, yet accessible from either side of the world. The Aspen Music Festival began on a high plane in 1949 by saluting the Goethe bicentennial. Sponsored by the Aspen Institute for Humanistic Studies, which is in session each June, July, and August, it has remained a superior event. While music is predominant at the festival, other stimulating activities might include international design conferences, discussions of labor and leisure and their significance for democracy and capitalism, domestic and foreign films, and a lecture-recital exploring problems in contemporary opera. The festival musicians who teach at the Aspen Music School's nine-week sessions perform concerts. In 1966, the Flamenco guitarist Carlos Montoya was a guest artist, the harpsichordist Fernando Valenti played sonatas by Domenico Scarlotti, and there was a full production in English of "The Play of Robin and Marion," by Darius Milhaud, who was in attendance for the Conference on Contemporary Music. The sponsors announced that for the first time non-western music would be played at the festival in 1967 when Ravi Shankar, the sitar player who is one of India's fine musicians, and two assisting artists, will give concerts of Indian classical music.

Medieval and modern music are played in May at the Ojai Festival, which started in 1947 at Ojai, Calif.

At Santa Barbara, Calif., the Music Academy of the West has been presenting a six-concert summer festival during July and August since 1947. Typical programs at the Lobero Theatre have featured the Academy Symphony Orchestra,

177

conducted by Maurice Abravanel; Grant Johannesen, pianist; Berl Senofsky, violinist; Verdi's "Falstaff" sung in English; and an evening of music by the faculty.

Since 1948, usually on Tuesdays in August, the Summer Music Festival at Ventnor, N. J., has featured pianists, violinists, dance groups, vocalists, and concerts by the Young Artists Symphony.

On or about the third Sunday in September a mass piano recital in which dozens of pianists play simultaneously is presented in the Outdoor Balboa Park Bowl, San Diego, Calif. The festival, originated in 1949, is supervised jointly by the Music Teacher's Association and the Thearle Music Co.

The most thoroughly star-studded rosters at any festival, year after year, are probably those of the Marlboro Music Festival, inaugurated in 1950 on the campus of Marlboro College, Marlboro, Vt. Often the brightest star on the list has been Pablo Casals, who has conducted both the Festival Orchestra and cello master classes. Rudolf Serkin is the artistic director of the festival which offers some sixteen concerts of works for chamber music ensembles on weekends during July and August. Programs are drawn from the works under preparation each week, and usually are not available in advance.

The Gibraltar High School Auditorium in Fish Creek, Wis., has been the site of the Peninsula Music Festival each August since 1952. Dr. Thor Johnson, Director of the Interlochen Arts Academy, Interlochen, Mich., is the founder-conductor of the Peninsula Festival. Vocalists, instrumentalists, ensembles, and dancers participate in typical programs.

At St. John's, Newfoundland, the Kiwanis Club has been sponsoring a music festival since 1952 to foster a greater interest in music and to discover and encourage musical talent, especially among the young. The Rotary Club, Corner Brook, Nfld., has pursued the same general course since about 1960.

178

A few years after the Shakespeare Festival at Stratford, Ont., was launched in 1953 a short musical program was introduced as a complementary attraction. It, too, caught on, so the festival committee eventually purchased the Avon Theatre, restored its original turn-of-the-century decor, added modern facilities for musical performances, and opened it in 1964. There, between July 8 to September 3, 1966, the Stratford Festival Opera Company presented Mozart's "Don Giovanni" in English, the Stratford Festival Company staged "The Dance of Death," William Kinsolving's "Nicholas Romanov," a new play about the last czar of Russia, and the Royal Winnipeg Ballet danced the world premiere of "Rose Latulippe."

A stalwart of the Alaska Festival of Music in Anchorage, Alaska, is Robert Shaw, choral and orchestra conductor. A consistent participant in the festival since it was inaugurated in 1956, Mr. Shaw still headed the list of guest artists in June, 1966. The quality of the festival in the far North is reflected in its programs which have included Verdi's "Requiem" and the Los Angeles String Quartet in a recital of chamber music. Since all aspects of the Alaska Festival of Music are considered educational, the University of Alaska, through its Anchorage Community College, offers undergraduate level credit for participation in the chorus or orchestra, private instruction with guest performers-teachers, and a master course in the work of Verdi.

Pablo Casals paid one of the nicest tributes an artist can pay to the memory of his mother when he, a native of Spain, established in 1957 at Puerto Rico, the birthplace of his mother, an annual Festival of Music. Now known as the Festivals Casals, and normally staged during the first two weeks in June, it attracts musicians, music lovers, and the curious. At the opening concert of the 10th annual festival in the University of Puerto Rico Amphitheater at Rio Piedras, near San Juan, June 1, 1966, Casals conducted the Festival

Orchestra through Beethoven's Symphony No. 5. The master also played the cello, while Mieczyslaw Howszowski played the piano and Alexander Schneider played the violin in a performance of Mendelssohn's Trio No. 2 for Piano, Violin, and Cello, on June 12th, and he conducted the Festival Orchestra, vocalists Justino Diaz, Olga Iglesias, and Leopold Simoneau and the chorus of the Conservatory of Music of Puerto Rico in a performance of Haydn's Oratorio "The Seasons" as the concluding offering of the festival. Other renowned musicians who participated in the 1966 festival were Artur Rubinstein, Victor Tevah, Igor Oistrakh, John Wummer, and Maria Esther Robles.

Since 1957, during the last week in July, a four-day music festival has climaxed the five-week training session for young, talented musicians at the Sewanee Summer Music Center, University of the South, Sewanee, Tenn. It includes concerts and student programs, a faculty concert, and concerts by the Sewanee Symphony and the Cumberland Orchestra.

Music at the vineyards in California sets a high standard and a good example for industrial participation in cultural activities. The annual three-part summertime program presented on the last weekends in June, July, and August, as a rule, was created in 1958 by the Paul Masson vintners. It has been staged with increasing success in the Masson vineyards 2,400 feet above sea level in the Santa Cruz Mountains near Saratoga, Calif. There are no commercials, unless the serving of free iced champagne to a capacity audience of 800 spectators is classed as commercial. A three dollar admission is charged, but proceeds go to the Music Scholarships Funds at San Francisco State College and San Jose State College because most of the audience comes from San Francisco, and San Jose State is near the vineyards. The 1966 program included a performance in English of Alessandro Scarlotti's opera buffo "Il Trionfo dell 'Onore" by the Opera Comique of San Francisco; the New York Chamber Soloists; an ensemble of strings, winds, and harpsichord; pianist Leo Smit and violinist Eudice Shapiro played works of Bach, Beethoven, Schubert, and Stravinsky.

At the University of Utah, Salt Lake City, Utah, since 1947 Summer Festival fare in the Stadium during July has been opera, musicals, plays, and ballets; a Festival of Contemporary Music inaugurated in 1960, and held in Kingsbury Hall each November and January, offers four concerts by the Utah Symphony on campus.

Some fourteen high school bands in a dozen southeastern states participated in the Music Festival at Virginia Beach, Va., in 1961, and staged during the second week in June. There are three days of competitions and parades at the oceanfront resort.

In 1966 the fourth Cabrillo Music Festival, a cooperative effort of the Cabrillo Guild of Music and Cabrillo College, Aptos, Calif., concentrated on classical symphonic works and opera during the last two weeks in August.

The Long Island Festival of the Long Island Arts Center offered variety at its fourth annual celebration during August, 1966, in "the world's largest theatre tent," C. W. Post College, Brookville, N. Y. Leonard Bernstein conducted the N. Y. Philharmonic, the Flemenco guitarist Carlos Montoya played, there were "Great Moments in Opera" by members of the Metropolitan Opera Company, Melissa Hayden and Jacques D'Amboise danced "Great Moments in Ballet," the Maria Alba Spanish Dance Company offered Latin dances, the L. I. Philharmonic played an all-Tchaikowsky program, Kurt Weil's "Threepenny Opera" was staged, Van Cliburn played classical piano music, and the Dave Brubeck Quartet and Peter Nero performed music in a lighter vein.

The Community Chorus and Orchestra of Muskogee, Okla., have been taking part in that city's annual Music and Arts Festival inaugurated in 1963. During the spring of 1966, audiences heard the music of Bach, Beethoven, Brahms, Mahler, and Mozart; jazz concerts; stage band music in the style of the 1930's and 1940's; a high school band concert,

181

and the Robert Shaw Chorale and an orchestra in a rendition of "The Messiah" in March and April.

The Peter Britt Music Festival, named for a pioneer who was popular in Jacksonville, Ore., was organized in that community in 1963 to promote fine music and art in Southern Oregon. There are concerts of classical and contemporary music during the last half of August.

The Shenandoah Valley Music Festival in the Woodstock-Orkney Springs, Va., area was launched in 1963 by a three-year-old institute for the training of young symphony orchestra conductors. The festival is sponsored by the American Symphony Orchestra League, the Shenandoah Valley Music Festival Committee, and the ninety-five-musician Symphony of the Valley. The six-concert festival in mid-August usually consists of chamber music, folk ballads, symphony, and young people's concerts.

During July and August, 1966, Southampton College of Long Island University, Southampton, N. Y., presented a series of concerts by the Kohon Quartet and Delia Calapai, lectures and films at its second summer fete.

Newly commissioned works by George Crumb and Mario Davidovsky, as well as performances of works by Rochberg, Schwartz, and Subotnick, commissioned in 1965, were heard at the second annual Contemporary Music Festival, Bowdoin College, New Brunswick, Me., in August, 1966. A progressive provision of the festival considers further performances of the commissioned works at Bowdoin, sponsored concerts in New York, through publication of much of the music by the Bowdoin College Music Press, and eventual recording of all the works for commercial distribution. The Aeolian Chamber Players were the resident ensemble at the first two festivals.

Sixteen concerts by the London Symphony Orchestra, three concerts by the London Chamber Players, and free admission to orchestra rehearsals for visitors were some of the attractions at the first Florida International Music Festival in Daytona Beach, Fla., July 28 to Aug. 21, 1966. Aaron Copland,

Richard Burgin, and Colin Davis conducted. In association with Stetson University, De Land, Fla., there was a Music Institute for gifted students (fifteen years-of-age and older) and music teachers. Members of the London Symphony Orchestra formed the nucleus of the faculty.

VOCALISTS

Sacred harp singing is still a musical specialty endemic in Alabama, Florida, Georgia, Mississippi, and Tennessee, just as it has been for generations in the southeastern United States. W. A. Parker, amanuensis for devotees of this type of devotional expression, reports that in 1966 there were an estimated 1,500 sacred harp singers in the five states, a schedule of at least 300 one-day singings, and some that lasted as long as three days. That amounted to a yearly average of about six singings a week. Approximately 80 songs were used at each one-day singing, which meant that some 24,000 renditions were heard during the year. Typical of the many sacred music festivals in the deep South is the one inaugurated at Birmingham, Ala., in 1961. The three-night songfest during the fourth week in November always includes Thanksgiving. It usually features one or two well-known guest singers, and attracts thousands of people from all parts of the state to the Municipal Auditorium. Sometimes on Thanksgiving there is gospel singing in Savannah, Ga., and the first Saturday in most months is the customary date of All Night Sings in Atlanta, Ga.

Soon after Carl Aaron-Swensson organized Bethany College at Lindsborg, Kan., in 1881, he and his bride concentrated on turning into reality a dream of his predecessor at Bethany Lutheran Church, Pastor Olsson. Once upon hearing Handel's "The Messiah" sung in London, the pastor had planned to have his congregation sing the oratorio, but before he had a chance to do so he was transferred to a larger field.

His successor, Rev. Swensson, created the first Easter Festival in Lindsborg in 1882. Mrs. Swensson accompanied the singers on the organ while they sang before a small audience in the sanctuary of the church. Now a chorus of several hundred voices and a symphony orchestra present a week-long festival in a 2,400-capacity auditorium of Bethany College. As a rule, the program begins on Palm Sunday afternoon with "The Messiah." St. Matthew Passion is sung on Good Friday night, and The Messiah is repeated Easter Sunday night. Customarily, concerts by the orchestra and an a capella choir go on during the remainder of the week, for in addition to the works of Bach and Handel the society also performs Haydn's "Creation," Mendelssohn's "Elijah," Rossini's and Dvorak's "Stabat Mater," and Carl Busch's "Pilgrims of the Prairie." An annual Midwest Art Exhibit became a part of Lindsborg's Easter Festival in 1889.

The name of an old song book, "Old South Harmony Festival," written and published by "Singin' Billie" Walker in 1835, became the name of a song festival when it was organized by James R. Lemon, a singing teacher, at Benton, Ky., in 1884. The people of Benton enjoyed the first songfest so much it has been an annual event on the fourth Sunday in May ever since. The festival also serves as a homecoming celebration, with many former harmonizers returning to meet their old friends at the courthouse, the focal point of the Big Sing.

What was known originally as the Tri-State Singing Convention of Linville, N.C., is now called "Singing on the Mountain," even though participants continue to come from all sections of North Carolina, Tennessee and Virginia. The songfest still takes place on the fourth Sunday in June, as it has since 1924, and it is probably the largest annual event in the mountains of the South. It is a king-size singing, preaching, family reunion, and Sunday school picnic, all rolled into one, and normally attracts some 25,000 people each year. In

184

1962 when Dr. Billy Graham was the principal speaker, the highway was crowded from Mation to Blowing Rock. The festival was founded by Joe Lee Hartley, who certainly knew what his neighbors liked when he planned a day-long program around sorrowful gospel hymns and the music of duets, trios, quartets, and choirs trained by the "song masters" of the region, as well as the rousing sermons of the best spell-binding preachers who rail against sin and the evils of liquor.

Since 1898, usually on the second and third weekends in May, music of Bach has been a familiar sound in the Chapel of Lehigh University, Bethlehem, Pa. The Mass in B-minor has been given in its complete form many times, and so has "The Passion According to St. Matthew." The singers are members of the 240-voice Bach Choir.

A Bach Festival has been held in the Kulas Musical Arts Building, Baldwin-Wallace College, Berea, Ohio, regularly since 1932. The major work at the 1966 festival was "The Passion According to Saint Matthew." Other works performed at the festival, May 20th and 21st, were Concerto in C Major for Two Claviers, Sonata No. 1 in G Major for Clavier and Viola da Gamba, the motet "Jesu, Priceless Treasure," Overture (Suite) No. 4 in D Major, Cantata No. 29, Brandenburg Concerto No. 3 in G Major, and Cantata No. 30.

The well-established Bach Festival in Carmel, Calif., which was inaugurated in 1935, now includes works of other masters. The 29th annual festival, staged for ten days during the third and fourth weeks of July, 1966, offered the first American performance of the Passion according to St. Mark, the first West Coast performances of Handel's "Athalia" and "The Play of Herod," the complete sonatas for violin and clavier of J. S. Bach, a performance of the complete Mass in B minor, and works by Caldara, Haydn, Mozart, and Vivaldi. Since 1956 Sandor Salgo has served as Music Director and Conductor of the Carmel Bach Festival. He has acquired a favorable reputation for his recreations of masterpieces of the Baroque era and the standard repertoire of the Classic and Romantic periods, as well as for his sympathetic approach to works of contemporary composers.

A Bach Festival inaugurated at Winter Park, Fla., in 1935, is still held there. On May 9 and 10, 1966, in the Memorial Chapel, Rollins College, a 40-piece orchestra and a 100-voice choir presented J. S. Bach's "Trauerode" Cantata, "Komm du suesse Todesstunde," and "Praise Jehovah"; five sacred songs by C. P. E. Bach; Mozart's "Requiem"; Handel's "Samson Oratorio"; and Locillet's B minor sonata for violin, flute, and harpsichord.

Missouri's summer musical theatre, the Municipal Opera staged in Forest Park, St. Louis, from early in June to Labor Day, began on June 16, 1919 with a performance of "Robin Hood." This pioneer among civic-sponsored musicals is said to have developed out of a "Masque and Pageant" staged in the park in 1914 as part of the city's sesquicentennial celebration. Representative of the musicals which have been staged there are "South Pacific," "Meet Me In St. Louis," "Guys and Dolls," "Here's Love," "110 in the Shade," "Little Me," "Cinderella," "The Student Prince," "High Button Shoes," "Flower Drum Song," and "Camelot."

The Summer Opera at the zoo in Cincinnati, Ohio, is the opera center for the Ohio Valley for five weeks in June and July. Inaugurated in 1920 with 200 chairs for spectators, it now boasts a covered pavilion which seats nearly 3,000. The 1966 season spanned the period June 22nd to July 24th. It featured "Madam Butterfly," "Cavalleria Rusticana," "Cinderella," "Cosi fan Tutti," "Don Pasquale," "Pagliacci," and "La Traviata."

Usually in July operatic performances have preceded a month of stage plays at Central City, Colo., since the Central City Opera House Association was formed in 1932 through the efforts of the late Anne Evans and the late Ida Kruse McFarlane, descendants of prominent Colorado pioneers. In 1931 the heirs of Peter McFarlane, who owned the theatre, had presented it to the University of Denver as a lasting memorial to the pioneers of Colorado. Many of the pioneers were such fun-loving people Central City became the entertainment center of "the richest square mile on earth" after the Gregory lode was discovered there in 1859. For some fifteen years, however, its theatre was a log structure, and after it burned down in 1874 it was replaced in 1878 by an opulent opera house in which such stars as Sarah Bernhardt, Salvini Mudjeska, and Joseph Jefferson played. When General Grant stayed next door at the Teller House—where the face on the barroom floor is a long established tourist attraction—the ebullient citizens of Central City promptly paved the path between the two buildings with solid silver blocks. However, in the late 1890's the colossal boom petered out. Celebrities and townsfolk alike deserted Central City, and for many years few performances were staged in the Opera House. As the house regained its old-time glory in the 1930's a gracious gesture of the romantic Victorian era was revived, at least on some opening nights. Then, during the last intermission, attractive sub-debs dressed in crinolines distribute to the audience red and white carnations. But the boutonnieres are not for wearing. They are to be tossed across the footlights as the actors take their curtain calls. In July, 1966, there were curtain calls following performances of "Ballad of Baby Doe," "Carmen," and "Italian Girl in Algiers."

The cost of staging a one-week run of a standard professional light opera out-of-doors in Cheesman Park, Denver, Colo., during July, has been borne for thirty-four summers by Helen G. Bonfils, the owner of *The Denver Post* and an established theatrical producer, as a friendly gesture to her neighbors and friends. Usually the principal roles are sung by members of the Metropolitan Opera Company. The admission-free show attracts as many as 25,000 spectators per night. In 1966, a production of "Kismet" featured Joshua Hecht, Nancy Killmer, and Lou Ann Wyckoff.

Although the Indiana University Opera Theater, Blooming-

187

ton, Ind., does not present an annual festival, since 1947 it has staged operas each Saturday night, October to May inclusively. Thus Bloomington is probably the only American city besides New York to offer opera weekly for seven months in the year. The 1966–67 season included Mozart's "Abduction from the Seraglio," Gounod's "Romeo and Juliet," Britten's "Albert Herring," "Rigoletto," "Cavalleria Rusticana," "Pagliacci," and Wolf-Ferrari's "The Four Ruffians." Sometimes "Parsifal" is performed on Palm Sunday. The Opera Theater's outdoor season was inaugurated in 1963 with "Aida." Since then the company has staged "Carmen," "Turandot," and "A Hoosier Tale."

The Gilbert and Sullivan Players of Oberlin College, Oberlin, Ohio, have been traveling to Falmouth, Mass., each summer since 1953 to stage as many as nine musicals a season at the Highfield Theatre. In July and August, 1966, the repertoire included Gilbert and Sullivan's "The Gondoliers," "H.M.S. Pinafore," "The Pirates of Penzance," "Ruddigore," and "The Yeomen of the Guard;" Menotti's "Amahl and the Night Visitors" and "The Old Maid and the Thief;" Offenbachs "La Belle Helene" and "The Gypsy Baron."

Dimitri Shostakovitch's "The Rose," and Hans Werner Hanzl's "Il re cervo," were given their first hearings in America in 1965 at the Santa Fe Opera, staged annually in July and August in Santa Fe, N. M., since 1957. In 1966 the repertoire included "Capriccio," "Cinderella," "Dialogues of the Carmelites," "Don Giovanni," "Rake's Progress," "Rigoletto," "Tosca," and "Wozzeck."

A repertoire of six operas presented in 1957 during the first New York Opera Festival at the 4,500-capacity Carter Barron Amphitheatre, Rock Creek Park, Wash., D.C., set the pattern for ensuing festivals. In 1966 the select six staged during the second week in July were "Aida," "Carmen," "La Boheme," "La Traviata," "Madame Butterfly," and "Rigoletto."

A Festival of Opera was incorporated at Laguna Beach, Calif., in January, 1962, and began entertaining audiences on three weekends that summer. In August and September, 1966, the company sang "Madame Butterfly," "Spanish Hour," and "Tales of Hoffman."

To celebrate its fourth season, the Lake George Opera Festival, which originated in Lake George, N. Y., in 1962, moved to an 875-seat Opera Festival Auditorium in Glen Falls, N.Y., in July, 1965. In July and August, 1966, the schedule included "Barber of Seville," "Butterfly," "Crucible," "Die Fledermaus," and "Taming of the Shrew."

The inaugural Sagamore Summer Festival at Milford, Pa., in July, 1966, offered "Die Fledermaus," "La Traviata," "Pirates of Penzance," "Tosca," "Madam Butterfly," and "Faust."

For the summer of 1966, the Metropolitan Opera Company, of New York, and the Newport Jazz Festival, Newport, R. I., worked out a novel exchange. The Metropolitan staged four operas—"Aida," "Carmen," "La Boheme," and "Lucia di Lammermoor"—as an added attraction at the popular Jazz Festival, and jazz ensembles performed at Lincoln Center for the Performing Arts, in New York. The opera entrepreneurs used the appearances of the singers in Newport as a tryout to learn whether or not a season of opera would prosper there. Apparently, they were convinced that it would, because after the experiment a ten-day opera festival was planned for the third and fourth weeks of August, 1967. Seven Verdi operas in concert form and various other cultural attractions were scheduled for Festival Field and such fabulous Newport mansions as The Breakers, The Elms, and The Marble House through the courtesy of the Preservation Society of Newport. The operas selected were "Aida," "Il Trovatore," "I Vespri Siciliani," "La Traviata," "Macbeth," "Otello," and "Rigoletto." Among the singers due to participate were Martina Arroyo, Grace Bumbry, Irene Dalis, Mignon Dunn, Tito Gobbi, Robert Merrill, Renata Tebaldi, Gabriella Tucci, Richard Tucker, Jon Vickers, and Virginia Zeani. Francesco Molinari-Pradelli and Thomas Schippers were to conduct. In addition to the concert version of the operas there was to be a chamber music series, connoisseur concerts, comic and serious operatic films, taped concerts of little known Verdi operas, a Verdi Exhibition, an opera bazaar, workshops, operalogues, musical analyses, and demonstrations. Rudolf Bing, General Manager of the Metropolitan Opera Company, has expressed the belief that the Newport Festival would offer a more intensive examination of Verdi than has ever been available in America; that in inaugurating the festival the Metropolitan Opera hopes it will become a musical event of international significance. Bing's judgment of a first rate cultural festival is reliable because he has been closely identified with them since the 1930's. In 1934 he helped John Christie, founder of the Glyndebourne Festival in England, organize its first season, and stayed on to manage it until World War II. When Glyndebourne was reactivated after the war, Bing resumed his former role with it. In 1947 he created the prestigious Edinburgh Festival in Edinburgh, Scotland, and supervised it until he became general manager of the Metropolitan in 1950. To insure the necessary financial base for the new undertaking in Rhode Island, Mrs. Claiborne Pell, wife of the Senator from that state, led the organization of a Newport Metropolitan Opera Festival Foundation. The Foundation contributed $75,000 to the Verdi festa, and Governor John H. Chafee and the state of Rhode Island contributed another $50,000.

The best-known folk music festival in Kentucky, and one of the most distinctive in the United States, is the American Folk Song Festival on the second Sunday in June. From the time it was inaugurated in 1930 until 1964 it was presented at "the Wee House in the Wood," also known affectionately as the Traipsin' Woman Cabin, in Ashland, Ky., on Mayo Trail, the route Daniel Boone is said to have taken when he explored Kentucky. However, because the festival outgrew its original site it was transferred in 1964 to Jenny Wiley State Park, then to Carter Caves State Park, Olive Hill, Ky., in 1966. There, as in its previous locales, tunes are extracted from banjos, corn stalk fiddles, dulcimers, and zithers by many performers who cannot read a note of music. The guiding spirit of the songfest has always been Mrs. Jean Thomas, who is called "The Traipsin' Woman" because she used to traipse around the Federal Judicial Circuit as secretary to the judge. Ashland is in the Big Sandy Country, battleground of the "feudin' " Hatfields and McCoys. They quit "feudin' " years ago, and in 1948 young Jack Hatfield and Rosanna McCoy, descendants of the former enemies, took part in a modern folkplay with music, "The Love of Rosanna McCoy." Even the music in that drama, like many of the old tunes heard in the Kentucky mountains, might well have been inspired by the Gregorian chants of the sixth century, or the Elizabethan tunes brought over here by the early settlers. Mountaineers supplied their own lyrics and gave the ancient melodies such American titles as "Boatin' Up Sandy," "Old Joe Clark," and "Down in the Valley."

The first national competition sponsored by the Society for the Preservation and Encouragement of Barber Shop Quartet Singing in America, or SPEBSQSA, took place at Tulsa, Okla. in June, 1939. Now regional qualifying competitions are held yearly in fifteen districts during March, April, and May, and they are followed by the annual international convention and contests at locations selected four years in advance. In 1966, it was known that SPEBSQSA would meet in Los Angeles in 1967, in Pittsburgh in 1968, in St. Louis in 1969, and in Atlantic City in 1970.

Each year since 1952 attractive single girls, aged seventeen to twenty-two, who are residents of Florida, compete during the Valentine Day weekend for the title "Jeanie With the Light Brown Hair." This is a natural highlight for a festive salute to Stephen Foster, the American composer. The contest is staged at the Foster Memorial, White Springs, Fla., on the Suwanee River, which the composer also made famous in song, even though he never saw the stream. It is assumed that he saw the original Jeanie, Jane McDowell Foster, although she is supposed to have had auburn tresses. The judges of the Jeanie Auditions do not insist that the contemporary Jeanies have light brown hair, nor that they sing only songs by Stephen Foster, but they do stress the fact that all the contestants must be attractive. Each girl is sponsored by a Federated Music Club. The winner, announced at the Jeanie Ball, receives a $1,000 scholarship to further her musical education. Four runners-up, designated as maids of honor, receive $200 scholarships.

The first Stowe Festival of Music, staged at Stowe, Vt., in August, 1965, honored the well-known Trapp Family Singers, who fled from Austria when the Nazis invaded that country in March, 1938, and established their famous music camp at Stowe in 1944. During the fourteen seasons the camp was operated many persons went there to sing classical, folk, and choral music, and perform folk dances. It closed in 1958, a year or so before the Rogers and Hammerstein hit musical about the Trapps titled "The Sound of Music" began a long run on Broadway, Nov. 16, 1959. At the 1966 festival "The Sound of Music" was reenacted, there were concerts, Tyrolean music and yodeling, and a Viennese Night Ball.

Charlottetown, Prince Edward Island, inaugurated its Festival in 1964, the same year it dedicated the city's spacious and attractive Confederation Centre in observance of the conference which resulted in self-government for Canada in 1867. As a rule, most of the entertainers at the festival in July and August are vocalists. They sing ballads, folk tunes, popular songs, and operatic arias.

The first Christmas Festival at St. Olaf College, Northfield, Minn., was sung in 1912. Now an estimated 16,000 persons attend the event in the college gymnasium on four nights early in December every year.

BANDS, INSTRUMENTALISTS

Some 30 states and the District of Columbia were represented by 127 bands in the 1966 Old Time Fiddlers' Convention at Union Grove, N.C., on the Friday and Saturday before

Easter. Those have been the traditional days for the convention since it was organized in 1924 by H. P. VanHoy, an old time fiddler, for the benefit of Union Grove School. On Friday evening there was informal picking, singing auditions, and group dancing. A parade of horses, mules, covered wagons, ox carts, buggies, surreys, antique autos, floats, and bands was staged Saturday morning. That afternoon and night there were band competitions. Modern string bands are now eligible to compete for cash, ribbons, and trophies. Fifty percent of net gate receipts are divided equally between musicians and the school.

A natural amphitheater at Lake Whippoorwill, Warrenton, Va., is the site of the National Championship Country Music Contest on the first weekend in August, as a rule. Inaugurated in 1951, it attracts bands, banjo pickers, fiddlers, vocalists, and miscellaneous entertainers who specialize in country and western music. In 1966 they competed for a total of $1,500 divided among six categories.

The National Oldtime Fiddlers' Contest and Folk Music Festival has been an annual event in June at Weiser, Idaho, since 1953. Competition for cash and trophies determines area champions, women's champion, and winners of junior, senior, and trick-fiddling contests.

The Tri-State Music Festival staged at Phillips University, Enid, Okla., for three days during the first week in May, began in 1933 as a Band Festival. Originally the states which made up the triumvirate were Arkansas, Kansas, and Oklahoma. Now these six are in the lineup: Louisiana, Mississippi, New Mexico, Oklahoma, Tennessee, and Texas. These festivals are annual educational projects, planned by the participating directors and produced for the benefit of schools and students who are intersted in comparison, in constructive criticism, and in improvement of school music organizations and individual musicians. Much of the continuity and sustained interest in Tri-State is attributed to the participation of prominent adjudicators.

The North Iowa Band Festival, staged annually in June at Mason City, Iowa, since 1936, is said to have inspired Meredith Willson's successful musical "The Music Man." Mason City is Willson's home town. Typical of the numbers played by the "76 trombones" and other instruments at the single concert early in June are "Pilgrim's Chorus," "High School Cadets," "Military Escort," "Let Me Call You Sweetheart." The band festival is sponsored by the local Chamber of Commerce as a reward and fun day for high school bands in North Iowa and southern Minnesota. As far as musical events are concerned it has no contest features for some 5,000 musicians in approximately eighty-five bands. Normally, an all-city elementary band starts the day with a concert about nine A.M. and a parade of bands, queens, and floats begins at ten A.M.; there are concerts in Central Park in the afternoon, and in the evening all the bands give a mass concert at Roosevelt Field, where often musicians fill the stands, and the spectators crowd the infield.

Some 4,500 young musicians usually respond when the sponsors of the All-Western Band Review in Long Beach, Calif., announce the date of this big annual event. The first band festival was held in 1937, with units being judged on showmanship, flash, color, rhythm, precision, tone, quality, volume, marching technique, cadence, general ability, and appearance as they march in the business district on a November Saturday.

A mass admission-free concert of approximately forty bands from high schools and military posts climaxes a mile-long Band Review, a regular event in National City, Calif., the first Saturday in May since 1948.

The annual Jazz Festival established at Newport, R.I., by Mr. and Mrs. Louis Lorillard in 1954, set the pace and inspired the vogue for this type of musical festivity. Ever since then probably all the great names in jazz have entertained thousands of enthusiasts and stirred the staid old resort community as it never expected to be stirred. Louis Armstrong,

194

Ella Fitzgerald, Stan Kenton, Billie Holiday, Benny Good-man, Errol Garner, Cozy Cole, Jack Teagarden, J. C. Hig-ginbotham, Kid Ory, Dave Brubeck, Chris Connor, Mahalia Jackson, Count Basie, and Sarah Vaughan are just a few of the many artists who jazzed things up at the Newport Casino or Freebody Park for eleven consecutive years during the first week in July. The celebration moved to a new 12,000-seat, 9-acre festival field about a mile from downtown Newport in 1965. A new attendance record of 54,000 was set at the 1966 festival. That year the lineup included the Florida Jazz Quin-tet, the Dave Brubeck Quartet, the Jimmy Smith Trio, and the Newport Jazz Festival All Stars, one of whom was pianist George Wein, the producer of the festival.

A new note in jazz festivals is being struck on campuses in the United States. While quite a number of college music schools are reported to have jazz bands, only a few jazz festivals are affiliated in any way with colleges or universities. Thus far jazz festivals have been swinging at Notre Dame, Notre Dame, Ind., since 1958; at Villanova University, Vil-lanova, Pa., since 1961; and the University of Kansas, Law-rence, Kansas, since 1964. The Villanova Intercollegiate Jazz Festival began as a class project in the winter of 1961. Since that time it has grown in stature. There are generally two or three semi-final rounds and finals during the two-day event, plus clinics and special attractions. Judges and advisors at the 1966 festival were Stan Kenton, Bob Share, Hal Cook, Dan Morgenstern, John Hammond, and Jack McKinney. The North Texas State Lab Band from Denton, Tex., was judged the best at the show.

Early in April, 1966, the first Mobile Jazz Festival attracted some of the top-flight collegiate jazz musicians and vocalists who competed for prizes and recognition in the Municipal Auditorium, Mobile, Ala.

Rutgers State University, New Brunswick, N. J., has be-come the guardian of a valuable collection of recordings, books, periodicals, manuscripts, photographs, films and, memorabilia on the development of jazz in America which was gathered by Dr. Marshall Stearns, a noted jazz historian, who founded the Institute of Jazz Studies, Inc., in 1952. Although the principal buildings of Rutgers are in New Brunswick, it is planned to install the jazz music archives in the new John Cotton Dana Library on the Newark, N. J. campus of the University, where they will be available to historians, musicians, scholars, and writers. Some of the money earned by a series of concerts at Carnegie Hall in New York City titled "Jazz in the Great Tradition" was prorated for development of the Institute as a center for jazz scholarships and a sponsor of jazz concerts.

A Jazz Festival was launched at Monterey, Calif., in 1958, and it has been thriving ever since. Five concerts are usually on the agenda during the three-day celebration around mid-September at the Monterey County Fairgrounds. The 1966 Festival saluted "Blues All the Way." Joining in the tribute were Jon Hendricks, host and narrator; the Monterey Jazz Festival All-Star Orchestra; Count Basie Orchestra; Paul Butterfield Blues Band; and Duke Ellington and his Orchestra.

The All-Texas Jazz Festival launched at Corpus Christi, Tex., in 1961, on a modest scale as the South Texas Jazz Festival, is a one-day celebration in mid-June. Among the units that took part in the 1966 festival were the Jazz Festival All Stars, Phil Timmons Quartet, Red Camp Quartet, Bob Sardo Trio, the Galvans, J. B. Floyd Trio, Shorty's Jazz Band, the Houstonians, Rudy Garcia's Latin Rhythms, Paul Guerrero Quintet, and Claudio Rosas and the Orchestra.

Pianist Rocky Cole headed up the third annual Savoy Jazz Festival over the Fourth of July weekend in 1966 in a tent on the banks of the Mohawk River at Rome, N. Y. The sponsor insists the emphasis is on "happy jazz," no far-out contemporary.

The Longhorn Jazz Festival was inaugurated at Disch Field, Austin, Tex., on the first weekend in April, 1966. It consisted of two concerts at night and a workshop in the afternoon. Some fifty well-known jazz musicians were present, among them the Dave Brubeck Quartet, the Miles Davis Quintet, the Pete Fountain Sextet, the Stan Getts Quartet, Teddy Wilson, and Gerry Mulligan. The North Texas State University Lab Band represented collegiate jazz.

Variety is the keynote of the Chicagoland Music Festival which has been sponsored by The Chicago Tribune one night in mid-August since 1930. Staged at Soldier Field, Chicago, Ill., it serves as a climax for a series of music festivals in various parts of the United States. There are selections by massed bands and performances by top-ranking professional singers and musicians. Sometimes as many as 500 Chicago area council Boy Scouts stage patriotic pageants and popular music is played by well-known orchestras.

The Forest Hills Music Festival brought popular music to the West Side Tennis Club, site of the Men's National Singles Championship each September at Forest Hills, a residential area of New York City. The Music Festival has been staged on weekends during July and August since 1960, after an experimental concert by the Kingston Trio in 1959. Among the performers participating in the 1966 festival were Ray Charles, Sammy Davis, Jr., the Supremes, and Andy Williams.

Sports Festivals

CHAMPIONSHIP SPORTS contests from auto racing to yachting, invariably generate high festive feelings. So, it is not surprising that full-fledged festivals now precede some sports fixtures. Since 1958, the International Automobile Speed Classic at Indianapolis, Ind., has been ushered in by several days of civic excitement known as the "500" Festival, because the granddaddy of all auto races has always been a 500-mile event. Inaugurated in 1911, it takes place on Memorial Day, May 30th, or on May 31st if the 30th is a Sunday. A series of time trials determines which thirty-three racing cars will be in the starting lineup. The inaugural race was won by Ray Harroun, who drove a Mormon for 6 hours, 42 minutes, and 8 seconds at an average speed of 74.59 miles per hour. In 1966, Graham Hill piloted an American Red Ball Special at the average rate of 144.317 miles an hour for 3 hours, 27 minutes, and almost 53 seconds. The record speed of 150.686 miles per hour for 3 hours, 19 minutes, and 5 seconds was established in 1965 by Jimmy Clark in a Lotus powered by Ford. The "500" Festival program might include an invitation golf tournament on the Speedway Golf Course, a coronation ball, memorial ceremonies at Monument Circle, street dancing, a classic car display, and a big parade.

Forty years after the Indianapolis 500-mile auto race was inaugurated in 1911, an annual twelve-hour endurance race was introduced at Sebring, Fla., in 1951. Staged on a Saturday in March, the Sebring Grand Prix is a grueling contest over a winding, five and two-tenths-mile course of bends, sharp turns, and straightaways that served as a bomber base during World War II. After a day devoted to qualifying runs and a motorcycle race, as many as seventy cars have been in position for the Le Mans start of the longest auto road race in the United States. In 1966, the enduro was won by Ken Miles and Lloyd Ruby in a Ford Roadster X6 that averaged 98.631 miles per hour.

One of the five events counting towards the world rally championship sponsored by the Royal Automobile Club of London, England, is the Canadian Car Rally which has stretched between Montreal, Que., and Vancouver, B.C., around the last week in April since 1961. It is called the 4000 Rally because it traverses some 4,200 miles between the starting point and the finish line. Most of the rally course is open to onlookers. Normally, only isolated areas are closed to them.

Boys eleven to fifteen from North America as well as from across the seas compete with each other on a Sunday in August when the All-American Soap Box Derby is staged at Derby Downs, Akron, Ohio. The unusual race sponsored exclusively for juveniles on the only course of its kind in the world originated in 1933 as a newspaper test promotional event in Dayton. Entrants compete in gravity powered cars which they are supposed to have built themselves. A four-year college scholarship is first prize at the competition.

Old cars, vintage 1896–1927, at least, converge on the Henry Ford Museum and Greenfield Village, Dearborn, Mich., around the second weekend in September to participate in the Old Car Festival, an annual event since 1951. Costumed drivers in search of prizes pilot chugging antique vehicles through the American museum area created by Henry Ford.

BASEBALL

When the Baltimore Orioles of the American League took four straight games from the Los Angeles Dodgers of the National League to win the Baseball World Series in 1966, that gave the American League a total of thirty-eight World Series victories against twenty-five for the National League since the title contests were played for the first time in 1903. The great American pastime is believed to have grown out of the English games of rounders or cricket beginning in the 1830's, at least. In the 1940's it was called the New York Game because the Knickerbockers and the New York Nine were its leading exponents. The National League was organized in 1876, and the American League in 1901. The World Series during the first week in October on the home grounds of the winning American and National League teams is the big baseball event of the year. The title goes to the first team to take four games out of a possible seven.

BOATING

High on the list of famous international yacht races is the one which has been sailed just twenty times since 1851, the America's Cup. Although the race is open to all classes of yachts from all over the world, thus far it has been a contest between American and British yachtsmen. The competition began as an added attraction at the London Exposition of 1851. The vessels traversed a sixty-mile course around the Isle of Wight, the only time this historic event was staged in British waters. The Americans won that race as well as the nineteen held since, and have defended off their own shores the trophy donated by the Royal Yacht Squadron of England. The race is called the America's Cup because the first yacht to win it was the United States yacht *America*. After the initial race in 1851, the challengers and defenders competed for the cup in

1870, 1871, 1876, 1881, 1885, 1886, 1887, 1893, 1895, 1899, 1901, 1903, 1920, 1930, 1934, 1937, 1958, 1962, and 1964. In 1964, the $700,000, thirty-seven-foot *Constellation* flying the Stars and Stripes vanquished the British yacht *Sovereign,* four races to none, off Newport, R. I.

For many years Newport, R. I., has set the pace for sailing in the grand manner. It is still the starting point for at least two major yacht races staged biennially. One is the well-known Newport-Bermuda contest which was first sailed in 1906, and is still scheduled during even-numbered years. The other is the 466-mile Newport-Annapolis race inaugurated in 1947 and staged during odd-numbered years.

The only four-day rowing regatta in North America is the Royal Canadian Henley, on the Welland Canal at St. Catherines, Ont., around the last week in July. Originated in the 1880's, and staged for the eighty-fourth time in 1966, the race also attracts contestants from the United States and overseas.

The top-ranking three-mile collegiate rowing event in the United States is the one inaugurated by the Intercollegiate Rowing Association on the Hudson River at Poughkeepsie, N. Y., in 1895. That year Columbia defeated Pennsylvania and Cornell. Now on a Saturday late in June the race is rowed on Onondaga Lake, Syracuse, N. Y. In 1966, Wisconsin's crew covered the distance in about sixteen minutes, three seconds, to win over Navy, Princeton, Brown, and Penn.

Around 1904 some workers in the fruit orchards of the fertile Okanagan Valley launched an aquatic meet on Lake Okanagan, hard by Kelowna, B. C. It has developed into the famous Kalowna International Regatta, an annual event in mid-August. The four-day festival attracts several hundred spectators from western Canada and as far south as California. Water sports include championship diving contests, water skiing, aqua kite flights, swimming, rowing, sailing, and power boat races. Also on the agenda are an art show, parade, and band concerts.

The President's Cup Regatta, staged on the Potomac River,

off Hains Point, Washington, D. C., in mid-June, was launched in 1926 during the Coolidge Administration. The feature race, one heat, five laps, is the President's Cup Special Inboard Invitation Free-for-all.

Until about 1905, what is now Salton Sea in the Imperial Valley of southeast California, was Salton Sink, some 280 feet below sea level. Then a levee of the Colorado River sprung a leak and spilled water into the sink for a couple of years before it was checked. Water from irrigation systems still seeps into Salton Sea and keeps its level as high as 245 feet below sea level. In November, 1966, the 6th annual Salton City 500-mile endurance boat race on the Salton Sea attracted racers from all over the United States as well as from foreign countries.

Until broad, paved highways were built among the bayous of Southwest Louisiana, pirogues were to the natives what autos have long been to other Americans. Slim, delicately balanced boats built especially to skim over shallow marshes and swamps, they are the bayou families' principal mode of transportation. Pirogues were commonplace around Barataria in the days of Jean Lafitte, the pirate, and since 1936 they have starred in their own Derby at Lafitte, on the second or third Sunday in May. Brawny, sun-tanned paddlers vie for cash, trophies, and goods as spectators line the banks or view the race from pleasure craft.

Women's surfing contests, matches for boys, and a men's senior surfing competition are standard events each December at the International surfing Championships at Makaha Beach, on the lee side of Oahu Island, Hawaii. In spring and summer the waves at Makaha Beach might be all right for beginners and intermediate surfers; but in autumn and winter the surf challenges the experts, so the contests are staged in November or December. Then, if the surf is right and rolling, visitors can thrill to performances on the thirty-five-foot waves which roar 300 to 400 yards before pounding onto the beach. The sport of riding a board down the slope of a wave in ski fashion originated with the old Hawaiians. Surfing was once the prerogative of the Alii, or chiefs, and Waikiki was their special surf run. In the Bishop Museum in Honolulu are two gigantic koa wood boards, one weighs 160 pounds and the other 148 pounds. They emphasize the point that surfing was the sport of strong men. Modern boards of balsa or other light woods are much lighter and much shorter.

A public luau is often a climactic attraction at the inter-island surfboard competition launched in 1960 and staged in June across the Auau Channel from Halepalaca, Lanai, to Lahaina, Maui, Hawaii. While the main nine-mile contest is underway, other Hawaiian sports events take place at the festival site in Lahaina.

The first Alaska Boating Festival was introduced as a week-long event in 1964. In June, 1966, the third annual edition at Petersburg offered seafood treats, glacier tours, fishing, sightseeing, boating, and prizes in a salmon derby.

CURLING

Curling, imported to North America from Scotland where it has been a popular winter sport since as long ago as the sixteenth century, is also a favorite pastime in New York, New England, and throughout Canada. The governing body of the sport is the Grand Caledonia Curling Club founded in Scotland in 1838. In 1966 the Scotch Cup, symbol of world supremacy in curling competition, was won at Vancouver, B.C., by curlers from Calgary, Alta., who also won the Macdonald's Briar Tankard at Halifax, N.S., that year. Also in 1966, the Gordon International Medal was won by representatives of the United States when they defeated Canadians by eighty-eight stones in Boston, and the U.S. Men's Championship played at Hibbing, Minn., was won by North Dakotans who defeated Minnesotans 5–3 in the final round. Since curling is becoming increasingly popular in Canada, the following Dominion Curling Association contests, in addition

to the Macdonald's Brier Tankard which the D. C. A. staged
for the first time in 1927, and the years they were inaugurated,
are of special interest: Canadian School Curling Championships, first held with all Canada taking part in 1950; National
Mixed Championships, two men and two women, first held in
Canada in 1964; and the National Seniors Championships for
men over fifty-five, first held in Canada in 1965.

FOOTBALL

In the first intercollegiate football game on an American
campus, Rutgers defeated Princeton, six to four at New
Brunswick, N. J., Nov. 6, 1869. Since then, football has
achieved such status among sports fans the Army-Navy Game,
played for the first time at West Point, N. Y., Nov. 29, 1890,
and now staged regularly in Philadelphia, Pa., on the Saturday
after Thanksgiving, might be classified as the nation's football
game. However, five intercollegiate contests which have
sparked festivals are the post-season games on New Year's
Day at Pasadena, Calif., Miami, Fla., New Orleans, La.,
Dallas and El Paso, Tex. The first Tournament of Roses
football game was played at Pasadena in 1902, when pro-
moters of the annual flower festival scheduled football in place
of chariot races, which had been standard entertainment at the
New Year's Day civic celebration. However, sports fans
turned thumbs down on the game and demanded the return of
chariot races the following year. So the football classic was not
really established in Pasadena until Jan. 1, 1916. The first few
contests were played at Tournament Park, but increased
attendance prompted the erection of a ninety thousand capacity Rose Bowl in 1923. A Junior Rose Bowl football game for
championship high school teams was launched in mid-
December, 1946.

Just a few thousand spectators saw the first Orange Bowl
Game at Miami, Fla., on Jan. 1, 1935, but the contest now
ranks as one of the major attractions on New Year's Day,

even though the contest has been shifted to nighttime. The Orange Bowl Festival begins as early as Dec. 21st with an admission-free tennis tournament, and usually includes such events as a North-South College All-Star Football Game, a junior golf tournament, basketball, junior and senior Orange Bowl parades, track and field meets, a pro football playoff, regatta, and fireworks.

The Mid-Winter Sports Association Festival in New Orleans, La., has been a huge success ever since it was launched with the first Sugar Bowl football game on Jan. 1, 1935. The contest comes naturally by its name, because in addition to being played in the nation's sugar bowl, the site of the stadium was once a sugar cane plantation owned and operated by Etiènne de Bore, who pioneered in sugar growing and refining. The sports festival usually begins the day after Christmas. During Christmas Week there are rowing regattas, tennis matches, golf tournaments, basketball, and other athletic contests.

The El Paso, Texas Sun Bowl football game is the crowning event of a week-long Sun Carnival introduced Jan. 1, 1935. Festive activities include inter-scholastic tennis tournaments, arts and crafts displays, a street carnival, square dances, concerts, and a parade.

In Dallas, Texas, the Cotton Bowl celebration first staged on Jan. 1, 1937, has been embellished with a week of festivities topped off by a parade since 1957.

The Grey Cup is the big prize in Canadian football. Placed in competition in 1892, it was once sought after by all teams. However, in 1936, the intercollegiate group withdrew because it objected to professionalism in other leagues. Now the Eastern Interprovincial champions play the Ontario Union winner, and the victorious team meets the Western Canada League champions for the trophy on the last Saturday in November. In 1966 the classic was staged in Vancouver, B.C.

GOLF

The U.S. Golf Association, New York, N.Y., inaugurated the U.S. Open, Amateur, and Women's Golf Championships in 1895. It has sponsored Public Links Championships since 1932, Junior Amateur Championships since 1948, and Girls Junior Championships since 1949. Tournaments are held during the summer in various parts of the country, the sites being determined on the basis of invitations the Association receives.

Three major golf tournaments in Canada, and the years they were inaugurated, are the Canadian Amateur, 1895; Women's Canadian Open Amateur, 1901; and the Canadian Open, 1904. Two international team matches in which Canadians and Americans participate teed-off in 1952. They are the Americas Cup matches among amateur golfers of Canada, Mexico, and the United States, and the Hopkins Cup Series for professional teams from Canada and the United States.

When Bobby Jones, the eminent American golfer, retired in 1930, he set out to build an ideal golf course. So, he and friends bought a 365-acre tract near Augusta, Ga., persuaded Dr. Alister MacKenzie, a famous Scotch architect, to supervise construction, and by 1934 the Augusta National Golf Club was ready for the first Masters Tournament. The big meet has taken place there each April since, except for three years during World War II.

Two renowned golf matches in California every winter are those named for Bing Crosby and Bob Hope. The Crosby contest is a standby at Pebble Beach, around the third weekend in January. The Hope Desert Classic about the first week in February utilizes four courses at Palm Springs.

HIGHLAND GAMES

Canada has been staging Highland Games almost as long as Scotland itself. One of the first Caledonian games on record in

Scotland took place in 1819, whereas Highland Games have been a Canadian attraction since 1838, when the Caledonian Club of Prince Edward Island was organized. A Scottish Festival is held in Charlottetown, P.E.I., during the second week in August, and often features the Gathering of the MacLeod Clan. The MacLeod Clan also holds a lawn party in Southport, P.E.I., in August, and that month there are Highland Games at Eldon. The traditions of athletics, dancing, and music still prevail at the annual Highland Games at Antigonish, N.S., as they did at the Highland Society's first games on Oct. 18, 1863. Now at Antigonish, around the third weekend in July, there are golf, bowling, concerts, and a ball.

The Gaelic Mod at St. Ann's, on Cape Breton Island, N.S., during the second week in August, also is redolent of Scotland. In addition to the traditional dancing and piping competitions, and competitive sports such as tossing the caber, at St. Ann's there are also a Highland Dance Instructors' course, and the only college in North America where Gaelic is taught.

There is a Gathering of the Clans and a Fisherman's Regatta at Pugwash, N. S., on July 1st, Dominion Day in Canada. A kilted piper, clad in the distinctive Nova Scotia plaid, delivers an official greeting in a sunken garden on Highway 2, not far from Amherst. Lobster canning factories along the shore of the River Philip identify a major economic activity there, and the inspiration for its fishing festivity. Visitors to the Gathering and the Regatta see and hear a parade of pipe bands, and watch floats, clowns, and briskly stepping drum majorettes. Then they head for Cyrus Eaton Park, donated to his birthplace by the community's most famous son, where he accepted a special Peace Prize from the Russians. During the afternoon amateurs and professionals compete in the complicated Sword Dance, the Highland Fling, pipe dancing, and playing bagpipes. Brightening the scene are tartans worn by Frasers, MacDonalds, MacDougalls, and Stewarts.

In Ontario Province, Highland Games and dancing contests

are staged in July at Embro, Fort Williams, Kincardine, St. Catharines, and Windsor; and in August at Cobourg, Dutton, Fergus, Maxville, and Orvillia.

Highland dances and bagpipe music enliven the summer in Vancouver and Victoria, B.C., and Seattle, Wash., a region to which many Scots gravitated in the nineteenth century.

The Caledonian Club of San Francisco, Calif., marked its 100th anniversary in 1965 by staging the U.S. Open Highland Dancing Championship and inviting all comers to toss the famous 125-pound, 17-foot Ballantine caber from Scotland, which has never been tossed successfully.

At Stamford, Conn., the Round Hill Highland Scottish Games have been an annual event since 1924, and on Mac-Rae Meadow, a shoulder of Grandfather Mountain, near Linville, N.C., Highland Games and Gatherings of the Scottish Clans have been yearly attractions around the second weekend in July since 1956. In 1965 the U.S. Air Force Bagpipe Band made its first appearance at Grandfather Mountain. Kilted bands from Carnegie Tech and Miami also played and paraded as costumed members of some 100 different clans and septs from throughout the United States, Canada, and overseas danced. In addition to caber tossing there was also sheaf toss, shot put, and wrestling.

HORSES

The title of one of the oldest annual thoroughbred horse races in North America changes with the reigning monarch of Great Britain. In 1860, when Queen Victoria was on the throne, the race began as the Queen's Plate. It was the King's Plate during the reigns of Edward VII, George V, Edward VIII, and George VI, and has been the Queen's Plate again since Queen Elizabeth ascended the throne. The race is run in June at Woodbine Track, Toronto, Ont. Traditional prize is 50 Guineas, about $150, plus a purse which varies in value.

The most famous horse race in the United States is the

Kentucky Derby. Run at Churchill Downs in Louisville, Ky., on the first Saturday in May since 1875, it also inspired a two-week festival which usually begins about April 25th. There are street dances, beauty contests, fireworks, parades, receptions, barbecues, concerts, stage shows, and a steamboat race on the Ohio River.

The Kentucky Derby, along with the Belmont Stakes, run in New York about the second Saturday in June, since 1867, and the Preakness, an annual event usually the third Saturday in May at Pimlico, near Baltimore, Md., since 1873, make up the Triple Crown, the most sought after horse racing prize in the United States. Eight horses and the years in which they won the Triple Crown were Sir Barton, 1919; Gallant Fox, 1930; Omaha, 1935; War Admiral, 1937; Whirlaway, 1941; Count Fleet, 1943; Assault, 1946; and Citation, 1948.

The twelve-furlong, $150,000 Washington, D.C. International, inaugurated in 1952 and run at Laurel Race Course, Laurel, Md., on November 11, is the American competition for "Horse of the World" hopefuls. The other two famous races which are a part of the "International Big 3" are the King George VI and Queen Elizabeth Stakes, inaugurated in 1951 and run at Ascot Heath, England, and the Prix de l'Arc de Triomphe, inaugurated in 1920 and run at Longchamps, Paris. The horse that wins the three top-quality events in a single year gains the mythical triple crown of international racing. Thus far no contender has achieved that distinction. Entries from the United States won seven of the first fifteen contests; horses from France won five; and those from Australia, England, and Venezuela, one each. The first time that the gold, purple, scarlet, and black silks of the Royal Family of England had been raced anywhere outside that country was in 1954 when Queen Elizabeth's horse, Landau, ran in the third Washington, D.C. International. It finished seventh in a field of seven. Russian horses began competing in Western world handicaps when two Russian horses, Garnir and Zaryad, came to the United States to race in the 1958 International.

They finished sixth and tenth, respectively, in a field of ten. In 1966 the French horse, Behistoun, won the fifteenth running of the International, and Aniline, the U.S.S.R. entry, finished second in a field of ten.

The famous Hambletonian Stakes for trotters, named for the celebrated family of trotters, was first run at Syracuse, N.Y., in 1926. Later it was moved to Good Time Park, Goshen, N. Y., and is now a major attraction at Du Quoin, Ill., around September 1st. In 1966, the three-year-old Kerry Way trotted in first to win a purse valued at $122,540.

In 1966, Romeo Hanover was the winner of the Little Brown Jug pacing classic named for a pacer that was famous in the nineteenth century. Inaugurated in 1946, this premier contest for three-year-old pacers is run during the Delaware County Fair, Delaware, Ohio, in September. The "Jug," the William H. Cane Futurity introduced in 1955 at Yonkers Raceway, N.Y., and the Messenger Stakes, raced for the first time in 1956 at Roosevelt Raceway, N. Y., comprise pacing's "Triple Crown." Thus far only three horses have won all three events: Adios Butler, 1959; Bret Hanover, 1965; and Romeo Hanover, 1966.

Medieval-type jousting tournaments have been presented regularly since 1821 on the third Saturday in August at Mt. Solon's Natural Chimneys, near Staunton, Va. Riders exhibit horsemanship, balance, and marksmanship by racing their mounts along the seventy-five-yard stretch in eight seconds and attempting to spear three rings suspended from cross arms as they ride. The largest ring is not more than two inches in diameter, the smallest about one inch. Ring posts are approximately thirty yards apart, six-and-one-half feet off the ground. Each rider makes three passes for a total of nine rings. Time-honored, courtly ritual adds glamour to every tournament, and the men who plan to ride regularly receive knightly titles.

Jousting is so popular in Maryland it is the official state sport. The season begins about the last Saturday in May, and usually ends with the state championship at Owings Mills, the last Saturday in September.

In South Carolina, jousting enthusiasts gather at Moncks Corner in April to stage a spring tournament, and in the Cedar Swamp community of Kingstree in November for their fall meeting. Normally, both tournaments are ridden in full regalia, and contestants are called knights.

Steeplechase races, which are believed to have started in Ireland in 1752 when the steeple of St. Leger Church served as the goal and a guide during a four-and-one-half-mile cross country race, have been particularly popular in Maryland and South Carolina at least since the 1890's. In both states Saturdays in April are the customary dates for the meets, which are also famous for picnics, reunions, and socializing in general. As a rule, in Maryland the traditional opener of the steeplechase season is My Lady's Manor, at Monkton, on the second or third Saturday; the Grand National, at Butler, and the Maryland Hunt Club, near Shawan, Worthington Valley, on the last Saturday. In South Carolina, the Carolina Cup Races attract steeplechase fans to Camden on the first Saturday in April, and the steeplechase at Aiken, on the second Saturday. Since 1947, North Carolinians have been trekking to Tryon, N.C., about the last Saturday in March to watch the Block House Steeplechase. The first Iroquois Steeplechase run at Nashville, Tenn., in 1941, is now raced annually on the second Saturday in May.

JUMPING FROG CONTESTS

California is the scene of the two top annual jumping frog competitions in the United States. Both are staged in spring, the senior of the two being at Angels Camp. It drew its inspiration from the famous story about the Jumping Frog of Calaveras County, which Mark Twain wrote after visiting the area in the 1860's. Now during the Calaveras County Fair in May, jumping frogs from all points of the compass jump for cash prizes. Other attractions might include historic parades, pageants, horse racing, a horseshoe pitching contest, and dances. The second jumping frog contest is staged in April at the Del Mar Fair Grounds, in Southern California. The best dressed frog is awarded a prize, and there are clown acts, a dog show, and a judo show.

KITE CONTEST

The beach front at Ocean Beach, Calif., is the site of the annual Kite Festival around the third Saturday in March. As many as a thousand youngsters parade through the streets, kites in hand, as they head for the communitywide competition.

RODEOS

Some ten million spectators attend approximately 600 rodeos in the United States and Canada each year to see cowboys go bull riding, bust broncs bareback or in a saddle, rope calves, and wrestle steers. On July 4, 1883, several cowhands were persuaded to compete in riding and roping contests in Pecos, Tex., and thus the first organized rodeo with prizes was born. Exactly five years later, July 4, 1888, the first rodeo with prizes for which admission was charged was staged at Prescott, Ariz. It was an added attraction at a typical Independence Day picnic which has been held regularly at Prescott since 1864. Today the yearly event, complete with rodeo, is called Frontier Days. The world's first indoor rodeo was a feature of the 1917 Southwestern Exposition and Fat Stock Show, and has been an annual event ever since. Indoor shows have become cool weather events at Madison Square Garden, New York City, in October and November since 1925, and at the Grand National Livestock Exposition, San Francisco, during the same period, since 1941. The oldest of the big three among rodeos in the United States these days is Frontier Days, Cheyenne, Wyo., an annual attraction during the last full week in July since 1897. The other two are the Pendleton Roundup, Pendleton, Ore., 1910, and the California Rodeo, Salinas, Calif., 1911. Parades of cowboys and cowgirls on horseback, and townsfolk in the period dress of pioneers riding vintage vehicles that blazed the trails westward, are often daily attractions there.

For the second consecutive year the National Finals Rodeo was held in Oklahoma City, Okla., late in 1966. That year Larry Mahan, Brooks, Ore., was named All Around Cowboy. He earned $40,358 piling up points. He was the third cowboy in the history of rodeo to earn more than $40,000 in one season. The other two were Jim Shoulders and Buck Rutherford.

The big time rodeo in Canada is the Calgary Stampede, staged in Calgary, Alta., during the second week in July. The Stampede was begun in September, 1912, by a young cowboy from Wyoming named Guy Weadick, who dreamed of gathering the finest crew of bronc busters and offering them king size purses in competitions. Indians from many miles away encamped around Calgary, and some 2,000 took part in the Frontier Days parade. That first three-day rodeo produced $125,000 gross profits, of which $20,000 went for prize money. The second Stampede was not put on until 1919, and the third in 1923, but since then it has been staged more regularly. Recently the Stampede has been credited with drawing 60,000 people who have spent some ten million dollars while in Calgary during the rodeo.

SOARING

The twenty-first annual Pacific Coast Mid-Winter Soaring Championship was staged the last week in February, 1966, above Torrey Pines Mesa, at San Diego, Calif. As the air currents strike the bluff and rise the sailplanes riding the ridge are carried aloft. The glider pilots compete in aerobatics, altitude distance, duration, and spot landing. Of all the trophies and prizes awarded at the meet the John J. Montgomery Memorial Trophy is the most important. Montgomery is believed to have made the first controlled flight by man when he flew a glider from a hillside at Otay Mesa, south of San Diego, for a distance of about six hundred feet in 1883. That was twenty years before the flight of the Wright Brothers at Kitty Hawk, N.C., in December, 1903.

SWIMMING

A grueling contest limited to experts, the Rough Water Swim inaugurated at La Jolla Beach, Calif., in 1925, usually attracts about 150 contestants about the third Sunday in August. It is a one-mile aquatic race over a triangular course.

TENNIS

The first Men's National Singles Tennis Championships opened to all comers and sanctioned by the U.S. Lawn Tennis Association, was held at the Casino, Newport, R.I., in 1881. The matches are now held annually at the West Side Tennis Club, Forest Hills, L.I., N.Y., late in August and early in September, as a rule.

WALKING

On the morning of the first Monday in September thousands of people take part in the annual Labor Day Mackinac Bridge Walk which was first staged in 1958 by a few dozen walking enthusiasts out for a recreational stroll led by Michigan's Governor G. Mennen Williams. Each year since then public interest in "the world's greatest walking event," as the Mackinac Bridge Authority refers to the walk, has increased.

So, the event, which begins at the St. Ignace end of the bridge, in Michigan, has begun earlier every year to avoid interfering with vehicular traffic.

Winter Carnivals

THE IDEA of staging winter carnivals in North America is believed to have been inspired by injured civic pride. During the winter of 1885, according to the report, the editor of a magazine published in New York is supposed to have sent a writer to Minnesota to gather material for an article abut that state. When the writer got off the train in St. Paul the temperature was considerably below zero, and the snow was piled higher than his head. So, he took the next train back to the East, and reported to his editor that St. Paul was a frozen hell unfit for human habitation. Soon the report got back to businessmen in St. Paul, and they decided to show the effete easterners that snow can be fun. The result: the first St. Paul Winter Carnival in 1886.

Winter carnivals can be fun! What's more, they are very photogenic, since the fields of snowy white provide excellent backgrounds for the colorful cold weather costumes now in vogue. Also, there usually is lots of action as skiers jump and glide, skaters race, and all manner of motorized vehicles speed across frozen lakes. Normally the St. Paul Winter Carnival lasts for ten days late in January. It is ruled by King Boreas, Custodian of the North Wind, and his consort, the Queen of Snows. Their mythical castle is an ice palace that is destroyed at festival's end by Vulcan, the Fire King, whose destructive antics symbolize the triumph of summer over winter. Before Boreas and his Queen are deposed, however, they and their subjects have a fancy final fling. Familiar fare are two big

215

parades, championship sports contests both indoors and outdoors. The St. Paul Winter Carnival hibernated sporadically between 1898 and 1938, when it was revived on a permanent basis. It was inactivated during World War II. Since it returned to a regular schedule in 1947 the carnival has pioneered several successful events. Among them are an ice fishing contest on White Bear Lake, mutt racing which spoofs the more serious husky contests, construction of a free public toboggan slide in the vicinity of the State Capitol, hot air balloon races which were popular in the 1930's, and a Snowmobile Rally. These attractions have proved to be so popular with spectators they have become regular features each year. The Snowmobile Rally is particularly exciting when contestants participate in a common start. They head for a narrow passage under a bridge leading to a creek bed, climb the bank to a hilly course in a park, then travel back over the same course to the finish line. "Fun 'n Frolic" is a typical theme of the snow show in St. Paul, which is launched with the coronation of King Boreas, and climaxed with sled dog races, ski jumping, and a performance of Ice Capades. Sandwiched in between those events are the National Majorette Contest, the National Outdoor Speed Skating Championships, a day parade, and a night parade, both of which wind up inside the auditorium where some 10,000 spectators sit and watch the floats go by in steam-heated comfort. The carnival is televized nationally.

Canadians created their winter carnival in Quebec in 1894, just to break the monotony of the long winter season. However, it did not flourish for too many years beyond 1900. The present series was inaugurated in 1954. Bonhomme Carnaval, "the only talking snowman in the world," is the symbol of the Quebec Show, a pre-Lenten feast that is climaxed on Mardi Gras, the day before Ash Wednesday, first day of Lent. When Bonhomme Carnaval is not cavorting with the crowds he holds court in a brightly lit translucent ice palace. Sometimes the carnival lasts almost three weeks, especially when Mardi

Gras arrives late in February or early in March. Among the more exciting sports events on Quebec's carnival agenda is the ice canoe race over and around ice floes drifting in the mighty St. Lawrence River. The contest developed naturally out of the necessity of transporting foodstuffs and mail in portable, hand-propelled craft when ice in the river prevented normal ferry service. Quebec also has its day and night parades, barrel-jumping contest, motorcycle races on ice, a pee-wee hockey tournament, ice and snow sculpture, a dog derby, and costumed balls. The carnival's budget for the first year, 1954, was $30,000. By 1964 it was $400,000. Some of the money is raised by a door-to-door "blitz" of candles. The candles sell at five cents each, or a bundle for $1. A buyer may become winner of a $100 prize if he discovers a capsule bearing a lucky number when the candle is burned. Popular subscriptions through the sale of candles and ballots to elect the Queen rose from $42,765 in 1954 to $140,146 in 1962. The sales of emblems which brought $6312 in 1954 brought $64,658 in 1963. In 1954 businessmen's contributions amounted to $18,842. In 1963 they rose to $52,102. Since the very beginning, the Municipal Government's contributions have been on an increasingly generous scale, the sponsors report. The Provincial Government, after making a small donation the first year and giving nothing for the next five years, is reported to have contributed $10,000 in 1960 and $20,000 in 1963, and sponsored production of a film which has been shown world-wide by Paramount Pictures. The Quebec Winter Carnival now requires some five dozen committees comprising almost 500 active members and a few thousand volunteer workers.

A collegiate version of the popular winter carnival was introduced at Dartmouth College, Hanover, N. H., in 1911. Since then, except during World Wars I and II when it was inactivated, it has been one of the foremost campus capers in North America. Photographs of the fantastic snow sculpture which adorns the lawns in front of dormitories and fraternity houses at Dartmouth have been a winter-time staple in newspapers, magazines, and other news media for more than half-a-century. Traditional programs include championship intercollegiate ski meets, basketball, hockey, and swimming contests, customarily on the first or second weekends in February. Elsewhere in New Hampshire in February there are winter carnivals at Nathaniel Hawthorne College, Antrim; the University of New Hampshire, Durham; New England College, Henniker; Colby Junior College, New London; Plymouth State College, Plymouth, and Franklin Pierce College, Rindge. Two other New England collegiate carnivals each February are those at Williams College, Williamstown, Mass., and Middlebury College, Middlebury, Vt. In New York, St. Lawrence University, at Canton, plays host to carnival revelers.

In February, 1936, Alaskans decided to publicize their animal pelts as well as their snow by naming their new winter carnival in Anchorage the Fur Rendezvous. In the 1930's there were an estimated 300 mink and fox ranches in the territory, which enhanced a market well supplied with pelts of wild animals. A northland novelty introduced by the Eskimos is the blanket toss, in which individuals are bounced high in the air from patch-quilts of walrus hides. World championship dog-sled races, a $5,000 sweepstakes, a fur-hat contest, jade auctions, skijoring, Chilkat Indian dances, an Eskimo show, a miners and trappers ball, day and night parades, art exhibitions, curling, hockey, a coronation pageant, a ball, and a Miss Alaska contest fill the bill.

In 1961 the people of Cordova, Alaska, created a distinctive trade mark for their new winter carnival: a 150-foot walking ice worm. Each year it has led the parade at the three-day Ice Worm Festival in February. To dramatize the fact that Alaska is not frozen as solidly in winter as most citizens of the South 49 imagine, there is a nighttime parade of decorated cruisers and sailboats.

Sourdough Rendezvous is the title of the three-day Winter Carnival at Whitehorse, Yukon Territory, late in February.

There usually is a Days of '98 Dance, Indian dances, a parade of beauty queens, dog team and snowshoe races, curling, hockey, and a ski meet.

Vernon, B. C., has been the locale of a ten-day Winter Carnival each February since 1961. Queen Silver Star reigns over the fete from a palace built of 40 tons of ice blocks. Reflections of colored lights enhance its appearance at night. Western Canada ski championships are a major attraction of the Vernon Carnival, and there are also a torchlight parade, Snowflake Ball, a pioneer parade, ice stampede, square dance jamboree, rock and gem show, curling, and skating.

A mukluk, traditionally an Eskimo boot, is now also the name of a Mardi Gras in Edmonton, Alberta, each February. Keeping the theme in tune with the Eskimo title, there are snowshoe and dog team races along the Saskatchewan River, a moccasin dance, and a giant igloo surrounded by ice sculpture.

Since the community of The Pas has the largest raw fur market in Manitoba, and some credit it with being the largest in Canada, it seems natural that the three-day Winter Carnival there each February should be known as The Trappers' Festival. To celebrate the fact that furs exported from Manitoba are valued at approximately $8 million annually, people of The Pas build their party around trappers' activities, such as dog racing among teams of huskies used regularly on trap lines, rat skinning, trap setting, ice fishing, bannock baking, tea boiling, flour packing, tree felling, log sawing, moccasin dancing, jigging, moose calling, snowshoe racing, and canoe portaging. There is also a beaver and lynx competition for the best pelts, prepared under the approved method of the Wildlife Trapper Education Program. The Handicraft Exhibition displays beaded buckskin articles by Indians or Metis, mixed bloods of either French-Canadian Indian, or English-Scottish Indian ancestry.

A torchlit float parade usually opens the annual Winter Carnival which takes place at Ottawa, Ont., during the first two weeks in February, and a Snowshoers Church Parade customarily closes it. Prizes are given for the best ice sculpture, and the city's importance as the nation's capital is saluted with the staging of international food events, international dog sled derbies, and international motorcycle races on frozen Dow's Lake in the center of the city.

The Laurentian Show Festival at Sainte Agathe, Que., usually spans the pre-Lenten period from early in January through Shrove Tuesday, or Mardi Gras, as the French prefer to call it. Inaugurated in 1947, the festival has dog sled races, hockey games, and other winter carnival competitions. It also has some fine do-it-yourself features, such as toboggan slides, sleigh rides, and dances at the ice palace on the shore of the Lac des Sables, curling matches on the lake, and a Snow Queen's ball. Ice sculpture adorns the streets.

Niagara Falls, New York, and Ontario scheduled their first joint Winter Carnival for eight weekends between mid-January and early March, 1965. The Canadians had staged their own festival in 1964, then courteously invited the Americans to join in the fun. Programs during the eight weekends, Friday nights through Sundays, include outdoor ice skating, dog sled races, indoor square dancing, and fashion shows.

By the time the first annual ten-day Winterfest in Boston, Mass., reached its climax in the huge, year-old War Memorial Auditorium late in February, 1966, the city had established a practical pilot festival which could be used as a guide by other communities which are looking for ways to use their new civic and cultural centers. The Winterfest was timed to coincide with the traditional week-long school holiday most young people in the Greater Boston area enjoy around Washington's birthday. Most of the daytime events were geared to the interests of elementary and high school students, but there were also seminars and workshops in which prominent authors, clergymen, designers, doctors, lawyers, and other professionals participated. On the list of seminars were "Urban Design or Urban Disaster," "City Lights, the Creation of an

220

Exciting Nightscape," "The Social and Ethical Reorientation of Churches in Our Time," "What Makes Modern Poetry Modern," "The Revolution in Criminal Justice," "Boston in the Age of John Fitzgerald Kennedy," "Art in Boston," and "On Understanding Contemporary Atheism." At night the entertainment included ballet, choral concerts, drama, films, poetry, and popular and symphonic music. Melissa Hayden and Jacques D'Amboise of the New York City Ballet headed a company of fifteen ballet dancers. There were performances by the Dance Circle of Boston, described as "the city's only modern dance group," and programs of folk dances from around the world for young people and adults. Two commissioned choral works were heard: "Sweet Freedom's Song," by Robert Ward, and "City Upon A Hill," a cantata by Jacob Avshalomov, who gained his inspiration from an address President Kennedy delivered to a joint convention of the two houses of the general court of Massachusetts on January 9, 1961. Most of the choral offerings were in a traditional vein, but "The Swallows of Salangan," by Morton Feldman, sounded as contemporary as electronic music. Obviously bewildering to many listeners, nevertheless the music of mass flight was pleasantly performed by the Brandeis University Choral Union and Tufts University Chorus. Martyn Green, regarded by some authorities as "the greatest living portrayer of Gilbert and Sullivan roles," was imported to star in an evening of dialogue about the world-famous collaborators interspersed with music. Other notable importations included the Eureka Brass Band and Storyville Ramblers from New Orleans, and Cleveland's celebrated Karamu Theater. The actors from Ohio performed Pinter's "The Birthday Party."

Annual Events in States, Provinces

Here is the what-where-when of some 2,000 events which take place regularly in the United States and Canada. The schedules for individual states and provinces are arranged by calendar. Within each month the host communities are listed alphabetically. Movable feasts are posted in the first month in which they could occur, i.e., Easter can occur in March or April, so activities pertaining to it are recorded in March. Any event which lasts longer than one month is reported in the first month in which its run begins. Persons who wish to know the exact date of a festival might ask for it by writing to the Chamber of Commerce where it will take place. Use a double postal card, and be sure to write a return address on one of them. Also, remember that dates are subject to change.

ALABAMA

January. Mobile: Senior Bowl Football. Montgomery: Cattle Show. Tuscaloosa: Camellia Show.

February. Birmingham: Camellia Show. Mobile: Mardi Gras. Opp: Rattlesnake Roundup. Tuscaloosa: Festival of Arts.

March. Cullman: Ave Maria Grotto Open House. Fairhope: Arts, Crafts Festival. Mobile: America's Jr. Miss Pageant; Azalea Trail; Mansion Candlelight Tour; Square Dance Festival. Montgomery: Southeastern Livestock Exposition. Moundville: Road to Calvary. Union Springs: National Shooting Dog Championship. Warren: Easter Sunrise Service.

April. Birmingham: Festival of Arts; Square Dance Ju-

222

bilee. Mobile: Jazz Festival. Tuscaloosa: Band, Choral Festival.

May. Bay Minette: Fishing Rodeo. Birmingham: Livestock Show. Selma: Spring Festival.

June. Clanton: Peach Festival. Tuscumbia: Art Show.

July. Bayou La Batre: Blessing of Shrimp Fleet. Fort Wayne: Potato Pageant. Tuscumbia: "The Miracle Worker."

August. Albertville: Broiler Festival. Mobile: Fishing Rodeo.

September. Eufaula: Water Festival. Florence: North Alabama Fair. Jasper: Northwest Alabama Fair. Selma: Central Alabama Fair.

October. Birmingham: Alabama State Fair. Dothan: National Peanut Festival. Florence: Art Show. Mobile: Gulf States Fair. Montgomery: South Alabama Fair. Oneonta: Horsepens 40 Festival. Tuscaloosa: West Alabama Fair.

November. Birmingham: Sacred Music Festival. Gulf Shores: Speckled Trout Rodeo.

December. Livingston: Costume March. Montgomery: Blue-Gray Football.

ALASKA

January. Fairbanks: Alaska Dog Mushers' Race. Kodiak and Sitka: Russian Orthodox Christmas Service.

February. Anchorage: Fur Rendezvous. Bethel: Arts, Crafts Show. Cordova: Ice Worm Festival. Willow: Winter Carnival.

March. Dillingham: Beaver Roundup. Fairbanks: Sled Dog Racing Championship. Juneau: Alaska Arts, Crafts Show. Sitka: Russian Easter Celebration.

May. Kodiak: King Crab Festival. Palmer: Colony Days. Petersburg: Little Norway Festival. Skagway: Days of '98 Show.

June. Anchorage: Alaska Music Festival. Barrow: Whaling Festival. Fairbanks: Midnight Sun Baseball. Nome: Mid-

223

night Sun Festival. Petersburg: Alaska Boating Festival. Point Hope: Whaling Festival. Sitka: Salmon Derby. Wainwright: Whaling Festival.

July. Fairbanks: Golden Days. Haines: Strawberry Festival. Homer: Halibut Derby. Juneau: Salmon Derby. Kodiak: Halibut Derby. Kotzebue: Eskimo Games; Whaling Festival. Mt. Alyeska: Midnight Sun Skiing. Seward: Mountain-climbing Race. Sitka: Alaskan Loggers' Championship. Soldotna: Progress Days.

August. Seward: Silver Salmon Derby. Valdez: Gold Rush Days; Silver Salmon Derby.

September. Palmer: Alaska State Fair. Skagway: Sourdough Days.

October. Sitka: Alaska Purchase Day.

December. Eskimo Games at Christmas.

ARIZONA

January. Sacaton: Mul-cha-tha All-Indian Show. Tubac: Art Festival.

February. Phoenix: Cactus Show; Citrus fruit blossom time; Open golf tournament. Scottsdale: Parada del Sol. Tucson: La Fiesta de las Vaqueros; Open golf tournament. Wickenburg: Gold Rush Days. Yuma: Silver Spur Rodeo.

March. Grand Canyon: Easter sunrise service. Laveen: St. John's Indian Festival. Phoenix: Easter sunrise services; Rodeo; Superstition Dutchman Lost Gold Mine Trek. Scottsdale: National Indian Arts Exhibition. Tucson: Livestock Show; Tucson Festival. Wickenburg: Easter sunrise service. Yuma: Square Dance Festival.

April. Phoenix: Indian Fair; Square Dance Festival.

May. Nogales: Fiesta Cinco de Mayo.

July. Flagstaff: All-Indian Rodeo; Navajo Craftsmen's Exhibit. Prescott: Frontier Days. Winslow: Hopi Rain Dance.

August. Prescott: Smoki Snake Dance. Winslow: Hopi India Snake Dance.

224

September.   Window Rock: Navajo Tribal Fair.
October.   Papago Indian Rodeo. Tombstone: Helldorado Celebration. Tucson: Intercollegiate Championship Rodeo.
November.   Phoenix: Arizona State Fair.

ARKANSAS

March.   Hot Springs: Easter sunrise service.
April.   Batesville: Dogwood Trail. Hot Springs: Arkansas Band, Choral Festival. Mountain View: Arkansas Folk Festival. Stuttgart: Grand Prairie Auto Race.
May.   El Dorado: Poultry Festival. Fort Smith: Rodeo. Springdale: Poultry Festival.
June.   Batesville: Poultry Festival. Mountain Home: Folk Festival. Warren: Pink Tomato Festival.
July.   Eureka Springs: Fine Arts Festival. Springdale: Rodeo.
August.   Batesville: Water Carnival. Newport: Rice, Cotton Festival. Texarkana: Four States Golf Tournament. Tontitown: Grape Festival.
September.   Fort Smith: Arkansas-Oklahoma Livestock Show. Pine Bluff: Arkansas Livestock Show. Texarkana: Four States Fair.
October.   Eureka Springs: Ozark Folk Festival. Huntsville: Crossbow Championship. Little Rock: Arkansas Livestock Show. War Eagle: Ozarks Arts, Crafts Fair. Yellville: Wild Turkey Calling Contest.
November.   Hot Springs: Christmas parade.
December.   Hot Springs: Christmas carols, tableaux. Stuttgart: Duck Calling Contest.

CALIFORNIA

January.   Pasadena: Rose Bowl Football; Tournament of Roses Parade. Pebble Beach: Crosby Golf Tournament.

San Francisco: Chinese New Year Festival; Japanese Art Festival.

February. Cloverdale: Citrus Fair. Holtville: Carrot Festival. Imperial: California Mid-Winter Fair. Indio: National Date Festival. Kernville: Whiskey Flat Days. La Habra: Highland Dancing, Piping Contest. Long Beach: International Beauty Pageant. Los Angeles: Olvera Street Mardi Gras. Niland: Tomato Festival. Oakland: Northern California Industrial Exposition. Oceanside: Abraham Lincoln Observance at Mission San Luis Rey; Surfing Championship. Palm Springs, Eisenhower Golf Tournament; Hope Desert Golf Classic. Paso Robles: Indian Cooking Day at Mission San Miguel. Ripon: Almond Blossom Festival. San Diego: Yacht Race to Acapulco, Mexico. Santa Monica: Underwater Film Festival. Solvang: Mardi Gras. Southern California: Citrus fruit blossom time. Temple City: Camellia Festival.

March. Fresno: Camellia Show. Healdsburg: Prune blossom time. Hollywood: Easter sunrise service. Holtville: Carrot Carnival; Swiss Schwingfest. Modesto: Peach Blossom Tour. Ocean Beach: Kite Festival. Oceanside: Art Day at Mission San Luis Rey. Palm Springs: Desert Circus. Paso Robles: Art Days at Mission San Miguel. Quartz Hill: Almond Blossom Festival. Riverside: Easter sunrise service. Sacramento: Camellia Festival. San Bernardino: National Orange Show. San Diego: Children's Easter Tournament of Wheels; Easter sunrise services; Glider Soaring Championships at Torrey Pines; Walking Tour of Old San Diego; Yellowtail Fishing Derby. San Francisco: Easter sunrise service on Mt. Davidson; St. Patrick's Day Parade. Winterhaven: Southwest Indian Pow Wow.

April. Berkeley: U. of California Junior Bach Festival. Carlsbad: Spring Holiday. Coronado: Flower Show. Del Mar: Jumping Frog Contest. Hemet: Romona Outdoor Pageant. La Jolla: Garden Tour. Lakewood: Pan American Fiesta. Lindsay: Orange Blossom Festival. Mill Valley: Easter floral display. Mt. Tamalpais: Easter sunrise service. Murphys:

226

Spring Festival. Oakland: California Spring Garden Show. Oceanside: Literature Days at Mission San Luis Rey. Pacific Grove: Wild Flower Show. Palmdale: Lilac Festival. Paradise: Gold Nugget Celebration. Pasadena: Festival of Arts. San Diego: Rose Show. San Francisco: Blossom, Wildflower Shows in Golden Gate Park; Junior Grand National Livestock Exposition. Sebastopol: Apple Blossom Tours. South Gate: Azalea Festival. Trinidad: Crab Feed.

May.   Angels Camp: Jumping Frog Jubilee. Antioch: Delta Festival. Arcata: Plaza Art Festival. Boonville: Wildflower Show. Calexico: Cinco de Mayo Parade. Corcoran: Cotton Festival. Delano: Cinco de Mayo. Escondido: Citricado Days. Fair Oaks: Fiesta. Fallbrook: Avocado Festival. Ferndale: Victorian Art Festival. Fillmore: May Festival. Fort Bragg: Rhododendron Show. Fresno: West Coast Relays. Garden Grove: Strawberry Festival. Hayward: American Indian Memorial Pageant. Indio: Cinco de Mayo. Julian: Wildflower Show. King City: Sacred Rose Garden in bloom at Mission San Antonio. Lompoc: La Purisima Mission Fiesta. Milpitas: Frontier Days. Mt. Tamalpais: Mountain Play. National City: Band Review. Oceanside: Madonna Festival at Mission San Luis Rey. Ojai: Music Festival. Pala: Corpus Christi Procession. Paramount: Festival. San Diego: Folk Festival. San Francisco: Latin American Fiesta; Rose Show; Spring Opera Season; U.S. World Trade Fair. San Jacinto: Ramona Outdoor Pageant. San Jose: Blue Ribbon Horse Show. San Luis Obispo: Fiesta de las Flores. Santa Barbara: Blessing of Animals at Mission Santa Barbara. Santa Rosa: Luther Burbank Rose Festival. Sonoma: Outdoor Art Show. Stanford: Stanford University Student Architecture Exhibition. Stinson Beach: Wild Flower Show. Watsonville: Antique Airplane Fly-in.

June.   Clearlake Highlands: Redbud Festival. Del Mar: Southern California Exposition. Dunsmuir: Railroad Days Homecoming. King City: Anniversary Fiesta at Mission San Antonio. Kingsburg: Swedish Festival. Lodi: Five Western

States Art Show. Lompoc: Flower Festival. Oceanside: Indian Dancers at Mission San Luis Rey. Oxnard: Spring Art Festival. Paso Robles: Indian Dancers at Mission San Miguel. Pleasant Hill: La Fiesta del Diablo. Ross: Art and Garden Fair, Sacramento: California State Fair Horse Show. San Diego: National Shakespearean Festival. San Fernando: Fiesta. San Francisco: Stern Grove Concerts. Santa Barbara: Semana Nautica. Saratoga: Music at the Vineyards. Sonoma: Bear Flag Day. Stanford: Stanford Summer Festival of the Arts; Stanford University Graduate Art Students Projects Exhibition.

July. Carmel: Bach Festival. Chula Vista: Fiesta de la Luna. Hollywood: Symphony Under the Stars. Huntington Beach: All Southern Bathing Beauty Pageant. Kingsburg: Watermelon Festival. Laguna Beach: Pageant of Masters. Oceanside: Fiesta at San Luis Rey Mission. Paso Robles: Indian Dances at Mission San Miguel. Pebble Beach: Concourse d'Elegance. Redlands: Concerts. Ross: Art and Garden Fair: Marin Shakespeare Festival. Salinas: California Rodeo. San Clemente: Fiesta La Cristianita. San Diego: Trek to the Cross on Presidio Hill. San Juan Bautista: Fiesta. Santa Barbara: Indian Dancers at Mission Santa Barbara; Music Festival; National Horse and Flower Shows. Willits: Frontier Days.

August. Aptos: Cabrillo Music Festival. Fort Bragg: Fuchsia Show. Glen Ellen: Art Festival. Julian: Desert Weed Show. King City: Junipero Serra Day at Mission San Antonio. Laguna Beach: Festival of Opera. LaJolla: Rough Water Swim. Los Angeles: Nisei Festival. Mill Valley: Dipsea Race. Mount Shasta: "I Am" Pageant. Oceanside: Junipero Serra Day at Mission San Luis Rey. Petaluma: Old Adobe Days. Sacramento: California State Fair. San Francisco: Flower Show. San Mateo: Floral Fiesta. Santa Barbara: Old Spanish Days. Santa Monica: Sports and Arts Festival. Santa Rosa: Championship Horse Show. Sonoma: Chess Festival.

Ukiah: Redwood Empire Fair. Yreka: Paul Bunyan Jubilee.
September.   Boonville: Apple Show. Boron: 20 Mule
Team Days Carnival. Delano: Mexican Independence Day.
Dinuba: National Raisin Festival. Fort Bragg: Paul Bunyan
Celebration. Guerneville: Festival of Fire Mountain. Indio:
Mexican Independence Day. King City: Display of Labor,
Arts, and Crafts at Mission San Antonio. LaJolla: Rough
Water Swim. Lancaster: Alfalfa Festival. Lodi: Grape Festi-
val. Los Angeles: Mexican Independence Day. Monterey:
Jazz Festival. Morro Bay: Rock-o-Rama. Paso Robles: Anni-
versary of Mission San Miguel. Pomona: Los Angeles County
Fair. Sacramento: California State Fair. San Diego: Mass
Piano Recital; Mexican Independence Day. San Francisco:
Fall Opera Season. San Gabriel: Mission Fiesta. San Rafael:
Autumn Festival; Concours d'Elegance. Santa Rosa: Cale-
donian Gathering and Games. Solvang: Danish Days. So-
noma: Grape Festival. Tehachapi: Mountain Fruit Festival.
Tulare: California Dairy Fiesta. Walnut Creek: Walnut Festi-
val.
October.   Anaheim: Community Halloween Festival.
Avalon: Bicycle Tour of Catalina; Scottish Highland Games.
Biola: Raisin Day Celebration. Delano: Harvest Holidays.
Julian: Apple Days Festival. Long Beach: Sea Festival. Mill
Valley: Arts Festival. Monterey: SCCA Grand Prix Road
Race. Oakland: Concours d'Antique. Pacific Beach: Surfing
Championship. Pala: Children's Festival. Paso Robles: Pio-
neer Day Parade. Ross: Flower Festival. Ridgecrest: Turtle
Races. Sacramento: California State Fair Beef Cattle Show;
Harvest Hoedown. San Anselmo: Grape Festival. San Diego:
Fiesta of Nations; Southern California Band Contest. San
Francisco: Blessing of Fishing Fleet; Chinese Double Ten
Celebration; Columbus Day Parade; Grand National Livestock
Exposition and Quarter Horse Show; International Film Festi-
val.
November.   Brawley: Cattle Call. Death Valley: 49ers

Encampment. El Cajon: Mother Goose Parade. Hollywood: Santa Claus Parade. King City: Document Days at Mission San Antonio. Long Beach: All-Western Band Review. Los Angeles: Great Western Exposition and Livestock Show. Oakland: Folk Dance Festival. Oceanside: Library Days at Mission San Luis Rey. Paso Robles: Document Days at Mission San Miguel. Pismo Beach: Clam Festival. Salton City, 500-mile Boat Race. San Diego: Band Review; Fiesta de la Cuadrilla. Whittier: Rose Spectacle.

December.   Corona: Band Jamboree. King City: Christmas Eve at Mission San Antonio. Lodi: House Tour. Naples: Christmas Water Pageant. Oceanside: Las Posadas at Mission San Luis Rey. Pala: Fiesta at Mission San Antonio de Pala. Pasadena: Junior Rose Bowl Football. Paso Robles: Las Posadas at Mission San Miguel. San Diego: Old San Diego Posada. San Francisco: East-West Shrine Football Game. Santa Barbara: Las Posadas at Mission Santa Barbara. Santa Rosa: Lighting of Luther Burbank Tree of Lebanon.

COLORADO

January.   Denver: Junior Livestock Sale; National Western Stock Show.

February.   Fort Collins: Colorado State University Opera. Leadville: Winter Carnival. Steamboat Springs: Winter Carnival.

March.   Colorado Springs: Easter sunrise service at Garden of the Gods. Morrison: Easter sunrise service at Red Rocks Amphitheater.

April.   Grand Junction: Drama Festival; Music Festival.

May.   Aspen: Schweitzer Convocation. Canon City: Blossom Festival. Grand Junction: National Junior College Baseball. Loveland: Huckleberry Finn Day.

June.   Aspen: Music Festival. Canon City: Buckskin Joe Melodrama. Grand Lake: Sunrise slalom.

July. Boulder: Opera. Central City: Opera. Denver: Post Outdoor Light Opera. La Junta: Koshare Ceremonials. Manitou Springs: Pikes Peak Auto Climb. Steamboat Springs: Dance and Drama Festival.

August. Boulder: Arapahoe Glacier Hike; Shakespeare Festival. Central City: Theatre Festival. Pueblo: Colorado State Fair. Rocky Ford: Watermelon Day.

September. Louisville: Fall Festival. Ouray: Fall Color Week. Windsor: Harvest Festival.

October. Carbondale: Potato Day. Rye: Aspencade.

November. Grand Lake: Salmon Snagging.

December. Colorado Springs: New Year's Eve Salute. La Junta: Winter Night Koshare Indian Ceremonials.

CONNECTICUT

March. Hartford: Autorama; Flower Show in Elizabeth Park.

April. Lime Rock: Sports car races.

May. Hartford: House and Garden Tour. Middletown: Homes Tour. Windsor: River Shad Derby.

June. Bridgeport: Barnum Festival. Brookfield: Craftsmen's Festival. Danbury: Boating Spectacular. New Haven: Starlight Festival of Music. New London: Yale-Harvard Rowing Regatta on Thames River. Norwich: Rose-Arts Festival. Stratford: American Shakespeare Festival.

July. Falls Village: String Quartet Concerts. Hartford: Festival of Music. Litchfield: Historic Homes Tour. New Canaan: Silvermine Chamber Music Festival. Niantic: Outdoor Art Show. Norfolk: Concerts. Stamford: Scottish Games. Waterbury: Arts Festival.

August. Mystic: Outdoor Art Show. New London: American Dance Festival. Stratford: Women's Softball Games. Torrington: Arts Festival. Westport: Auto Concourse.

September. Stratford: Men's Softball Games.

October.　　Bristol: Chrysanthemum Festival.
November.　　Willimantic: Arts and Crafts Festival.
December.　　Greenwich: Christmas Antique Bazaar.

DELAWARE

March.　　Newark: Delaware Play Festival at U. of Delaware Dramatic Center.
April.　　Wilmington: Photography Show. Winterthur: Gardens open at du Pont Winterthur Museum.
May.　　Dover: Dover Day. Newark: Folk and Square Dancing. New Castle: A Day in Old New Castle. Wilmington: Garden Day.
July.　　Harrington: Delaware State Fair.
August.　　Georgetown: Farm and Home Field Day. Rehoboth Beach: Art Colony House Tour.
September.　　Wilmington: Art Festival.

FLORIDA

January.　　Miami: Orange Bowl Football. St. Petersburg: Ringling Bros. Barnum and Bailey Circus premiere. Tarpon Springs: Epiphany Cross Day Greek Orthodox Church ceremonies. White Springs: Stephen Foster Week.
February.　　Boca Raton: Mardi Gras. Fort Myers: Pageant of Light; Island Shrimp Festival. Fort Pierce: Sandy Shoes Festival. Homestead: Frontier Days. Kissimmee: Livestock Show. Lake Wales: Black Hills Passion Play. Miami: Orange blossom time. Naples: Swamp Buggy Days. St. Augustine: Fiesta de Menendez. Tampa: Florida State Fair; Pirate Invasion. White Springs: Jeanie Auditions. Ybor City: Latin Fiesta.
March.　　Bradenton: De Soto Festival. Clearwater: Fun 'n Sun Festival. Hollywood: Fiesta Tropicale. Jacksonville Beach: Easter sunrise service, parade. Moore Haven: Chalo Nitka Indian Festival. Palatka: Azalea Festival. Plant City:

232

Strawberry Festival. New Port Richey: Chasco Fiesta. St. Augustine: Easter Festival. St. Petersburg: Festival of States. Sanibel Island: Shell Fair. Sarasota: King Neptune's Frolic. Sebring: Grand Prix Auto Race. Tarpon Springs: Greek Easter Week. Winter Haven: Florida Citrus Exposition.

April.   Sarasota: Sailor Circus.

May.   Crestview: Old Spanish Trail Festival. Miami Beach: Miss USA Pageant. White Springs: Florida Folk Festival. Winter Park: Bach Festival.

June.   Daytona Beach: Dixie Frolics. Fort Walton Beach: Billy Bowlegs Festival. Miami: Royal Poinciana Fiesta. Pensacola: Fiesta of Five Flags. St. Augustine: "The Cross and the Sword." Sarasota: Summer Music Festival.

July.   Arcadia: All-Florida Championship Rodeo. Coral Gables: Southern Shakespeare Repertory Theatre. Daytona Beach: Florida International Music Festival; Miss Dixie Contest. Miami: Miss Universe Beauty Pageant. Sarasota: Asolo Theatre Festival. Tampa: Theatre Repertory Festival.

September.   Kissimmee: Boat-a-Cade. St. Augustine: Day in Spain Fiesta.

October.   Perry: Pine Tree Festival.

November.   Fort Lauderdale: Beaux Arts Promenade. Naples: Swamp Buggy Days.

December.   Jacksonville: Gator Bowl Football. Miami: Orange Bowl Festival.

GEORGIA

January.   St. Simons Island: Camellia Show. Thomasville: Camellia Show. Tifton: Camellia Show. Waycross: Camellia Show.

February.   Atlanta: Emory Creative Arts Festival Series. Augusta: Camellia Show. Cairo: Camellia Show. Macon: Fine Arts Festival. Savannah: Camellia Show; Georgia Day Celebration.

March.   Atlanta: "500" Stock Car Race; Lenox Easter

Parade with Atlanta Symphony. Augusta: Fine Arts Week. Callaway Gardens: Easter sunrise service. St. Simons: Homes and Gardens Tour. Savannah: Homes and Gardens Tour. Sea Island: Homes and Gardens Tour. Statesboro: First District Music Festival. Sylvania: Livestock Festival. Thomasville: Homes Tour.

April.   Atlanta: All Night Sing; Country and Western Show; Dogwood Festival; 4-F and FFA Cattle Show; Homes Tour. Augusta: House and Garden Tour; Masters Golf Tournament. Macon: Gospel Sing. Savannah: Coastal Empire Arts Festival. Thomasville: Rose Festival. Waycross: Flower Show.

May.   Augusta: Rose Show. Brunswick: Blessing of Shrimp Fleet. Clarksville: Mountain Laurel Festival. Swainsboro: Pine Tree Festival. Waycross: Forest Festival.

June.   Calloway Gardens: Florida State University Circus.

July.   Alma: Tobacco auctions. Atlanta: Watermelon Day. Cornelia: Fine Arts Festival. Hazelhurst: Tobacco auctions. Statesboro: Tobacco Festival Parade. St. Simons: Sunshine Festival. Waycross: Tobacco auctions.

August.   Atlanta: Dixie 400 NASCAR Race. Hiawassee: Georgia Mountain Fair. Waycross: All Night Gospel Sing.

September.   Atlanta: Southeastern Fair. Clarkesville: Livestock Fair and Horse Show. Gainsville: Northeast Georgia Fair.

October.   Atlanta: Southeastern Fair. Cedartown: Art Festival. Clarksville: Harvest Festival. Cleveland: Harvest Festival. Macon: Georgia State Fair. Rising Fawn: Plum Nelly Clothesline Art Show. Waycross: Georgia State Championship Rodeo. Woodbury: Pimento Festival.

November.   Cornelia: Tour of Homes. Ocilla: Sweet Potato Festival. Savannah: Gospel Singing.

December.   Athens: Christmas in Georgia for visitors from other lands.

January. Honolulu: Chinese New Year Festival; Hula Bowl football; Narcissus Festival.

February. Honolulu: Cherry Blossom Festival.

March. Honolulu: Easter sunrise service at Punchbowl National Memorial Cemetery; Kamehameha Schools Song Contest.

April. Hilo: Merry Monarch Festival. Honolulu: Flora Pacifica at East-West Center of University of Hawaii. Waikiki: Buddha Day.

May. Honolulu: Lei Day; University of Hawaii Ka Palapala Beauty Pageant and Racial Beauty Contest. Kona Coast: Capt. Cook Festival. Waikiki: Hawaiian Song Festival.

June. Honolulu: Fiesta Filipina; King Kamehameha Day. Kauai: Rodeo Week. Lahaina and Maui: Surfing Festival.

July. Hilo and Hawaii, Orchid Show. Honolulu: Hawaii State Fair. Kailua Kona: Hawaii Billfish Tournament.

August. Honolulu: Bon Odori Season; Hula Festival.

October. Honolulu: Aloha Week; Orchid Show. Kauai: Aloha Week. Maui: Aloha Week. Molokai: Aloha Week.

November. All Islands: Makahiki Festival. Lahaina and Maui: Whaling Festival.

December. Honolulu: Bodhi Day. Makaha Beach and Oahu: International Surfing Championship. Waikiki: Festival of Trees.

IDAHO

January. Boise: Basque Festival.

February. Fruitlands: Ground Hog Festival. Homedale: Basque Dance. Lewiston: Old Time Fiddlers' Jam Session.

March. Boise: Cranston Cup Ski Race. Marsing: Easter sunrise service at Lizard Butte.

235

April. Priest Lake: Fishing Derby.

May. Hayden Lake: May Festival. Kendrick: Locust Blossom Festival. Nampa: Art Festival. Payette: Apple Blossom Festival.

June. Coeur d'Alene: Forest Festival. Emmett: Cherry Festival. Idaho City; Gold Rush Days. Meridian: Dairy and Stock Show; Tater Cup Races. Weiser: National Oldtime Fiddlers' Contest.

July. Boise: Basque Festival; Raft Race on Boise River. Buhl: Antique Festival Theatre Plays. Gibson: Sacred Sun Dance of Shoshone-Bannock Indians. Grangeville: Border Days. McCall: Idaho Square Dance Festival. Moscow: Summer Music Festival. Nampa: Snake River Stampede. Priest River: Loggers' Celebration. Salmon: Salmon River Days. Shoshone: Old Time Fiddlers' Jamboree.

August. Boise: Western Idaho State Fair. Corral: Mannie's Jamboree. Parma: Old Fort Boise Days.

September. Blackfoot: Eastern Idaho State Fair. Midvale: Idaho Fiddlers' Jamboree. Mountain Home: Air Force Appreciation Days. Orofino: Lumberjack Days.

October. Boise: Basque Farmers' Dinner. Lewiston: Steelhead Fish Derby. Riggins: Oldtime Fiddlers' Jam Session.

November. Boise: Basque Bazaar; Fairyland Parade.

December. Boise: Basque Christmas Festival; Christmas Music Festival.

ILLINOIS

January. Antioch: Ice Fishing Derby.

February. Springfield: Abraham Lincoln's Birthday, pilgrimage. Urbana: Contemporary Arts Festival.

March. Alto Pass: Easter sunrise service on Bald Knob Mountain. Bloomington: American Passion Play. Chicago: St. Patrick's Day Parade. Lebanon: Easter sunrise service in Horner Park. Peoria: Easter Lily Show.

April. Arlington Heights: Kite Karnival. Galena: U.S.

Grant Pilgrimage. Peoria: Arts Festival. Princeton: Homes Tour. Springfield: Ceremonies on anniversary of the death of Abraham Lincoln at his tomb.

May. Carbondale: S.I.U. Spring Festival. Chicago: Blossomtime in Grant Park; Norwegian Independence Day Parade; Polish Independence Day Parade. Galesburg: Knox College Fine Arts Festival. Lombard: Lilac Festival.

June. Chicago: German Day Celebrations; Lithuanian Song Festival. Danville: House and Gardens Tour. Elgin: "Song of Hiawatha." Geneva: Swedish Festival. Harvard: Milk Day. Plainfield: Music Festival. Ravinia: Music Festival. Rockford: Scandinavian Midsummer Festival. Springfield: Rose Show.

July. Alton: Blessing of Fleet. Collinsville: Kahok Indian Dances. Dixon: Petunia Festival. Farmersville: Irish Day Picnic. Melrose Park: Italian Feast. Wyoming: Spoon River Days.

August. Aurora: Corn Boil. Carmi: Thresherman's Reunion. Chicago: Lakefront Festival; Tribune's Chicagoland Music Festival. DuQuoin: Hambletonian Trotting Classic. Harvey: Irish Feis. Mendota: Sweet Corn Festival. New Salem State Park: "Abe Lincoln in Illinois." Rock Island: Lantern Parade. Springfield: Illinois Farm Sports Festival; Illinois Gladiolus Show; Illinois State Fair. Wapella: Corn and Bean Festival. Winchester: Burgoo Picnic.

September. Chicago: Mexican Independence Day Parade. Galena: Homes Tour. Hoopeston: Sweet Corn Festival. Murphysboro: Apple Festival. Nauvoo: Wedding of Wine and Cheese. Pontiac: Threshermen's Reunion. Rock Island: Indian Pow Wow. Kewanee: Hog Capital Festival. Zion: Jubilee.

October. Chicago: Chinese Independence Day; Columbus Day Parade; Holiday Folk Fair. Sycamore: Pumpkin Festival.

November. Chicago, Army-Air Force Football; Christmas Parade; Chrysanthemum Show; Harper Theater Dance Festival; International Film Festival; International Livestock

237

Exposition. Golconda: Deer Festival. Peoria: Chrysanthemum Show.

December.   Chicago: Christmas Flower Show. Rockford: Lucia Festival.

INDIANA

February.   Rockville: Maple Sugar Festival.
May.   Fort Wayne: Fine Arts Festival. Indianapolis: "500" Festival. Oldenburg: Corpus Christi Procession. St. Meinrad: Corpus Christi Procession.
August.   Peru: Old-time Circus Festival. Tell City: Schweizer Fest.
September.   Indianapolis: Indiana State Fair; National Drag Championship Races. Mitchell: Persimmon Festival.
October.   Bloomington: Opera. Rockville: Covered Bridge Festival. Troy: Lincolnland Fall Foliage Tour. Vincennes: Wabash Valley Folk Festival.

IOWA

March.   Emmetsburg: St. Patrick's Day Celebration.
April.   Des Moines: Drake Relays.
May.   Mount Vernon: May Music Festival. Orange City: Tulip Festival. Pella: Tulip Festival.
June.   Burlington: Steamboat Days. Decorah: Sangerfest. Hampton: Dairy Day. Mason City: North Iowa Band Festival. Ottumwa: National Sport Parachute Meet.
July.   West Point: Sweet Corn Festival.
August.   Britt: Hobo Day. Cedar Rapids: All-Iowa Fair. Des Moines: Iowa State Fair. Elkader: Sweet Corn Festival. Gladbrook: Corn Carnival. Marion: Old Settlers Day. Marshalltown: Central Iowa Fair. Mason City: North Iowa Fair. Montrose: Watermelon Day. Nashua: Marriage Reunion Sunday at Little Brown Church. Oskaloosa: Southern Iowa Fair. Ottumwa: Midwest Square Dance Festival. Reinbeck:

Sweet Corn Day. Sidney: National Tractor Rodeo; Cowboy Rodeo. Tama: Indian Pow Wow.

September. Carroll: Iowa Beef Festival; Western Iowa Band Festival. Jefferson: National Plowing Matches. Missouri Valley: Goose Calling Contest. Mt. Pleasant: Threshers Reunion. Waterloo: National Dairy Cattle Congress.

October. Algona: Band Festival. Clarinda: Southwest Iowa Band Jamboree. Waterloo: National Dairy Cattle Congress.

November. All-State Music Festival; Foreign Food Fair. Marion: National Corn Picking Contest.

KANSAS

January. Wichita: Beef Show.

February. Liberal: Shrove Tuesday Pancake Race.

March. Lindsborg: Easter Music Festival.

April. Abilene: National Coursing Meet. Dodge City: Square Dance Festival. Fort Hays Experimental Station: Cattleman's Roundup. Lawrence: Kansas Relays.

May. Dodge City: Arts Festival. Lindsborg: Fine Arts Fair. Topeka: Rose Week.

June. Topeka: Kansas High School Rodeo.

July. Hutchinson: National Jalopy Races. Mayetta: Indian Pow Wow. White Cloud: Indian Pow Wow. Wichita: Kansas Baseball Tournament.

August. Topeka: Accordion and Guitar Festival. Wichita: National Baseball Congress.

September. Chanute: Mexican Fiesta. Horton: Kickapoo Indian Pow Wow. Hutchinson: Kansas State Fair. Topeka: Mid-America Fair.

October. Arkansas City: Arkalallah. Ashland: U.N. Weekend Show. Hiawatha: Halloween Festival. Independence: Newollah. Wichita: Kansas National Junior Livestock Show.

November. Wichita: Square Dance Festival.

December. Garden City: Christmas Parade.

February. Louisville: National Polled Hereford Show.
March. Louisville: Aberdeen Angus Sweepstakes; National Short-horn Show. Paducah: National Amateur Quail Championship.
April. Benton: Tater Day. Berea: Mountain Folk Dance Festival. Lexington: Keeneland Race Meeting. Louisville: Kentucky Derby Festival.
May. Adairville: Strawberry Festival. Benton: Old South Harmony Festival. Greenville: Strawberry-Coal Festival. Hardin: Sailing Regatta for Governor's Cup. Louisville: Kentucky Derby; National Guernsey Show. Pineville: Mountain Laurel Festival.
June. Bardstown: "The Stephen Foster Story." Harlan: Poke Sallet Festival. Harrodsburg: "The Legend of Daniel Boone." Louisville: Shakespeare in Central Park. Olive Hill: American Folk Song Festival. Pineville: The Book of Job.
July. Auburn: "Shakertown Revisited." Carlisle: Blackberry Festival. Lexington: Junior League Horse Show. Warsaw: Water Festival.
August. Cloverport: Sacajawea Festival. Hickman: Emancipation Proclamation Day. Jamestown: Big Singing. Lexington: Angus Livestock Show. Louisville: Kentucky State Fair. Mount Sterling: Festival.
September. Bedford: Hydroplane Regatta. Berea: Mountain Folk Dance Festival. Elkhorn City: Song Festival. Fulton: Homecoming Banana Festival. Lexington: Band Contest. Princeton: Western Kentucky Band Festival.
October. Barbourville: Daniel Boone Festival. Hardin: Watkins Cup Regatta. Louisville: Brown Swiss Cattle Show. Mt. Sterling: Court Day. Russellville: Tobacco Festival. Shelbyville: Tobacco Festival.
November. Lexington: Blessing the Hounds; 4-H and FFA Cattle Show. Paris: Tobacco Festival.

240

December.   Bethlehem: Living Nativity Pageant. Paducah: Quail Championship Invitational.

LOUISIANA

January.   New Orleans: Sugar Bowl Football.
February.   Lafayette: Mardi Gras. New Orleans: Mardi Gras.
March.   Baton Rouge: L.S.U. Livestock Show, Rodeo.
April.   Breaux Bridge: Crayfish Festival in even numbered years. Hammond: Dairy Festival. New Orleans: Spring Fiesta. Shreveport: Holiday in Dixie.
May.   Barataria: Pirogue Races. Grambling: Broiler and Swine Show. Walker: Pine Tree Festival.
June.   Ruston: Peach Festival.
July.   Baton Rouge: Fundora.
September.   Bastrop: Cotton Festival. Haynesville: Dairy Festival. Jonesville: Soybean Festival. Leesville: Forestry Festival. Marksville: Pasture Festival. Morgan City: Shrimp Festival. New Iberia: Sugar Cane Festival.
October.   Abbeville: Louisiana Dairy Festival. Baton Rouge: Horse Show. Crowley: International Rice Festival. Delcambre: Shrimp Festival. Opelousas: Yambilee Festival. Shreveport: Louisiana State Fair.
November.   Baton Rouge: National Quarter Horse Show.
December.   Natchitoches: Christmas Festival.

MAINE

July.   Bar Harbor: Clothes Line Exhibit. Belfast: Broiler Festival. Bernard: House and Garden Tour. Cumberland: Maine Dairy Goat Show. Dresden: Yankee Peddler Day. Fort Fairfield: Potato Blossom Festival. Orono: U. of Maine Arts Festival. South Paris: Bean Hole Bean Festival. Stratton: Tall

Timber Days. Vinalhaven: Bay Festival. Winter Harbor: Lobster Festival. Yarmouth: Festival. York: Twins Day.

August. Boothbay: Lobster Festival. Bristol: "Yankee Traveler." Buxton: Old Peabody Pew. Ellsworth: Downeast Festival. Kittery-Portsmouth: Whaleback Ocean Race. New Brunswick: Contemporary Music Festival. Rockland: Maine Seafood Festival. Union: Blueberry Festival. Windham: Old Home Days. York: Canadian Friendship Day.

MARYLAND

January. Annapolis: Governor's Open House. Cambridge: Outdoor Show.

April. Butler: Grand National Steeplechase. Monkton: My Lady's Manor Steeplechase. Shawan: Maryland Hunt Club Steeplechase. Upper Marlboro: President's Cup Sports Car Races.

May. Baltimore: Flower Mart; Maryland House and Garden Pilgrimage; Preakness Horse Race.

June. Annapolis: Fine Arts Festival; Newport Sailing Race in odd numbered years. Baltimore: Historic Homes Tour.

August. Annapolis: Clam Festival.

September. Baltimore: Defender's Day. Crisfield: National Hard Crab Derby. Owings Mills: State Jousting Championship. Timonium: Maryland State Fair.

October. Annapolis: Heritage Month. Princess Anne: Olde Princess Anne Days.

November. Laurel: $150,000 Washington, D.C. International.

December. Fruitland: Wild Holly Auction.

MASSACHUSETTS

February. Boston: Winterfest.
March. Boston: St. Patrick's Day Celebration.
April. Boston: Patriot's Day.

242

May. Gloucester: Feast of Corpus Christi.

June. Gloucester: Dory race to Lunenberg, N.S.; St. Peter's Fiesta. Lee: Jacob's Pillow Dance Festival. West Springfield: Music Fair.

July. Chatham: Strawberry Festival. Falmouth: Gilbert and Sullivan Season by Oberlin College Players. Ipswich: Castle Hill Festival. Lenox: Berkshire Music Festival at Tanglewood. Marblehead: Race Week for boats. Newburyport: Yankee Homecoming. Pittsfield: South Mountain Concerts. Stockbridge: Berkshire Theatre Festival. Yarmouth: Clambake.

August. Dennis: Festival. Hyannis: Clothesline Art Show. Plymouth: Pilgrim Progress.

September. North Adams: Foliage Festival. West Springfield: Eastern States Exposition.

October. Worcester: Worcester Music Festival.

MICHIGAN

January. Bay City: Speed Skating Championship. Charlevoix: Winter Sports Carnival. Harbor Springs: Folk Festival. Lake City: Sport Car Races on Ice. Petoskey: Speed Skating Championship; Winter Sports Carnival.

February. Detroit: Speed Skating Championship. Grayling: Winter Sports Carnival. Marquette: Winter Carnival.

March. Detroit: Flower Garden Show. Iron Mountain: National Ski Jumping Championship.

April. Kalkaska: National Trout Festival. Vermontville: Maple Syrup Festival.

May. Ann Arbor: May Music Festival. Benton Harbor-St. Joseph: Blossomtime Festival. Holland: Tulip Time. Lake City: Mushroom Days. Traverse City: Blessing Cherry Blossoms; Cherry Blossom Festival; Square Dance Festival.

June. Frankenmuth: Bavarian Festival. Interlochen: National Music Camp. Mackinac Island: Lilac Festival. Manistee: Buckskin Rendezvous.

243

July.   Crystal Falls: Bass Festival. Detroit: Hydroplane Race; International Freedom Festival. Gaylord: Alpine Festival. Ironwood: Hiawatha Festival. Manistee: Forest Festival. Muskegon: Seaway Festival. Port Huron: Blue Water Festival. Quincy: Fine Arts Festival. The Tawases: Tourist Festival. Traverse City: National Cherry Festival.

August.   Detroit: Michigan State Fair. Grand Haven: Coast Guard Festival.

September.   Dearborn: Old Car Festival. Mackinaw City-St. Ignace: Mackinac Bridge Walk. Mt. Clemens: Oktoberfest.

October.   Ann Arbor: Dance Festival. Kalkaska: Fall Round-up.

November.   Grayling: Red Coat Roundup.

December.   The Tawases: Parade of Fish Shanties.

MINNESOTA

January.   St. Paul: Winter Carnival. White Bear Lake: Ice Fishing Contest.

February.   Ely: Snowmobile Races.

May.   St. Paul: Festival of Nations, staged triennially, 1964, '67, '70. St. Peter: String Quarter Festival at Gustavus Adolphus College.

June.   Brainerd: Paul Bunyan Carnival. Cook: Timber Days. Granite Falls: State High School Championship Rodeo. Minneapolis: Svenskanas Day. Montevideo: Fiesta Days. Mountain Lake: Pow Wow. Redwood Falls: Inventors' Congress. Rochester: Festival of Arts.

July.   Bemidji: Paul Bunyan Water Carnival. Bigfork: Lumber-jack Day. Crane Lake: Voyageur Day Celebration. Henderson: Sauerkraut Days. Hopkins: Raspberry Festival. Minneapolis: Aquatennial. Pipestone: Song of Hiawatha Pageant.

August.   Deer River: Wild Rice Festival. Duluth: International Folk Festival. Lake of the Woods: Sailing Regatta.

244

Le Sueur: Corn-on-the-Curb Days. Montgomery: Kolacky Day. St. Paul: Minnesota State Fair. Sandstone: Harvest Festival. Young America: Stiftungsfest.
September. Amboy: Corn Festival. Tracy: Box Car Days. Windom: Scandinavian Festival Days. Worthington: King Turkey Day.
October. Owatonna: Pumpkin Day.
December. Northfield: Christmas Festival at St. Olaf College. St. Paul: Christmas Choral Pageant.

MISSISSIPPI

January. Jackson: Square Dance Festival.
February. Biloxi: Mardi Gras. Jackson: Livestock Show.
March. Biloxi: Garden Clubs Pilgrimage along Gulf Coast. McComb: Lighted Azalea Trail. Natchez: Old Homes Pilgrimage. Vicksburg: "Gold in the Hills"; Old Homes Pilgrimage.
April. Holly Springs: Homes and Gardens Pilgrimage. Jackson: Homes and Gardens Pilgrimage.
June. Biloxi: Shrimp Festival.
July. Greenville: Water Carnival.
August. Oxford: Old Homes Pilgrimage. Philadelphia: Choctaw Indian Fair.
October. Jackson: Mississippi State Fair.

MISSOURI

May. Hermann: Maifest.
June. Camdenton: Dance Festival. Carthage: Dairy Days. Lathrop: Friendship Festival. St. Louis: Festival; Summer Musical Theatre.
July. Hannibal: Tom Sawyer Days.
August. Crane: Broiler Festival. Kansas City: Indian

Pow Wow. Ste. Genevieve: Tourist Festival. Sedalia: Missouri State Fair. Springfield: Ozark Empire Fair.

September. La Plata: Soybean Festival. Pineville: Gospel Singing Show. St. James: Grape Festival.

October. Branson: Ozarks Craftsmen's Festival. Caledonia: Historical Tour. Gainsville: Folk Festival. Kansas City: American Royal Dairy Show; Livestock Show. Princeton: Calamity Jane Day. St. Clair: Folk Festival. St. Louis: Veiled Prophet Parade. Savannah: Corn Picking Contest.

November. Charleston: Soybean Contest. Kansas City: Christmas Parade.

MONTANA

April. Helena: Vigilante Parade and Square Dance Festival.

May. Deer Lodge: O-Mok-See. Kalispell: Canadian Days. Lewistown: Music Festival. Missoula: Square Dance Festival. Red Lodge: Yellowstone Days. Sidney: Flag of Honor Ceremony.

June. Custer Battlefield: Reenact Custer's Last Stand. Harlem: Chuckwagon Days. Helena: Arts Festival. Red Lodge: Music Festival.

July. Browning: North American Indian Days. Deer Lodge: Match of Champions Rodeo. Libby: Logger Days. Roundup: Montana High School Rodeo. Wolf Point: Wild Horse Stampede.

August. Crow Agency: Crow Indian Celebration. Great Falls: Montana State Fair. Livingston: National Fresh Water Trout Derby. Red Lodge: Festival of Nations.

September. Culbertson: Threshers' Show.

NEBRASKA

February. Lincoln: Fine Arts Festival.

April. Dodge: High School Music Festival. Lincoln:

246

Arbor Day; Nebraska Wesleyan U. Fine Arts Festival.
McCook: Tri-State Soaring Meet. Scottsbluff: Five-state Art
Show.

May. Brownville: Spring Festival. Kearney: State Craftsman's Fair. Lincoln: Square Dance Festival.

June. Clarkson: Czech Festival. Harrison: Nebraska
Championship High School Rodeo. Schuyler: Czech Festival.

July. Dwight: Czech Festival. Winnebago: Indian Ceremonial Pow Wow.

August. Brownville: Old-time Fiddlers' Country Music
Contest. Fairbury: Echoes of Oregon Trail Pageant. Wilber:
Czech Festival.

September. Brainard: Old Home Town Festival. Lincoln: Nebraska State Fair. North Loup: Popcorn Days.
Omaha: Livestock Show.

October. Dodge: Kids' Halloween Costume Parade.

December. Minden: Christmas Pageant.

NEVADA

March. Las Vegas: Trans-Mississippi Senior Golf Tournament. Reno: State Band Festival.

April. Las Vegas: National American Roadrace Championship.

May. Boulder City: Lake Mead Flotilla. Las Vegas:
Helldorado. Reno: Square Dance Festival.

June. Fallon: Pioneer Days. Las Vegas: Golf Gold Cup
Finals. Reno: Rodeo.

July. Boulder: Damboree. Genoa: Pioneer Day. Reno:
Grand Ole Opry.

August. Ely: Nevada Fair of Industry.

September. Las Vegas: Outrigger Races. Reno: Championship Air Races.

October. Carson: Nevada Day. Las Vegas: $111,111.11
Golf Tournament. Nevada City: Fall Color Spectacle; Trade
Fair.

November.   Beatty: Wild Burro Races. Las Vegas: Miss Rodeo America Pageant. Nevada City: Artists' Christmas Fair.

NEW HAMPSHIRE

February.   Hanover: Dartmouth Winter Carnival.
May.   Peterborough: Apple blossom trail.
June.   Gilsum: Rock Swap. Hanover: Dartmouth College Congregation of the Arts. Manchester: Dairy Festival.
July.   Littletown: Book Sale. Pike: Seven Arts Festival. Portsmouth: Strawberry Banke Days. Salem: $75,000 Rockingham Park Special. Sanbornton: Old Homes Tour.
August.   Meredith: New Hampshire Music Festival Symphony Concerts. Mt. Sunapee State Park: N.H. Arts and Crafts Fair. Newport: Library Festival. Pike: Cracker Barrel Americana. Rochester: N.H. Drum, Bugle Corps Competition. Sanbornton: Old Home Day.
September.   Intervale: Swap, Talk, and Brag Day. Salem: $250,000 Sweepstakes.
October.   Concord: Tri-State Collectors' Exhibition. Warner: Fall Foliage Festival.

NEW JERSEY

March.   Atlantic City: Easter bonnet fashion parade.
May.   Fair Lawn: Art Festival. Wildwood: State Marbles Championship. Woodbury: Historical Home Tour.
June.   Allaire: Festival. Atlantic City: Canadian Week. Cape May: Bluefish Festival. Cape May: Fishing Festival. Red Bank: Art Festival. Wildwood: National Marbles Tournament.
July.   Asbury Park: Book Fair; Monmouth Opera Festival. Atlantic City: Hydrangea Trail. Cape May: Art Festival; Shakespearean Festival. Hammonton: Religious Pilgrim-

248

age. Ocean City: State Shuffleboard Championship. Ocean Grove: Choir Festival. Ringwood: Music, Folk Dance Festival.

August. Asbury Park: Life Guard Tournament. Atlantic City: Skills Day. Avalon: Baby Parade. Cape May: National Clamshell Pitching Contest. Ocean City: Baby Parade. Perth Amboy: Choral and Folk Dance Festival. Sea Isle City: Baby Parade. Stone Harbor: Baby Parade. Ventnor: Music Festival. Wildwood: Baby Parade.

September. Atlantic City: Miss America Pageant. Cape May: Baby Parade. Hammonton: Miss Blueberry USA Contest. Trenton: New Jersey State Fair.

October. Irvington: Chrysanthemum Show. Madison: Drew University Chrysanthemum Show. Newark: Columbus Day Parade.

November. Atlantic City: Catch a Cod Tournament.

NEW MEXICO

January. All Indian Pueblos install Governors on Jan. 6.

March. Santo Domingo Pueblo: Easter ceremonial dances.

April. Roswell: National Go-Kart Endurance Race. Tularosa: Rose Festival.

May. Portales: Eastern New Mexico University Opera; Industrial Arts Fair. Santa Fe: Corpus Christi Procession. Taos Pueblo: San Ysidro Procession.

June. Albuquerque: Arts and Crafts Fair. San Juan Pueblo: San Juan Day Dances. Santa Fe: Rose Show. Taos: St. Anthony Procession of Lights.

July. Las Vegas: Old Town Fiesta. Mescalero Apache Reservation: Fiesta and Devil Dance. Santa Fe: Opera Festival.

August. Gallup: Inter-Tribal Indian Ceremonial. Lincoln: "The Last Escape of Billy the Kid."

249

September. Albuquerque: New Mexico State Fair. Clovis: Steer Roping Contest. Laguna Pueblo: Fiesta and Dances. Santa Fe: Fiesta. Taos: Fiesta de San Geronimo.
October. Cloudcroft: Aspencade. Clovis: Cattle Festival. Santa Fe: Aspen Tours; Feast of St. Francis of Assisi.
December. Albuquerque: Luminario Tour. Cloudcroft: Winter Carnival. Jamez Pueblo: Matachines. Las Cruces: Tortugas Indian Pilgrimage. Mesilla: Posadas. Santo Domingo Indian Pueblo; Christmas Ceremonials. Taos: Our Lady of Guadalupe Procession; Cedar Torch Procession; Matachinas.

NEW YORK

January. Lake Placid: Snowmobile Championships. New York: Chinese New Year Festival. Niagara Falls: Winter Carnival. Saratoga Springs: Eastern States Speed Skating Championship.
February. Cooperstown: Winter Carnival. Lake Placid: Bobsled Championship. Malone: Winter Carnival. Old Forge: Winter Carnival. Saranac Lake: Winter Carnival.
March. Corning: New York State Theatre Festival. New York: Easter fashion parade; St. Patrick's Day Parade; World Dance Festival at Columbia U.
April. Jefferson: Maple Festival. Woodridge: Catskill Mountain Shakespeare Festival.
May. Albany: Tulip Festival. Kingston: Historic Walking Tour. New York: Outdoor Show in Greenwich Village.
June. Bronx: Irish Feis. Katonah: Caramoor Music Festival. Newark: Rose Festival. New York: Belmont Stakes; Lincoln Center Festival; New York Is A Summer Festival; St. Anthony Italian Fiesta; Shakespearean Festival in Central Park. Niagara Falls: Maid of the Mist Festival. Sag Harbor: Whalers Festival. Syracuse: Intercollegiate Rowing Regatta.
July. Brooklyn: Italian Fiesta. Brookville: Dance Program. Chautauqua: annual Chautauqua. Cooperstown: Baseball Hall of Fame game. Elmira: Eastern Open Soaring Cham-

pionship. Forest Hills: Music Festival. Glens Falls: Lake George Opera Festival. Lake Placid: Water Ski Tournament. Liverpool: Feis. Massena: Seaway Festival. New York: Forest Hills Music Festival. Ogdensburg: Seaway Festival. Palmyra: Mormon Pageant. Rome: Savoy Jazz Festival. Saratoga Springs: Saratoga Festival of Ballet, Music. Schroon Lake: Adirondack Music Festival. Utica: Arts Festival. Woodstock: Maverick Concerts.

August. Brookville: Long Island Festival. Canandaigua: Pageant of Steam. Ithaca: York State Craft Fair. New York: Harkness Foundation Dance Festival; Tennis Championships at Forest Hills. Old Chatham: Shaker Museum Festival. Seneca Falls: Aqua Festival. Southampton: Fine Arts Festival. Tupper Lake: Woodsmen's Field Day. Watkins Glen: "500" Championship Sports Car Races.

September. Lake George: Powerboat Races. Naples: Grape Festival. New York: International Film Festival; Labor Day Parade; Outdoor Art Show in Greenwich Village; San Gennaro Italian Fiesta. Pine Island: Onion Festival. Rochester: Clothesline Art Show. Syracuse: New York State Fair. Watkins Glen: U.S. Grand Prix Auto Road Race.

October. Monroe: Fall Festival. Syracuse: Square Dance Festival.

November. Elmira: Snowbird Soaring Meet. New York: Thanksgiving Day Parade.

December. Christmas Tree Party in Rockefeller Center.

NORTH CAROLINA

January. Asheville: North Carolina Artists' Exhibition. Pinehurst: Field Trials. Rodanthe: Old Christmas Celebration.

February. Whiteville: Camellia Show. Wilmington: Camellia Show.

March. Elizabeth City: Camellia Show. Hillsborough: Grand National Stock Car Race. Hoffman: National Amateur Field Trials. Salem: Moravian Easter sunrise service.

Tryon: Block House Steeplechase. Union Grove: Old-time Fiddlers' Convention.

April. Asheville: Mountain Youth Jamboree. Fontana Village: Square Dance Festivals. Southern Pines: Stoneybrook Steeplechase. Wilmington: North Carolina Azalea Festival.

May. Chadburn: Strawberry Festival. Charlotte: "World 600" late model auto race. Fontana: Square Dance Fun Fest.

June. Bakersville: Rhododendron Festival. Boone: "Horn in the West." Cherokee: "Unto These Hills." Hendersonville: Hobby Crafts Show. Linville: Singing on the Mountain. Manteo: "The Lost Colony." Wilson: Eastern Carolina Singing Convention.

July. Asheville: Southern Highland Crafts Fair. Brevard: Music Festival. Elkin: Fiddlers' Convention. Linville: Highland Games on Grandfather Mountain.

August. Asheville: Mountain Dance and Folk Festival. Hendersonville: North Carolina Apple Festival. Spruce Pine: Gems and Minerals Festival.

September. Benson: Mule Day. Cary: Gourd Festival. Cedar Island: Pony Penning. Charlotte: Festival in the Park. Fontana: Square Dance Fun Fest. Hendersonville: West North Carolina Fair.

October. Charlotte: 500 Stock Car Race. Raleigh: North Carolina State Fair. Rockingham: 500 Stock Car Race.

November. Charlotte: Carolinas' Carrousel. Elizabeth City: Rock Fish Rodeo.

December. Kitty Hawk: Anniversary of Wright Brothers' flight.

NORTH DAKOTA

July. Bottineau: Water Carnival. International Peace Garden: Choral and Dance Sessions. McClusky: Old Settlers Day. Minot: North Dakota State Fair.

August. Bismarck: Band and Choir Concerts.

September.　　Hazen: Harvest Festival. Page: State Tractor Pulling Contest. Williston: Amateur State Finals Rodeo.
November.　　Bismarck: Art Show.

OHIO

January.　　Cleveland: Folk Festival.
March.　　Chardon: Maple Festival.
May.　　Berea: Bach Festival.
June.　　Burton: Butter Churn Festival. Cincinnati: Summer Opera. Middlefield: Swiss Cheese Festival. Versailles: Poultry Days Celebration.
July.　　Quaker City: Ohio Hills Folk Festival.
August.　　Akron: Soap Box Derby Finals. Columbus: Ohio State Fair. Nelsonville: Parade of the Hills.
September.　　Burton: Rug and Craft Show. Cleveland: One World Day. Delaware: Little Brown Jug Pacing Classic. Jackson: Apple Festival. Milan: Melon Festival. Millersport: Sweet Corn Festival. Portsmouth: River Days Festival. Sugarcreek: Ohio Swiss Festival.
October.　　Burton: Apple Butter Festival. Circleville: Pumpkin Show. Jackson: Apple Festival. Middleburg: Antique Festival.

OKLAHOMA

March.　　Alva: Livestock Show. Anadarko: Livestock Show: Antlers: Livestock Show. Cherokee: Livestock Show. Chickasha: Livestock Show: Clinton: Livestock Show. Duncan: Livestock Show. Edmond: Livestock Show. El Reno: Livestock Show. Enid: Livestock Show. Guthrie: Livestock Show. Hobart: Livestock Show. Lawton: Easter Pageant. Madill: Livestock Show. McAlester: Livestock Show. Muskogee: Livestock Show; Music and Arts Festival. Oklahoma City: Livestock Show. Vinita: Livestock Show. Weatherford: Livestock Show. Woodward: Livestock Show.

253

April. Guthrie: Land Rush Anniversary. Muskogee: Dogwood Trail Tour. Okeene: Rattlesnake Hunt. Pawnee: Music Festival. Prague: Kolache Festival. Waurika: Rattlesnake Hunt.

May. Enid: Tri-State Music Festival. Guymon: Organic Act Day. Oklahoma City: $57,000 Open Golf Tournament. Stilwell: Strawberry Festival.

June. Clinton: Indian Pow Wow. Cushing: Inter-Tribal Pow Wow. El Reno: Indian Pow Wow. Madill: Sand Bass Festival. Pawnee: Free Pawnee Indian Pow Wow.

July. Anadarko: All-Indian Show. Okmulgee: Indian Pow Wow. Stroud: International Brick and Rolling Pin Throwing Contest.

August. Anadarko: Plains Indians Ceremonials. Rush Springs: Watermelon Festival. Shawnee: Sac and Fox Indian Pow Wow. Tulsa: Indian Pow Wow Campout.

September. Enid: Cherokee Strip Celebration. Oklahoma City: Oklahoma State Fair. Perry: Oklahoma Strip Celebration.

October. Salina: Oklahoma Historical Day. Vinita: $5,000 Steer Roping Finals.

November. Veterans Day.

December. Stillwater: Oklahoma Choral Festival.

OREGON

March. Chiloquin: All-Indian Basketball Tournament.

April. Corvallis: Arts Festival. Eugene: International Festival. Medford: Pear Blossom Festival. Portland: Flower and Garden Show. Salem: Contemporary Arts Festival.

May. Brookings: Azalea Festival. Florence: Rhododendron Festival. Milton-Freewater: Pea Festival. Tygh Valley: All-Indian Rodeo.

June. Lebanon: Strawberry Festival. Portland: Rose Festival. Rogue River: Rooster Crowing Contest. Tillamook: Timber Festival.

254

July.   Albany: Timber Carnival. Ashland: Oregon Shakespearean Festival. Springfield: Broiler Festival.

August.   Jacksonville: Peter Britt Music Festival. Prineville: Round-up. Salem: Oregon State Fair.

September.   Cave Junction: Illinois Valley Jubilee. Pendleton: Round-up.

October.   Portland: International Livestock Exposition.

December.   Salem: Christmas Choral Concert at Willamette University.

PENNSYLVANIA

January.   Harrisburg: Pennsylvania Farm Show. Philadelphia: Mummers' Parade.

February.   Uniondale: Winter Carnival.

March.   Grove City: Easter Choral Concert. Meadville: Easter Play. Philadelphia: Spring Flower Show. Pittsburgh: Easter sunrise service. Williamsport: Inter-collegiate Music Competition.

April.   Bloomsburg: Arts Festival. Erie: Ballet Festival. Glenside: Student Art Festival. Kutztown: Pennsylvania Dutch Fersommling. Meadville: Maple Camp Tours. Selinsgrove: Shakespeare Festival.

May.   Bethlehem: Bach Festival. Gettysburg: Apple Blossom Festival; Dogwood and Redbud Blossom time; Memorial Day Services at Gettysburg National Cemetery. Hanover: Heritage Days. Langhorne: Book Fair. Philadelphia: Arts Festival; Folk Fair. Pittsburgh: Three Rivers Art Festival. Scranton: Art Festival. Seagartown: Tulip Festival. Wilkes-Barre: Fine Arts Fiesta. York: Blossom time.

June.   Brookville: Laurel Festival. Manheim: Red Rose Payment. Philadelphia: Elfreth's Alley Day. Wellsboro: Pennsylvania State Laurel Festival.

July.   Ephrate: Musical Drama. Erwinna: Tinicum Art Festival. Kutztown: Pennsylvania Dutch Folk Festival. Milford: Festival. Philadelphia: Fourth of July celebration at

Independence Hall. Stroudsburg: Art Show. Tionesta: Indian Festival. Wernersville: Musical Festival.

August. East Stroudsburg: Pennsylvania Craft Fair. Hershey: Pennsylvania Dutch Days. Kinzers: Reunion and Steam Show. Ligonier: Highland Games.

September. Bangor: Welsh Day. Stahlstown: Flax Scutching. West Grove: Red Rose Rent Payment.

October. Bedford: Fall Foliage Festival. Bethlehem: Arts Festival. Clarion: Autumn Leaf Festival. Clearfield: Fall Foliage Tour. Du Bois: Fall Foliage Festival. Harrisburg: Pennsylvania National Horse Show. Johnstown: Flaming Foliage Festival. Lancaster: Harvest Days. Renovo: Flaming Foliage Festival. West Chester: Open House Tour.

November. Gettysburg: Anniversary of Lincoln's famous address. Harrisburg: Livestock Exposition. Philadelphia: Army-Navy football; Thanksgiving Day Toy Parade. Unionville: Hunt Cup Race.

RHODE ISLAND

February. Providence: Flower Show.

March. Pawtucket: Trade Fair. Tiverton: Easter sunrise service.

April. Cranston: Ceramic Show. North Kingstown: New England Folk Festival. Providence: Music Festival.

May. Cranston: Original May Day Breakfast. Pawtucket: Craftsmen's Show. Providence: Arts Festival; Bach Music Festival; Declaration of Independence; Tours of historic homes. Warwick: Gaspee Day Celebration.

June. Kingston: University of Rhode Island Theatre Festival. Newport: House Tour; Newport-Bermuda Yacht Race in even-numbered years.

July. Bristol: Independence Day celebration. Manville: Mahrajan, a Syrian religious celebration. Narrangansett: Art Festival. Newport: Folk Festival; Jazz Festival. Wickford: Art Festival.

256

August.   Charlestown: Indian Pow Wow; Old Fiddlers' Concert. Cumberland: Polish harvest festival. East Greenwich: Handtub Muster; Rocky Hill State Fair. Narragansett: Outdoor Art Show. Newport: Metropolitan Opera Festival; Outdoor Art Festival; Tennis Tournament at Tennis Hall of Fame. Wakefield: Outdoor Art Show. Warren: Festival.
September.   Galilee: Tuna Tournament. Newport: Military Reviews. West Kingston: Indian Memorial Pilgrimage.

SOUTH CAROLINA

March.   Johnsonville: Folk Music Festival. Myrtle Beach: Canadian-American Days.
April.   Aiken: Steeplechase. Camden: Carolina Cup Steeplechase. Charleston: Historic Homes Tour. Columbia: Spring Festival. Edgefield: Homes Tours. Georgetown: Historic Homes Tour. Greenville: Arts Festival. Moncks Corner: Jousting. Rock Hill: Come-See-Me Week.
May.   Moncks Corner: Striped Bass Derby. Myrtle Beach: Fishing Rodeo.
June.   Greer: Peach Festival. Myrtle Beach: Sun Fun Festival.
July.   Beaufort: Water Festival. Columbia: Jazz Festival. Gilbert: Peach Festival. Mountain Rest: Hillbilly Day.
September.   Darlington: Southern 500 Festival. Westminster: Apple Festival.
October.   Columbia: South Carolina State Fair. Fountain Inn: Horse and Buggy Festival.
November.   Kingstree: Jousting.

SOUTH DAKOTA

February.   Huron: State Crop Show. Watertown: Winter Farm Show.
April.   Brookings: Fine Arts Festival. Yankton: Jazz and Folk Festival.

May.   Sioux Falls: Fine Arts Week; Dakota Relays; Syttende Mai.

June.   Bison: Gala Days. Deadwood: Trial of Jack McCall. Hot Springs: Crazy Horse Pageant. Spearfish: Black Hills Passion Play. Tabor: Czech Days.

July.   Belle Fourche: Black Hills Roundup. Custer: Gold Discovery Days. Vermillion: Intercollegiate Rodeo.

August.   White River: Frontier Days.

September.   Huron: South Dakota State Fair. Mitchell: Corn Palace Festival.

October.   Aberdeen: Gypsy Day. Brookings: Hobo Day. Huron: Pow Wow Day. Sioux Falls: Tepee Days. Spearfish: Viking Days. Yankton: Pioneer Day.

TENNESSEE

February.   Grand Junction: Grand National Field Trials.

April.   Cosby: Ramp Festival. Gatlinburg: Wildflower Pilgrimage. Knoxville: Dogwood Arts Festival. Nashville: Homes and Gardens Pilgrimage.

May.   Humboldt: Strawberry Festival. Memphis: Cotton Carnival. Nashville: Iroquois Steeplechase.

June.   Roan Mountain: Rhododendron Festival.

July.   Maryville: Hillbilly Homecoming. Savannah: Catfish Derby. Sewanee: Music Festival.

August.   Shelbyville: Walking Horse Celebration.

September.   Nashville: Tennessee State Fair.

October.   Gatlinburg: Southern Highlands Crafts Fair.

November.   Nashville: Miss Teen-Age America Pageant.

TEXAS

January.   Abilene: Fat Stock Show. Amarillo: Fat Stock Show. Dallas: Cotton Bowl football. Donna: Lamb and Sheep Exposition. El Paso: Sun Bowl football. Fort Worth: Southwestern Exposition. Houston: Livestock Show. San Antonio: Junior Livestock Show; Los Pastores.

February. Brownsville: Charro Days. El Paso: Southwestern Livestock Show and Rodeo. Houston: Livestock Show and Rodeo. Laredo: Citrus fruit blossom time; Washington's Birthday Party. Mission: Texas Citrus Fiesta. San Antonio: Livestock Show and Rodeo.

March. Buchanan Dam: Bluebonnet Trail Festival. Dallas: Flower and Garden Show. Fredericksburg: Easter Fires. Houston: Azalea Trail; Spring House and Garden Pilgrimage. Junction: Easter Pageant. McAllen: Spring Fiesta. Plainview: Fat Stock Show. San Angelo: Fat Stock Show and Rodeo. Sweetwater: Rattlesnake Roundup. Woodville: Dogwood Festival.

April Abilene: Fine Arts Festival. Austin: Flower Show; Longhorn Jazz Festival; Texas Relays. Brenham: Bluebonnet Trails. Castroville, Alsatian Homes Pilgrimage. Corpus Christi: Buccaneer Days. Ennis: Bluebonnet Trails. Houston: Flower Show; San Jacinto Day. Kaufman: Cotton Festival. Killeen: Arts and Crafts Festival. La Grange: Tour of Historic Homes and Places. Laredo: Fair. Marlin: Bluebonnet Photo Fiesta. McKinney: Cotton Festival. Palestine: Dogwood Trails. Poteet: Strawberry Festival. Raymondville: Music Festival; Onion Fiesta. San Antonio: Fiesta San Antonio. Stephenville: State Singing Convention. Sweetwater: Industrial Art Competition. Tyler: Flower Show. Yoakum, Wildflower Trail.

May. Athens: Old Fiddlers Reunion. Brenham: Maifest. Columbus: Magnolia Homes Tour. Corpus Christi: Cinco de Mayo. Fort Worth: Pioneer Days. Laredo: Cinco de Mayo. San Antonio: Cinco de Mayo.

June. Aransas Pass: Shrimp Festival. Brownsville-Port Isabel: Shrimp Festival. Corpus Christi: All-Texas Jazz Festival. Crockett: Fiddler's Festival. Hallettsville: High School Championship Rodeo. Hillsboro: Arts and Crafts Show. Houston: Summer Concerts. San Antonio: Fiesta Noche del Rio.

San Augustine: Tour of Homes. Stockdale: Watermelon Jubilee.

July. Burnet: Old Fiddlers' Contest. Corpus Christi: All Texas Jazz Festival. Fort Worth: Roller Skating Championship. Port Aransas: Fishing Roundup. Port Mansfield: Redfish Fishing Tournament. Pecos: Rodeo. Stamford: Cowboy Reunion. Winnsboro: Old Fiddlers' Contest.

August. Austin: Aqua Festival. Buchanan Dam: Art Festival. De Leon: Peach and Melon Festival. Kemah: Blessing of Shrimp Fleet. Palacios: Blessing of Shrimp Fleet. Pharr: Aquatic Games. Abilene: West Texas Fair.

September. Brownsville: Cotton Carnival. Corpus Christi: Mexican Independence Day. Denton: North Texas Fair. El Paso: Fiesta de las Flores. Laredo: Mexican Independence Day. Lubbock: Panhandle-South Plains Fair. Marble Falls: Bass Tournament. San Antonio: Mexican Independence Day. Tyler: East Texas Fair.

October. Amarillo: Arts Fiesta. Beaumont: South Texas Fair. Dallas: Football in the Cotton Bowl; Pan-American Livestock Exposition; SMU Festival of the Arts; Texas State Fair. Eastland: Peanut Bowl football. Floresville: Peanut Festival. Gilmer: East Texas Yamboree. Grapeland: Peanut Festival. Lubbock: Chrysanthemum Colorama and Pilgrimage. Nocona: Pecan Show. Plainview: Cotton Festival. Sinton: Old Fiddlers' Contest. Tyler: Texas Rose Festival. Waco: Square Dance Festival.

November. Austin: Fine Arts Festival at University of Texas. Salado: Scottish Clans Festival.

December. Abilene: Pecan Bowl football. Dallas: All-Star Rodeo. El Paso: Southwestern Sun Carnival. Houston: Blue Bonnet Bowl football. Mission: Poinsettia Show.

UTAH

January. Salt Lake City: Contemporary Music Festival in even-numbered years.
February. Mountain Meadow Ranch: Dog-sled Derby.

Salt Lake City: Chamber Music Festival at University of Utah.
Springville: Utah Art Exhibit.
March.   Salt Lake City: Inventors' Exposition.
April.   Whiterocks: Ute Indian Tribal Bear Dance.
May.   Logan: Dairy Festival. Promontory: Reenact
Golden Spike Ceremony. Spanish Fork: Junior Livestock
Show. Vernal: Junior Livestock Show.
June.   Green River: Canyon Country River Marathon.
North Salt Lake: Junior Fat Stock Show. Pleasant Grove:
Strawberry Days. Provo: Music Festival. Salt Lake City:
Theatre Festival at University of Utah; Utah Art Exhibit.
July.   Aspen Grove: Hike up Mt. Timpanogos. Bluff:
Navajo Indian Festival. Cedar City: Shakespearean Drama
Festival at College of Southern Utah. Ogden: Pioneer Days.
Orem: Celebration. Nephi: Ute Stampede. Salt Lake City:
Days of '47; Summer Festival. Spanish Fork: Fiesta Days.
Whiterocks: Ute Tribal Sundances.
August.   Brigham City: Indian Pow Wow. Mendon:
Threshing Bee. Ogden: Music Festival. Roosevelt: Ute Indian
Pageant.
September.   Brigham City: Peach Days. Cedar City:
4-H and FFA Livestock Auction. Green River: Melon Days.
Midway: Swiss Days. Payson: Harvest Days. Roy: Festival.
Salt Lake City: Utah State Fair.
October.   Spanish Fork: Harvest Festival.
November.   Ogden: Golden Spike National Livestock
Show. Salt Lake City: Utah Folk Song Festival.
December.   Salt Lake City: "The Messiah," in the Mor-
mon Tabernacle.

VERMONT

January.   Ludlow: Winter Carnival.
February.   Manchester Center: Washington's Birthday.
Middlebury: Winter Carnival. Northfield: Winter Carnival at
Norwich University.
March.   Burlington: UVM Choir Concert. Killington:

Easter costume race. North Troy: American Hahnenkamm Race. Stowe: Easter sunrise service, fashion parade. Waitsfield: Easter costume parade.

April. Stowe: Sugar Slalom.

May. Burlington: UVM Horticultural Farm Display. Jamaica: White Water Canoe Slalom.

June. Arlington: Rose Show.

July. Burlington: Champlain Shakespeare Festival. East Poultney: Old Song Fest. Marlboro: Music Festival. Middlebury: Homes Tour. Morrisville, Air Show. Newbury: Cracker Barrel Bazaar.

August. Essex Junction: Champlain Valley Exposition. Lake Dunmore: Lumberjack Roundup. Stowe: Music Festival.

September. Barnet Center: Foliage Festival. Cabot: Foliage Festival. Groton: Foliage Festival. Marshfield: Foliage Festival. Peacham: Foliage Festival. Stowe: Folk Music and Dance Festival. Walden: Foliage Festival.

October. South Woodstock: Fall Foliage Ride.

November. Killington: Homecoming.

VIRGINIA

January. Williamsburg: Antiques Forum.

February. Fredericksburg: Washington's Birthday.

March. Monterey: Maple Sugar Festival. Williamsburg: Colonial Home and Garden Symposium.

April. Charlottesville: Dogwood Festival. Norfolk: International Azalea Festival. Richmond: Deep Run Hunt Races; Historic Garden Week.

May. Winchester: Apple Blossom Festival.

June. Richmond: Festival of Arts. Virginia Beach: Music Festival. Wiliamsburg: "The Common Glory."

July. Abingdon: Arts and Crafts Festival; Barter Theater Festival. Chincoteague: Wild Pony Roundup. Millboro: Jousting Tournament. Norfolk: Arts Festival. Virginia Beach: Boardwalk Art Show; Lotus Festival.

August.   Galax: Old Fiddlers' Contest. Staunton: Jousting. Virginia Beach: Surfing Carnival. Warrenton: National Championship Country Music Camp. Woodstock-Orkney Springs: Shenandoah Valley Music Festival.
September.   Crewe: Virginia Folk Music Festival. Emporia: Peanut Festival. Richmond: Virginia State Fair. Roanoke: Harvest Festival.
October.   Abingdon: Tobacco Festival. Fredericksburg: Dog Mart. Richmond: Autumn Pilgrimage; Tobacco Festival. South Hill: Harvest Festival. Urbanna: Oyster Festival.
November.   Arlington: Veterans' Day. Richmond: Thanksgiving Celebration.
December.   Williamsburg: Old English Christmas.

WASHINGTON, D. C.

March.   Flower, Garden Week.
April.   National Cherry Blossom Festival.
May.   American Music Festival. Armed Forces Day. Memorial Day.
June.   Flag Day. President's Cup Regatta. Summer Jubilee.
July.   Independence Day at Washington Monument. New York Opera Festival.
November.   Veterans' Day at Arlington National Cemetery, Arlington, Va.
December.   Pageant of Peace.

WASHINGTON

March.   Tacoma: Puyallup Valley Daffodil Festival. Wapato: Indian Trade Fair.
April.   Toppenish: Livestock Show. Yakima: Sports Festival.
May.   Bellingham: Blossomtime Festival. Buckley: Fine Arts Festival. Grand Coulee: Festival of Lights; Rodeo. Port

Townsend: Rhododendron Festival. Shelton: Forest Festival. Spokane: Lilac Festival. Wenatchee: Washington State Apple Blossom Festival.
June. Bellingham: Highland Games. Buckley: Finn Festival. Marysville: Strawberry Festival. Montesano: Dairy Day Celebration. Republic: Prospectors' Day. Spokane: Father's Day, where it originated. Wapato: All Indian Rodeo. White Swan: All Indian Encampment.
July. Cle Elum: Loggers' Festival. Seattle: Seafair; Pow Wow. Sedro-Woolley: Loggerodeo. Toppenish: Pow Wow.
August. Norton: Loggers' Jubilee. Port Townsend: Salmon Derby.
September. Connell: Fall Festival. Leavenworth: Autumn Leaf Festival. Port Angeles: Salmon Derby. Puyallup: Western Washington Fair. Spokane: Interstate Fair. Walla Walla: Southeastern Washington Fair. Yakima: Central Washington Fair.
October. Newport: Festival.

WEST VIRGINIA

March. Oglebay Park: Easter sunrise service.
April. Charleston: Creative Arts Festival. Charles Town: House and Garden Tour. Harpers Ferry: House and Garden Tour. Martinsburg: House and Garden Tour. Shepherdstown: House and Garden Tour.
May. Charleston: West Virginia Student Craftsmen Fairs. Davis: Wildflower Pilgrimage. Grafton: Mother's Day. Grantsville: Wood Festival. Huntington: Band Festival. Morgantown: Greater West Virginia Weekend. Petersburg: Golden Trout Festival.
June. Buckhannon: Strawberry Festival. Cedar Lakes: Mountain State Art and Crafts Fair. Glenville: West Virginia Folk Festival.
July. Moorefield: Poultry Festival. Mt. Nebo: Gospel Singing Convention.

August. Clarksburg: West Virginia Glass Festival. Lewisburg: West Virginia State Fair. Moundsville: Corn Festival.

September. Hinton: Water Festival. Kingwood: Buckwheat Festival. Lost River State Park: Garden Club Field Trip. Moorefield: House and Garden Tour. Mt. Nebo: Labor Day Sing. New Martinsville: Regatta. Princeton: Art and Crafts Festival.

October. Elkins: Mountain State Forest Festival. Grafton: Apple Festival. Milton: Harvest Festival. Spencer: Black Walnut Festival.

November. Wheeling: Chrysanthemum Show. Logan: Majorette Festival.

WISCONSIN

April. La Crosse: Square Dance Festival.

May. Aniwa: Maple Syrup Pancake Festival. Arcadia: Broiler Days. Langlade: White Water Canoe Races. Milwaukee: Folk Dance Festival. Stoughton: Syttende Mai.

June. Alma Center: Strawberry Festival. Elkhart Lake: Sports Car Road Races. Ephraim: Fyr Bal Fest. Hayward: Musky Festival. Lake Geneva: Guitar Festival. Menomonie: Red Cedar Days. Milwaukee: Arts Festival. New Glarus: Swiss Fun Weekend. Plymouth: Cheese Festival.

July. Baraboo: Circus City Festival. Bayfield: Tri-State Arts and Crafts Fair for Michigan, Minnesota, and Wisconsin. Beaver Dam: Steam Antique Engine Show. Eagle River: Floatarama. Franksville: Kraut Festival. Hayward: All-Tribes Indian Pow Wow; Log-rolling, Lumber-jack Championship. Keshena: Menominee Indian Homecoming. Milwaukee: Old Milwaukee Days. Pulaski: Polish Sausage Festival. South Milwaukee: Spectacle of Music.

August. Boulder Junction: Musky Jamboree. Chippewa Falls: Northern Wisconsin Fair. Fish Creek: Peninsula Music Festival. Middleton: Good Neighborhood Festival. Milwau-

265

kee: Wisconsin State Fair. New Glarus: Holiday in Heidiland, Swiss Volkfest. Sheboygan: Bratwurst Day. Sun Prairie: Sweet Corn Festival. Washington Island: Scandinavian Festival. West Allis: 200-mile big car race.
September. Elkhart Lake: 500 and 200 Sports Car Road Races. Janesville: Thresheree. Milwaukee: Air Show. Monroe: Green County Cheese Days, staged sporadically. New Glarus: William Tell Pageant. Northern Wisconsin Counties: Northwoods Colorama. Waterloo: Weiner, Kraut Day.
October. La Crosse: Oktoberfest. Ogema: Christmas Tree Festival.
November. Milwaukee: Holiday Folk Fair.

WYOMING

February. Pinedale: Winter Carnival. Saratoga: Winter Carnival.
March. Pinedale: Cutter Racing Championship.
June. Jackson Hole: Snake River Float Trips. Lander: Pioneer Days.
July. Cheyenne: Frontier Days. Cowley: Pioneer Day Celebration. Green River: Green River Rendezvous. Jackson Hole: Fine Arts Festival. Laramie: Jubilee Days. Sheridan: All American Indian Days.
August. Casper: Central Wyoming Fair. Douglas: Wyoming State Fair. Riverton: Arapahoe Pow Wow. Sheridan: All American Indian Days. Thermopolis: Gift of the Waters Pageant.

AMERICAN SAMOA

March. Pago Pago: Easter Visits.
April. Pago Pago: Flag Day.
October. Pago Pago: Children's White Sunday.

266

GUAM

March.   Agana: Discovery Day.
July.   Agana: Liberation Day.
December.   Agana: Religious Festival.

PUERTO RICO

January.   San Sebastian: Patron Saint Day. Throughout the island, Kings Day.
February. Arecibo: Carnival. Mayaguez: Sugarcane harvest bonfires. Rio Piedras: Tropical Flower Festival. San Juan: Mardi Gras.
March.   Loiza Aldea: St. Patrick's Day. San Juan: Feast of San Jose. Throughout the island, Abolition of Slavery Day.
April.   San Juan: Commonwealth Game Fishing Tournament; Puerto Rican Theatre Festival.
May.   Arecibo: Feast of San Felipe. Bayamon: Feast of Santa Cruz. Dorado Beach: Piano Contest.
June.   Ceiba: Feast of San Antonio de Padua. Rio Piedras: Casals Festival. San Juan: Feast of San Juan Bautista.
July.   Loiza Aldea: Feast of Santiago Apostal. Throughout the island, Commonwealth Constitution Day.
August.   San Juan: Feast of Santo Cristo de la Salud.
September. Cabo Rojo: Feast of San Miguel Arcangel. Hormigueros: Feast of Nuestra Senora de la Monserrate.
October.   Rio Piedras: Feast of La Virgen del Pilar.
November. Throughout the island, All Saints Day; Discovery Day.
December.   Ponce: Feast of Our Lady of Guadalupe.

U. S. VIRGIN ISLANDS

January.   Three Kings Day.
February. Donkey Races.

267

March. Transfer Day.
April. St. Thomas: Carnival.
May. Whit Monday.
June. Organic Act Day.
July. St. John Island: Festival. Supplication Day, for deliverance from hurricanes.
August. August Monday yacht races.
September. Labor Day yacht races.
October. Hurricane Deliverance Thanksgiving.
December. St. Croix: Christmas Festival.

CANADA

ALBERTA

January. Calgary: Curling Championship.
February. Edmonton: Mukluk Mardi Gras. Lethbridge: Alberta Dance Festival.
April. Jasper: Marmot Ski Derby.
May. Edmonton: Northwest Canadian Trade Fair; Ukrainian Bandurist Chorus. Jasper: Highland Dancing and Piping Competition; May Festival.
June. Calgary: Spring Field Trial.
July. Banff: Indian Days. Calgary: Stampede and Exhibition. Edmonton: Klondike Days. Jasper: Frontier Days. Lethbridge: Exhibition Fair. Medicine Hat: Exhibition and Stampede. Red Deer: Cavalcade.
August. Cardston: Blood Indian Sundance Festival. Lethbridge: Square Dance Festival. Red Deer: Exhibition and Fair; Horticultural Show.
October. Edmonton: Livestock Show.

BRITISH COLUMBIA

January. Vancouver: Chinese New Year Festival.
February. Dawson Creek: Outdoor Speedskating Cham-

pionship; Winter Carnival. Vancouver: Curling Championship. Vernon: Winter Carnival.

March. Penticton: Curling Bonspiel. Trail: Ski championship. Vancouver: Spring Carnival.

April. Abbotsford: Plowing Contest. Pine Pass: Ski championship. Vancouver: Canadian Car Rally.

May. Creston: Blossom Festival. Prince George: May Days. Trail: Silver City Fiesta. Victoria: Agricultural Exhibition.

June. Vancouver: Sea Festival. Williams Lake: Stampede.

July. Kamloops: Overlanders Day. Kelowna: Powerboat Races. Nanaimo: Highland Games. Princeton: Racing Days. Sooke: All Sooke Day. Vancouver: Film Festival; Highland Games; Vancouver Festival. Victoria: Highland Games; Vintage Car Run.

August. Abbotsford: Air Show. Kelowna: International Regatta. Penticton: Peach Festival; Square Dance Festival. Prince George: Exhibition. Vancouver: Pacific National Exhibition.

September. Armstrong: Interior Provincial Exhibition. Kelowna: Harvest Festival. Nelson: Highland Games.

November. Vancouver: Grey Cup football.

December. Victoria: Olde English Christmas.

MANITOBA

January. Winnipeg: Curling Bonspiel.

February. Beausejour: Winter Carnival. Brandon: Winter Carnival. The Pas: Trappers' Festival. Winnipeg: Outdoor Speed Skating Meet.

March. Winnipeg: Indoor Speed Skating Meet.

April. Brandon: Winter Fair.

June. Winnipeg: Red River Exhibition.

July. Austin: Threshermen's Reunion. Brandon: Provincial Exhibition. Dauphin: Ukrainian Festival. Flin Flon:

Trout Festival. Winnipeg: Scottish Highland Games.
August. Gimli: Islendingadagurinn. Winnipeg: Flower Show.
October. Winnipeg: Ukrainian Celebration.

NEW BRUNSWICK

February. Fredericton: University of New Brunswick Winter Carnival.
May. McAdam: Fishing Derby.
June. New Denmark: Danish Folk Festival.
July. Grand Falls: Potato Festival. Hartland: Potato Festival. Memramcook: Strawberry Festival. Rothsay: Highland Games.
August. Newcastle: Miramichi Folksong Festival. Saint John: Atlantic National Exhibition. Shediac: Lobster Festival. Woodstock: Old Home Week.
September. Fredericton: Exhibition and Livestock Show.
November. Moncton: Curling Bonspiel.

NEWFOUNDLAND

February. St. John's: Canadian Schoolboy Curling Championship.
June. Provincewide: Discovery Day on anniversary of Cabot's landfall.
July. Harbour Grace: Regatta.
August. Cappahayden: Old-time celebration. Holyrod: Festival Week. Renews: Old-time Celebration. St. John's: Regatta.
September. Harbour Grace: Agricultural and Homecrafts Exhibition.
October. St. John's: Homecraft Exhibition.

NORTHWEST TERRITORIES

March. Yellowknife: Caribou Carnival.
May. Frobisher Bay: Toonik Times Spring Festival.
June. Yellowknife: Midnight Golf Tournament.

NOVA SCOTIA

February. Antigonish: Winter Carnival. Halifax: Winter Carnival.
March. Halifax: Curling Championship.
April. Halifax: Music Festival.
May. Kentville-Grand Pré Area: Blossom Festival.
June. Cambridge: Square Dance Jamboree. Cape North: John Cabot's Day.
July. Annapolis Royal: Natal Day. Antigonish: Highland Games. Coxheath: Highland Gathering: Parrsboro: Old Home Week. Pictou: Lobster Fisheries Carnival. Port Hawkesbury: Festival of the Strait. Pugwash: Gathering of Clans.
August. Bridgewater: Exhibition. Church Point: Acadian Festival. New Glasgow: Festival of the Tartans. St. Ann's: Gaelic Mod. Tatamagouche: Nova Scotia Festival of Arts. Truro: Nova Scotia Provincial Exhibition. Yarmouth: International Tuna Cup Match.
September. Lunenburg: Fisheries Exhibition and Fishermen's Reunion. Windsor: Exhibition.
October. Halifax: Atlantic Winter Fair.

ONTARIO

January. Niagara Falls: Winter Carnival.
February. Kingston: Winter Carnival. Ottawa: Winter Carnival. Peterborough: Figure Skating Championship. Sault Ste. Marie: "Bon Soo" Winter Carnival.
March. Cobourg: Curling Bonspiel.

271

April.   Peterborough: Kiwanis Music Festival.
May.   Niagara Falls: Blossom Festival. Ottawa: Canadian Tulip Festival; Dominion Drama Festival; Festival of Performing Arts; Films on Art Festival.
June.   Stratford-on-Avon: Shakespearean Festival. Toronto: Queen's Plate horse race.
July.   Embro: Highland Games. Fort Williams: Highland Games. Maxwell: Highland Games. Kincardine: Highland Games. Niagara-on-the-Lake: Shaw Theatre Festival. St. Catharines: Highland Games; Royal Canadian Henley Rowing Regatta. Stratford: Musical Programs. Stroud: International Brick and Rolling Pin Throwing Contest. Windsor: Highland Games; International Freedom Festival.
August.   Brantford: Six Nations Pageant. Cobourg: Highland Games. Dutton: Highland Games. Fergus: Highland Games. Maxville: Highland Games. Orvillia: Highland Games. Toronto: Canadian National Exhibition.
September.   Milton: Steam-Era. St. Catharines: Grape and Wine Festival. Toronto: Canadian Opera Company Season.
October.   Ottawa: Winter Fair. Seaforth: International Plowing Matches.
November.   Ottawa: Remembrance Day. Toronto: Royal Winter Fair; Toy Parade.

PRINCE EDWARD ISLAND

July.   Charlottetown: Music Festival. Lennox Island: St. Ann's Day. Montague: Strawberry Festival. North Rustico: Scottish Festival. Souris: Fisheries Exhibition. Summerside: Lobster Festival.
August.   Charlottetown: Old Home Week; Provincial Exhibition; Scottish Festival. Eldon: Scottish Games. Tyne Valley: Oyster Festival.
September.   Dundas: Plowing Match. Summerside: Livestock Show.

QUEBEC

January.   Magog: Winter Carnival. Ste. Agathe: Laurentian Snow Festival.
February.   Chicoutimi: Carnival. Montreal: Winter Carnival. Quebec City: Canadian Winter Games; Winter Carnival.
March.   Mt. Tremblant: Quebec Kandahar Race.
April.   Montreal: Beethoven Festival; Shell 4,000 Car Rally to Vancouver.
June.   Alma: Quananiche Festival. Grand-Mère: Amateur Bands Festival. Joliette: Festival of Nations. Montreal: Quebec Music Festival; St-Jean-Baptiste Celebration. Quebec City: Choral Competition. Sherbrooke: Summer Festival.
July.   Grande Riviere: Lobster Festival. La Tuque: Swimming Relay Race. Montreal: International Film Festival. Provincewide, Tour du Saint-Laurent Bike Race. Val d'Or: Festival d'Ete. Valleyfield: Speedboat Regatta.
August.   Mistassini-Dolbeau: Blueberry Festival. Montreal: Montreal Festival.
September.   Quebec City: Provincial Exhibition.
October.   Alma: "Maria Chapdelaine" Festival.
December.   La Perade: Fishing-through-ice Season begins.

SASKATCHEWAN

February.   Prince Albert: Winter Carnival.
June.   Regina: Summer Festival. Saskatoon: Pion-era Days; Threshermen's Reunion.
July.   Saskatoon: Exhibition. Swift Current: Frontier Days.
August.   Regina: Exhibition.
September.   Regina: Festival of the Arts.

October.   Prince Albert: Festival of Arts. Yorkton: International Documentary Film Festival.
November.   Prince Albert: Folk Festival.

YUKON TERRITORY

February.   Whitehorse: Sourdough Rendezvous.
May.   Whitehorse: Victoria Day.
June.   Whitehorse: Midnight Sun Car Rally.
July.   Whitehorse: Klondike Trail of '98 Carnival.
August.   Dawson City: Discovery Day.

Index

275